TWINS!

TWINS!

Expert advice from two practicing physicians on pregnancy, birth, and the first year of life with twins

CONNIE L. AGNEW, M.D., ALAN H. KLEIN, M.D.,

AND JILL ALISON GANON

Illustrations by Victor Robert

Quill

A HarperResource Book

An Imprint of HarperCollins *Publishers*

CREDIT FOR APPENDIX B CHARTS:
Adapted from Hamill PVV, Drizd TA, Johnson CL. Reed RB, Roche AF, Moore WM: Physical growth: National Center for Health Statistics percentiles. AM J CLIN NUTR 32:607-629, 1979. Data from the National Center for Health Statistics (NCHS), Hyattsville, Maryland © 1982 Ross Laboratories

HarperCollins books may be purchased for educational, business, or sales promotional use. For information, please write to: Special Markets Department, HarperCollins Publishers, Inc., 10 East 53rd Street, New York, New York 10022.

FIRST EDITION

Designed by Elina D. Nudelman

Library of Congress Cataloging-in-Publication Data
Agnew, Connie, L., 1957–
   Twins! : expert advice from two practicing physicians on pregnancy, birth, and the first year / Connie L. Agnew, Alan H. Klein, Jill Alison Ganon.
     p. cm.
   ISBN 0–06–273460–1
   1. Twins. I. Klein, Alan H., 1946– . II. Ganon, Jill Alison, 1952– . III. Title.
RG525.A34   1997   97–14657
649'.144–dc21   CIP

02 03 04 05 ❖/RRD 20 19 18 17

This book is dedicated to:

My parents; my husband, William Brien; and my children,
William Jr., Brent, Kelly and Ashley

–Connie Agnew

My father, Don Klein; my daughters Laura and Rachael Klein;
and to the memory of my mother, Lois Klein

–Alan H. Klein

My mother and father, my husband David Arnay and my son Miles

–Jill Alison Ganon

Contents

ACKNOWLEDGMENTS / *ix*

INTRODUCTION / *1*

SECTION ONE: PREGNANCY AND BIRTH

1   What Are Twins? / *7*

2   Prenatal Care / *13*

3   Diagnosis: It's Twins! / *29*

4   4 to 8 Weeks / *42*

5   8 to 12 Weeks / *62*

6   12 to 16 Weeks / *75*

7   16 to 20 Weeks / *85*

8   20 to 24 Weeks / *98*

9   24 to 28 Weeks / *111*

10   28 to 32 Weeks / *123*

11   32 to 36 Weeks / *131*

12   Labor and Delivery to Postpartum / *137*

SECTION TWO: THE FIRST YEAR OF LIFE

13   Ready . . . Set . . . Twins! / *161*

14   Preparing for Delivery and Birth / *177*

15   Going Home / *196*

16   Settling in at Home / *209*

17   Your Twins from Birth to Two Months / *222*

18   Your Twins from Three to Four Months / *237*

19   Your Twins from Five to Six Months / *250*

20   Your Twins from Seven Months to One Year / *261*

APPENDIX A
    Immunization Schedules / *271*

APPENDIX B
    Growth Charts / *273*

APPENDIX C
    Midtrimester Risk for Chromosome
    Abnormalities / *279*

APPENDIX D
    Resource Guide / *281*

INDEX / *293*

Acknowledgments

The authors gratefully acknowledge the following families for their wisdom, humor, and the generous gift of their time in the preparation of this book:

The Copsis family–Judy, Peter, John, and Henry

The King family–Julie, Curt, Kevin, and Steven

The Mandel family–Nidia, Harold, Max, and David

The Moffat family–Susan, Donald, Samantha, Michael, and the memory of Brian

The Varblow family–Paula, Larry, Paul, and Robert

The Meizensahl family–Annie, Paul, Ben, Emily, Molly, and Jeff

The Timiraos family–Carol, Vince, Alex, and Nick

We also want to thank our agent Angela Rinaldi for her great instincts, faith in this project, and hard work on our behalf. Thanks for bringing us together for this book and those still to come.

To Patty Leasure at HarperCollins, thank you for looking at a proposal and seeing a book there.

To Tricia Medved, our editor at HarperReference, we appreciate your patience and support in shepherding our book from infancy to adulthood.

To our illustrator Victor Roberts, thank you for your beautiful and imaginative drawings.

To Marge at The Busy Key for transcribing many hours of tape that were so important in the creation of this book.

Dr. Agnew and Dr. Klein want to thank all their patients for helping them to continue to grow as physicians.

OUR FASCINATION WITH TWINS

As the Roman myth comes to us, Romulus and Remus were born to Mars, the God of War, and Rhea Silvia, one of the Vestal Virgins. After the birth of her two healthy boys, Rhea Silvia's wicked uncle Amulius had them placed in a basket and thrown into the Tiber River, so as to remove any potential threat to his throne. The twins were rescued and nursed by a she-wolf on the slope of the Palatine Hill and later discovered by the shepherd Faustulus and reared by his wife. When the brothers grew to manhood, they deposed Amulius and placed their grandfather Numitor on the throne. Then they decided to build the great city that we know today as Rome.

Romulus and Remus, Castor and Pollux—stories of twins and their unique positions in society appear in Greek and Roman mythology as well as the literature of the Old Testament. Even before there was any written documentation about the miracle of twinning, there were drawings of twins and twin births. We have ancient evidence of an incredible range of cultural responses to the phenomenon of twinning, as well as equally seasoned documentation of exceptional behavior attributed to twins.

Every culture has its own unique relationship with this phenomenon. It is the structure of each society, from its day-to-day function to its most profound view of life and death, that ultimately informs attitudes toward twinning. Economic conditions undoubtedly influence custom. Anthropologists tell us that in the well-supported economy, twins pose no threat to the survival of the family. But if poverty—with its devastating lack of adequate nutrition and shelter—is more prevalent, twins may represent an unbearable burden to the struggling family.

As we'll discuss later on, there is a racial component to the incidence of twinning. Twinning is most common among the black population. Outside Lagos, Nigeria, there is a temple dedicated to twin deities. Members of the Ibex tribe of Africa erect a statue to honor a twin who dies at birth. The statue is carved and raised to watch over its twin. The surviving twin cares for the statue and lives in close proximity to it, reminded forever of the absent brother or sister. The Mojave Indians of North America believe a twin represents the return of some beloved and highly esteemed family member who is honoring them with a reincarnation here on earth. For the Indians of British Columbia, Canada, the birth of a twin into the tribe heralds plentiful hunting and fishing in the year to come. Interestingly, in Asia, where the incidence of twinning is lowest, twins have not traditionally been welcomed. In modern China, there are strict rules governing a family's limit to have only one child. Certainly the birth of twins is not viewed positively by the state.

The significance of birth order carries implications in every culture. In some societies, twins have been viewed as an aberration, a punishment for some known or unknown wrongdoing on the part of the mother, father, or both. There are examples in primitive cultures of the community, bewildered by the question of twin paternity—This unfaithful woman has lain with another man!—making outcasts of the mothers of twins. While we can say with some certainty that this was probably not the case, there is a very rare phenomenon in twinning that can be the result of two different fathers. This extraordinary event can occur if a woman ovulates two eggs that are fertilized within a short period of time by sperm from two men. Not your everyday twins.

We seem to have an abiding fascination with the miracle of twin birth. Apparently there is no end of curiosity regarding the laws of nature as they apply to multiple births. Media coverage of high-order multiple pregnancies is relentless. Every year, thousands of twins congregate for a Twins Day Festival in Twinsburg, Ohio, where they revel in one another's company and pick and choose from among the many researchers who vie for their attention. Scientists have long been interested in exploiting the uniqueness of twins in an attempt to differentiate between the influence of genetic and environmental factors as they apply to our health and emotional well-being. There is fascinating data confirming our suspicion that we have a lot to learn about twins. From medical journals to television talk shows, there are demonstrations of uncanny similarities in the lives and habits of twins raised apart since earliest childhood. Social anthropologists, psychologists, and educators view twins as a sort of miraculous living laboratory—an invaluable tool for the examination of the effects of environment, parenting, and shared genetic material. Researchers have used twins to study the impact of certain pollutants when one identical twin has been exposed and the other has not. The perception that twins share some special ability to communicate has been noted since primitive times. Identical twins, more rare by far, hold an even firmer grip on our collective intellect and imagination, holding a mirror up to the face of society and asking us to explore the very idea of consciousness, and to what degree (if any) our genetic information figures into the development of the individual psyche.

But for a parent, the discovery that you are pregnant with twins is like being an explorer at the mouth of a beautiful, unexplored river. There is the shock of discovery, quickly followed by speculation about the unknown. Will the river be wild at times? Is your craft sturdy enough to navigate this uncharted territory? How about your crew . . . and supplies. Can you *afford* to take the voyage? If the rich, miraculous experience of parents who have already begun their expeditions is any measure, you can't afford not to. So, safe travels to you and your unborn twins. You're starting out on a truly epic journey.

PREGNANCY AND BIRTH

Chapter 1

WHAT ARE TWINS?

Fraternal and Identical Twinning

The miracle of conception takes place when an egg is fertilized by a sperm to become an embryo. Twins are defined as the simultaneous development of two embryos in a woman's uterus. After fertilization takes place, the fertilized ova enters the uterine cavity and implantation occurs. This phenomenon results in early differentiation of cells in each embryo: some develop into the extraordinary organ we know as the placenta, and other cells form the membranous, two layered sacs that will house each embryo. (On rare occasions, both embryos will reside in one sac.) The outer layer of the membrane is the chorion, and the inner layer is the amnion. Sounds pretty straightforward, right? But this is just the beginning. This book will talk about the two types of twinning: fraternal and identical.

Scientists refer to fraternal twins as *dizygotic*, the union of two eggs with two sperm to create two embryos. Dizygotic twins are by far the most common form of twinning, and are two completely separate individuals who are as genetically similar as any siblings born at any time to the same parents.

Monozygotic (identical) twins occur when one egg is fertilized by one sperm.

Dizygotic (fraternal) twins occur when two eggs are fertilized by two sperm.

diamnionic/monochorionic twins with one placenta (fused placenta)

diamnionic/dichorionic twins with separate placentas

Identical, or *monozygotic*, twins are the result of one egg that has been fertilized by one sperm. At some point in the very early stages of cell division, the developing cell group splits in two and develops as two separate embryos. This rare and remarkable twinning creates two embryos who share the complete complement of each other's genetic information; their DNA is identical. The point at which the split occurs will determine which of four possible developmental scenarios will develop for the babies.

This is a good time to talk about the difficulties in diagnosing identical twins. Contrary to what you may have heard, it *is* possible for two embryos to appear to be completely independent of each other within the uterus and still be genetically identical. In the majority of twin pregnancies, the embryos develop with a minimal amount of shared placenta, and that is the best scenario you and your practitioner can hope for. The placenta is magnificently suited to supply your twins with everything they need throughout their gestation. Under the best of circumstances it generously provides for the transfer of oxygen, water, and nutrition from the mother to each of her developing fetuses. There are rare situations in which the placenta appears to provide a preferential supply of nutrition to one fetus over the other. This can result in discordancy and while it may be very subtle, it can often be identified early, allowing practitioners to optimize outcomes for both babies.

It is interesting to note that the prevalence of twins occurring at conception is substantially higher than the birth rate would indicate, but due to a phenomenon called *vanishing twin syndrome*, one of the embryos may fail to develop and be resorbed by the body even before the diagnosis of pregnancy is made. We'll discuss that in more detail later on in this book.

The Factors That Influence Twinning

The first thing that captures our interest when we discuss twins is the incidence of twinning itself. Naturally, when we look at birth rates, the occurrence of twinning falls within a limited range. But if you look at the most recent data in the medical journals, the frequency of *fraternal* twinning in the overall population is about one in fifty live births. Interestingly, *identical* twins make their rare and thrilling appearance without regard to any of the factors that impact the incidence of their fraternal counterparts. Identical twinning occurs quite randomly throughout the population, but we are able to isolate and examine several variables that factor into the likelihood of a couple having fraternal twins:

monoamnionic/monochorionic twins with one placenta

• **Race**

Many people are amazed to learn that there is a racial component to the incidence of twinning in the world population. Twins occur in decreasing numbers within the Black, Caucasian, Hispanic, and Asian populations, respectively. And even within that demographic breakdown, the incidence of twinning among the Yoruba tribe of Western Nigeria is a stunning forty-five per thousand live births. This represents a rate of twinning that is four times that of the overall population! When we measure the naturally occurring hormone levels present in the Yoruba women we find levels that are equal to those in women receiving clomiphene citrate (Clomid) to stimulate their ovaries to produce multiple eggs. We have not yet seen a study that definitively explains the extraordinary fertility of Yoruba women, but speculation ranges from genetics to nutrition to environmental considerations.

diamnionic/monochorionic twins with separate placentas

• Mother's Age and Obstetric History

We also know that maternal age factors into the incidence of twinning. Mother Nature, with her droll sense of humor, visits twins upon mothers of increasing age and, as if that were not enough, the forty-year-old mom who already has children is more likely to conceive twins than her forty-year-old neighbor who has never had children. So far, the scientific community is at a loss to explain this. We know that in order to conceive fraternal twins, the mother must release more than one egg at a time. Yet we do not have data that absolutely suggest that a woman releases more eggs per cycle as she gets older. This increased rate of twinning for older moms does seem to drop off after the early forties, showing Mother Nature's ability to temper her humor with a little common sense.

• Genetics

The role of genetics in twinning remains open to continued investigation. It is commonly accepted that there may be an inherited trait on the maternal side that contributes to an increase in twin births, though a mother who is a twin has no guarantee that she will give birth to twins. There is, however, no equally compelling data to suggest a similar influence may come from the father.

• Infertility Treatments

The final factor known to influence twinning is treatment for infertility. It is accurate to say that for as long as we've marveled at the workings of nature, we've made attempts to improve upon it. Today, in the United States, one out of every fifty births is twin. One in fifty! Until very recently, medical texts cited the numbers of twins occurring in live births as about one in eighty. The current phenomenal statistic owes a large debt to the medical miracle of ovarian stimulation.

The approach to a couple struggling with infertility involves an evaluation of the woman's anatomy, as well as an assessment of the husband's ability to produce viable sperm. If ovulation irregularities appear to be the limiting factor in a couple's failure to conceive, medication to stimulate the ovaries is then considered. These medicines frequently stimulate multiple follicles to develop within the ovaries, which subsequently ovulate multiple eggs. Clomid, the mildest medication available at this time, is associated with an incidence of multiple pregnancies that can be as high as 20 percent. A physician may advise a woman to stay with the Clomid for as many as ten cycles. The next possibility is the use of stronger hormonal medications, called gonadotropins. The gonadotropins, such as Pergonal, stimulate the ovaries more significantly, resulting in a multiple birth rate of between 18 and 40 percent.

For the last twenty years, hormonal stimulation of the ovaries has been an extraordinarily effective method for increasing the incidence of twinning. But correcting the ovulatory problem may not be enough to ensure successful conception. The use of medication will hopefully supply an ample number of eggs, but a blocked fallopian tube may prevent the proper movement of the eggs from the ovary to the fallopian tube, where the sperm and eggs must meet for fertilization to take place. In that event, there are four techniques that may be called upon to achieve pregnancy:

- in vitro fertilization (IVF)
- gamete intra-fallopian transfer (GIFT)
- zygote intra-fallopian transfer (ZIFT)
- ovum transfer

Simply stated, these procedures involve the harvesting of a woman's eggs for fertilization outside her body:

• IVF

A woman's eggs are placed in a laboratory dish and sperm is introduced. The fertilized eggs are then placed in the uterus.

- **GIFT**

  During laparoscopy, the egg and sperm are separately placed in the fallopian tube to undergo fertilization.

- **ZIFT**

  The egg and sperm are introduced to each other in the lab and the fertilized eggs are then placed in the fallopian tube.

- **Ovum Transfer**

  Eggs are harvested from one donor woman, fertilized in the lab, and transferred via IVF into the uterus of a second woman who is attempting to become pregnant.

None of these methods are as much fun as the traditional method of conception, but are effective nonetheless. Egg and sperm are mixed together and when fertilization happens, an embryo results. The fertilized embryos, whether placed in the woman's uterus or in her fallopian tube, begin their valiant attempt at implantation. The cost of the procedure and the stress to prospective parents has made it common practice to harvest and place as many eggs as the doctor deems appropriate, thereby opening the portal to multiple pregnancy. While the parents of babies achieved through various fertility practices can attest to the miraculous nature of assisted conception, it is a remarkably straightforward and mechanical process. Ovaries are stimulated excessively, the resultant eggs are mixed with sperm, and because one egg might not turn into an embryo, doctors—with the blessings of hopeful would-be parents—use multiple embryos and hope for success. This fraternal twinning, two eggs fertilized by two sperm, is the norm for women who give birth to twins following fertility treatment. The average woman with no need of fertility enhancement will ovulate one egg during each menstrual cycle. In the event that she drops more than one and both are fertilized, she has a naturally occurring twin pregnancy: no family history, no hormone stimulation, just the luck of the draw.

Chapter 2

PRENATAL CARE

Before the Twins Are a Twinkle in Your Eye

While it is likely that many couples reading this book already know they are pregnant with twins, it is very important to discuss the importance of pre-conceptual counseling. If—as a result of fertility treatment, genetic predisposition, or just plain old-fashioned luck—you are one of the increasing number of couples who will become parents of twins, it is important that you become an advocate for your own prenatal health. Any couple contemplating pregnancy can take appropriate steps to prepare, long before they consult a health-care practitioner. The first thing to do is evaluate your life and the life of your partner for any risky behavior in which you might be participating.

Do you smoke, use any recreational drugs, or drink alcohol?

It is almost inconceivable that a person living in the United States today would be unaware of the health risks associated with smoking. For a woman contemplating pregnancy, the stakes are about as high as they get.

- Tobacco is associated with low birthrate.

- Smoking is also associated with a rate of miscarriage that is twice the rate of the general population.

- There is a high degree of risk of placental problems and low—birth-weight babies.

- There is some evidence to suggest that the incidence of sudden infant death syndrome (SIDS) is higher in the homes of smoking families than nonsmoking families.

The protocol here is very clear: Stop. Albert Einstein might very well have been right when he told us that God does not play dice with the universe. But mother nature is not above the occasional game of craps when it comes to your fetus' exposure to potentially harmful substances. There are always examples of someone who defies the odds. We all know of at least one hard-drinking, chain-smoking, ninety-nine-year-old granny who died peacefully in her sleep after winning a bundle at the track. But we also know that our hospitals and nursing homes are filled with prematurely aged men and women whose lives have been laid to waste by the ravages of smoking.

There is substantial improvement in individual pregnancies when mothers stop smoking. There are many support programs for people who want help in putting an end to their addictive habits, and there is no greater gift you can give your unborn (even unconceived) babies than a commitment to be tobacco- and drug-free. More subtle, but equally important, is dad's willingness to commit to a smoke-free environment. We know that secondhand smoke has potentially ruinous effects on infants and logic tells us that it could be damaging to a pregnant woman. Before you even begin to worry about the harmful effects of tobacco on your babies, you need to make a healthy commitment to yourselves and each other.

As far as alcohol is concerned, if you are used to the occasional social drink, or wine with dinner, anticipate giving it up for the duration of your prenatal prep time as well as your pregnancy. If alcohol is a serious problem for you, it falls into the tobacco and recreational drug category and you should seek whatever help you need in becoming sober before you become pregnant.

What, if any, prescription or over-the-counter drugs are you taking?

The Food and Drug Administration (FDA) categorizes drugs as to the degree of risk they pose to a fetus:

- **A**

  indicates there is no demonstrated risk to a human fetus

- **B**

  cautions that while animal studies do not appear to show risk to the fetus, we do not yet have good studies for humans

- **C**

  clearly indicates that the drug has had some affect in animal studies, but nothing definitive with humans

- **D**

  shows positive evidence of risk to humans, but it might be appropriate in certain situations considered to be life threatening to the mother

- **X**

  should never, under any circumstance, be used by a pregnant or possibly pregnant woman.

The majority of drugs fall within the B or C classifications. The impact of most medicines and substances is greatest between day thirty-one and seventy-one of your pregnancy, which corresponds roughly to four and one-half weeks to ten weeks.

A drug or substance which has the effect of possibly or most definitely producing birth defects or anomalies in growing embryos or fetuses is called a teratogen and is to be avoided during the pre-pregnancy planning time, as well as throughout your pregnancy. Always consult with your practitioner before taking any drug if you are pregnant or planning a pregnancy. Below, you'll find a list of a few common drugs that have been identified as teratogenic and are to be avoided. Be sure to speak with your doctor for a more comprehensive survey of drugs or substances that are teratogenic.

- **Accutane (class X)**

   Taken orally as a treatment for certain skin conditions, Accutane is highly associated with structural defects to the fetus. Dermatologists are likely to prescribe it for treatment of various skin conditions. It is one of a handful of drugs that is known to consistently cause birth defects. If there were ten pregnant women in a room who had all consumed Accutane during the first trimester of their pregnancy, one of them would have a baby with a serious problem. Any woman who is considering becoming pregnant should avoid orally prescribed Accutane for at least six months prior to conception. When used topically, Retin-A (class B), a related drug, is not associated with any ill effects on fetal development.

- **Danazol (class X)**

   Danazol is a type of steroid and is often used in the treatment of endometriosis. It is a testosterone derivative and has been reported to cause masculinization of a female fetus.

- **Vitamin A (class D)**

   There have been birth defects associated with megadoses of vitamin A (25,000 units daily).

- **Valproic Acid (class D)**
  Dilantin (class D)
  Phenobarbital (class D)
  Tegretol (class D)

These drugs are all anticonvulsant drugs, prescribed in the treatment of seizures in diseases such as epilepsy. Women taking anticonvulsant drugs have approximately twice the risk of having babies with fetal defects as occurs in the general population. Most physicians agree that under certain circumstances the benefits of therapeutic use of these drugs outweigh the risks, because seizure activity itself can be dangerous for a pregnancy. Some women who have been seizure-free for at least two years may be able to stop taking their medicine and become pregnant. Such a step would require a thorough assessment by the patient's neurologist and should never be undertaken without medical supervision.

- **Aspirin (and Ibuprofen)**

The woman who takes an aspirin for a headache and discovers a week later that she is pregnant need not be concerned about any ill effects. We do not see evidence of risk to the fetus in cases where women used aspirin for pain relief a few times early in pregnancy. But there is evidence of a condition called premature closure of the ductus arteriosus in babies exposed to aspirin and nonsteroidal antiinflammatories in the third trimester of pregnancy. It can also alter uterine contractility, causing the uterus to relax–not a great idea if one is going through labor. Aspirin also slows blood clotting and can contribute to excessive bleeding in mother and babies at delivery.

Ibuprofen (Motrin, Naprosyn, Advil, etc.), a frequently used aspirin substitute, should be treated with the same caution as aspirin. If you have a headache, acetaminophen (Tylenol, etc.) appears to be safe in pregnancy, but always ask your practitioner before taking any drug during your pregnancy.

Are you overweight or underweight? Do you have a history of or currently experience any eating disorder?

As the conduit through which all nutrition will pass to your babies, a woman's body is the first line of defense when it comes to protecting and nurturing fetal well-being. Physical health, as well as informed attitudes about food and your own body, are all important in the pre-pregnancy planning stage. For many women, the joy of pregnancy holds the added bonus of a little indulgence. For the woman expecting twins who is used to eating well and staying fit, that ice cream cone on a hot August night may be just what the doctor ordered. But if you are one of the legion of women in this country who wage a daily battle against the bulge, pregnancy presents a whole new challenge. Perhaps you have been on a weight-loss diet. It is not unusual for a woman to become pregnant inadvertently while she is dieting. Naturally, it's daunting for the woman who has literally worked her fanny off for a year to look at the prospect of regaining the weight she has struggled to lose. Which is not to say she isn't thrilled to be pregnant; she may very well be. But it is not unusual for a woman diagnosed with a multiple pregnancy to express concern about managing her weight. The first thing your practitioner is likely to tell you is that a weight-loss diet is not recommended during pregnancy. You certainly can choose nonfat milk over heavy cream in your tea or a lean cut of beef over those fatty ribs, but you must maintain adequate levels of caloric intake to nourish your growing babies.

There are specific concerns for the very young woman who may become pregnant with twins. Anyone who has ever observed the eating habits of teenagers left to their own nutritional devises will concur—there are reasonable concerns about the diets of male and female teens. A poll of the teen population accounts for an impressive amount of pizza, French fries, and potato chips, but the incidence of eating disorders among young women is also alarmingly high.

The good news is that women and their physicians, therapists, and support groups report very positive news about their ability to manage healthy pregnancies while continuing to battle their dietary demons. Women struggling with dietary problems that range from a mild obsession with chocolate to life-threatening bulimia and anorexia can have healthy babies. But it is very important to be frank with yourself, your mate, and your health practitioner when it comes to handling food issues and your pregnancy.

What is the extent of your exposure to environmental hazards such as common household chemicals, radiation, or hazardous chemicals in your work environment?

Even the woman who has shunned cigarettes all her life may be vulnerable to less obvious environmental risks. If you read the labels on some very effective but noxious household cleaning products, you'll find that they carry warnings about toxicity and the importance of avoiding contact with your skin, or of using in a well-ventilated area. Now is the time to really pay attention to those warnings. Careful use of pesticides (use the natural ones if you can) and fertilizers out in the garden is equally important. Basic precautions for the home gardener will go far when it comes to ensuring your health and the health of your babies—wear your gardening gloves, wash your hands as soon as you're done, be sure to use sunscreen, and wear a hat.

Since it is possible for a pregnancy to go undiagnosed until after a considerable amount of fetal development has occurred, it is very wise to limit exposure to toxins in the workplace well before you try to conceive. The occasional Sunday gardener should wear gloves while handling pesticides or fertilizers, but she need not curtail her hobby. But an agricultural worker, exposed daily to chemical pesticide spray, may want to rethink her working status.

Painting a room in your house is fine as long as there is adequate ventilation, but if your job entails daily exposure to painting, you might want to look for alternative employment. Prolonged exposure to paint or any chemical fumes is unwise. Educate yourself about your work environment so you can make informed decisions about prenatal health.

A cross-continental airplane flight up to your twentieth week of pregnancy should be fine, but we are exposed to additional radiation from the sun while flying. The closer to the poles one flies, the greater the dose of radiation. Pilots, flight attendants, and women making very frequent long business trips should consult their local Federal Aviation Authority (FAA) guidelines as to risks attendant to particular routes and frequency of travel.

When did you last have a comprehensive physical and dental exam?

A woman in good health is already advocating for her as yet unconceived child. Prenatal considerations should also include any significant radiological evaluations that need to be performed. Now is the time to have any dental work done that you think might otherwise require attention in the coming year. If you've been putting off your mammogram, do it now. There is always the possibility that an X ray will be necessary during your pregnancy. Diagnostic X-ray doses are exceedingly low in most situations, and if there is a possible fracture of your ankle, the consequences of failing to have the X ray are potentially devastating. Always tell the examining physician as well as the X-ray technician that you are pregnant, or that you *may* be pregnant, so you can effectively cover your pelvis and abdominal area with a lead shield.

What form of birth control are you using?

The decision to try for a baby can be as simple as tossing your diaphragm in the trash and lighting some candles, or it can require a little more planning. It is recommended that a woman using birth control pills allow her body to go through two or more regular menstrual cycles before attempting to become pregnant. The most dependable form of birth control to use during this waiting period is a condom. The IUD is a terrific method of birth control that is far safer now than it was twenty years ago. It does not appear to interrupt the reproductive cycle, so you can in theory have your IUD removed in the afternoon and conceive that very night! If condoms and spermicide have been your birth control method of choice, you do not need to enforce any waiting period before attempting to conceive.

But there are more subtle questions about your life that are equally deserving of thoughtful consideration. It is the rare couple who is able to take stock of their situation and proclaim that "this is the perfect time for us to start our family." And it is more rare still for that couple to march into the bedroom, firm in their resolve, and have the extraordinary good fortune to immediately conceive their baby (or babies, as the case may be). The decision to have children, whether your first or fourth, is often made as a sort of good-faith agreement between couples who wish to reaffirm their shared desire to move forward, together, into the next phase of their lives. There are no guarantees in this agreement and the only absolute is that there is no absolute. It is probably wise to take some time to look at your relationship as a couple.

- If there are fertility problems, are you in synch about exploring your options?

- Have you thought about the implications of becoming parents as far as your careers and finances are concerned?

- Are you prepared to delay exotic travel plans or even modest vacations if need be?

- Are you living in a place that is suitable to raising a family?

- Have you read your health-insurance policy and determined that you have adequate coverage?

After thinking about these things, it is time to see your practitioner for an evaluation of your medical history. This is the time to speak with your mother, sisters, or grandmothers about their obstetric and genetic histories. Any established inherited genetic disorders should be made known to your physician prior to pregnancy to determine your level of risk for passing on a problem to your child. Now is the time for your grandmother to tell you if she is aware of any history of twinning in the family. And most important, if it is possible, sit down with your mother and learn what you can about her reproductive history. It is particularly important for your practitioner to know if *diethylstilbestrol* (DES) was prescribed for your mother during her pregnancy. DES was prescribed in the '50s for women who were thought to be at risk for miscarriage. Women born to DES mothers frequently have unusually shaped reproductive tracts, so their pregnancies can be a bit complicated.

Determine if anything in your family medical history puts you in a different risk category than you may have anticipated. Is it responsible to contemplate pregnancy, or are there risks associated to your own health that must be managed and carefully monitored? Far from discouraging you, your physician should be eager to work with you to control any pre-existing conditions that might put you or your babies at risk:

- diabetes
- hypertension
- certain forms of arthritis
- anemia
- hypothyroidism/hyperthyroidism
- asthma
- systemic lupus erythematosus (SLE)

All of these conditions should be evaluated prenatally in order to develop the most effective regime for their control during pregnancy. Any known infection is best treated before becoming pregnant so as to reduce concerns about antibiotic use. That would include sexually transmitted diseases as well as an infection of the sinus or urinary tract.

There are also screening tests that can be done to determine if a patient or her fetuses might be at risk for problems that could compromise an otherwise healthy pregnancy:

• Rubella is highly associated with birth defects to the fetus and can be screened easily by measuring the antibodies in a patient's bloodstream. Look into your own history of childhood illnesses. Remember that rubella can be devastating to your fetus. If found never to have been exposed, a woman should be vaccinated so as not to be at risk of contracting the disease during her pregnancy.

• Genetic screening for racially associated health risks such as *sickle cell anemia* among the Black population (and in rare cases, some Mediterranean populations); *Tay-Sachs disease* among Ashkenazi Jews; *Thalassemia* in people of southern Mediterranean or Asian descent; and *cystic fibrosis* in the Caucasian population. In each of these cases, the disease is caused by a recessive gene and can have a devastating effect on the fetus if both parents pass on the same recessive gene.

Every woman contemplating pregnancy should have her obstetrical and gynecological surgical history assessed. *Gravity* describes the number of pregnancies experienced and *parity* indicates the number of natural births or C-sections, the number of children delivered, and whether they were premature or full-term. Documenting a miscarriage, elective termination, or ectopic pregnancy is equally important in assembling a complete reproductive history. If this is not your first pregnancy, sharing any history of bleeding during pregnancy, as well as noting the size of your babies, will be beneficial in helping your practitioner assess any likely risks to you or your unborn children. Certainly these issues will come up in any initial visit to a practitioner once a woman knows that she is pregnant. But it is valuable to have that information on hand before pregnancy occurs.

Eating for Two . . . or Three: Nutrition for While You're Planning and When You're Pregnant

There is a great deal of information to support the time-honored tenet that you are indeed what you eat. Medical literature is filled with observational studies that link pregnancy outcome to maternal nutrition. Surely there is enough anecdotal evidence of that theory. Well-fed women have an uncanny proclivity toward making healthy babies with high birth weights. The classic studies in the medical literature are observational studies that record the birth weights of babies born to a specific segment of previously well-fed European women during the nutritionally deprived years of World War II. When the women were eating well, their babies were bigger and healthier at birth. During the war, when food was in short supply, the birth weights dropped and after the war they rose again. Very simple, and hard to refute.

It seems clear from our more recent and sophisticated research that while good nutrition is important for maternal health in the first trimester of pregnancy, it doesn't have a proportional impact on the weight of the babies at birth. This is great news to twin moms who may experience considerable nausea and/or vomiting during their first trimester. The fact that your appetite is compromised need not compromise the health of your babies. You'll have plenty of time after your symptoms disappear to regain a great appetite for healthy food.

Many mothers of twins are concerned about weight gain. They want to provide their babies with the best possible start, but they are not eager to gain more weight than is necessary. Keep in mind that once you are pregnant, a weight-loss diet is out of the question. If you are overweight and considering pregnancy, a healthy diet can go a long way toward helping you to shed unwanted pounds. If you are overweight and discover you are pregnant with twins, your metabolism will go into high gear and the weight you gain can all go toward making healthy babies. Women who are underweight can get excellent guidance from their practitioners on how to supplement their diets throughout pregnancy. Remember, it is never too late to start eating right. For any woman, pregnant or contemplating pregnancy, it is important to keep several basic concepts on the table at all times:

- The quality of your food is more important than the quantity. A healthy woman can certainly indulge every once in a while, but as a rule you'll want to avoid the empty calories of sugary snacks. Fill your home with fruits, vegetables, and other healthy snacks. If you are the only person trying to eat healthfully, the temptation to indulge may prove to great. Get your husband and children on track with you.

- You are likely to feel more comfortable all the way through your pregnancy if you get used to eating six small meals a day instead of three large ones.

- Avoid the American dining tradition of eating progressively larger meals as the day goes on. Along with the bonus of an additional baby, mothers of twins are prone to additional gastrointestinal distress. You will eventually discover that going to bed with a very full tummy is not a good idea.

- Chronic constipation in pregnancy is associated with inadequate fiber and fluid intake. Daily servings of fresh vegetables, whole-grain products, fruit, and at least eight glasses of water daily are a requirement for every mother of twins. If you begin to get constipated, get in the habit of carrying around a bottle of water and drinking the equivalent of a glass of water each hour. Moms of twins need to be superhydrated during pregnancy.

- Proteins contain amino acids, which are fundamental to the creation of human cells. A diet low in protein has been associated with low birth weight in babies. A healthy diet makes efficient use of each of its sources. Fat, for example, is an inefficient source of calories, while protein is highly efficient.

- Mood swings are associated with fluctuations in our levels of blood sugar. In case the empty calories of sugar are not enough reason to minimize it in your diet, the last thing a mom of twins needs is the sugar-related highs and lows associated with candy bars and too many cookies. Also keep in mind that sugar is associated with increased risk of gestational diabetes and, as a mother of twins, that is already something you're watching out for.

- Complex carbohydrates—such as those found in whole grains, brown rice, and legumes—are rich sources of B vitamins, protein, and trace minerals. It's not the whole-wheat bread that adds unwanted calories, it's the thick pat of butter you put on top of it !

- Avoid foods that are highly processed or filled with additives whose names you can't pronounce. It is possible to eat a lot of food and still be malnourished. Too many empty calories will help you to put on weight but you still may be seriously deficient in the vitamins and minerals necessary for your twins' development.

- Unless your practitioner tells you otherwise, do not go on a salt-restricted diet. Your body needs salt to retain all the water needed for the increase in blood volume, as well as additional fluids required for your changing breast tissue and amniotic fluid. So while you should not add salt to your food, don't restrict it either.

Having discussed the need for a healthy, well-balanced diet, the following is a general guideline of how you might approach great nutrition for yourself and your babies:

- Four to five servings of complex carbohydrates, simple carbohydrates, and starch each day.

  whole-grain breads; whole grains such as wheat, barley, oats, rice, corn and millet; soy; whole-grain cereals; whole-grain pastas; potatoes; beans such as navy, red, black, lima, soy, and lentils; and green peas

- Three to four servings of milk and milk products each day.

  low-fat or nonfat milk, yogurt, cottage cheese and buttermilk; hard cheeses such as Swiss, cheddar, and Jarlsburg

- Three to four servings daily of protein from meat or other sources.

  liver, dark poultry meat, cooked oysters, and sardines are also very high in iron. All the milk products listed above, eggs, poultry, tofu, fish, shellfish, meat, and nuts

- Three servings of iron-rich green, leafy vegetables or yellow fruits each day. They are also rich in vitamin A, beta-carotene, vitamin E, folic acid, vitamin B_6, calcium, and trace minerals.

  spinach, kale, Swiss chard, mustard, beet or collard greens, broccoli, cantaloupe, carrots, apricots, mango, papaya, winter melons, pumpkin, dark lettuces

- Two to three servings of fruit provide vitamin C and all the sugar you are likely to need. If you are concerned about sugar, fruit juices can be cut with carbonated water (check labels for hidden sodium) or water. Grapes and pineapples are great but are very high in sugar, so don't go overboard.

  citrus juice; fruits such as grapefruit, orange, lemon, tangerine, and lime; berries such as strawberries, blackberries, and raspberries

- Substitute with these fruits for sources that are very rich in vitamin A, potassium, and magnesium.

  cantaloupe, apricots, mangos, nectarines, peaches, and bananas

Vitamin supplementation is uniformly embraced as a good idea for pregnant women. There has been a tremendous amount of discussion in the medical literature about the beneficial effects of folic acid in decreasing the risk to fetuses of certain neural tube defects such as spina bifida. It appears that folic acid supplementation is most important prior to pregnancy and in the early weeks post-conception when the spine is developing. The recommended dose for women contemplating pregnancy is 0.4 mg per day. Women who have a personal history of neural tube defect or who have already given birth to a child with a neural tube defect are advised to increase their folic acid supplement to 4.0 mg per day.

A healthy, well-balanced diet comes pretty close, but in addition to folic acid supplements, the woman who is pregnant with twins should also have about 1,800 milligrams of calcium daily—and that may be hard to manage without a vitamin supplement. The other supplement that may be appropriate for a twin pregnancy is iron. The strain on the multiple mom to increase her blood supply makes her vulnerable to anemia. You may also want help getting your fifty milligrams of iron each day. Talk to your practitioner about your diet and any recommended vitamin and mineral supplements.

Recommended Dietary Allowances for Pregnant and Nonpregnant Women

Nutrient	Nonpregnant	Pregnant	Percent Increase	Dietary Sources
Energy (kcal)	2,200	2,500	+13.6	Proteins, carbohydrates, fats
Protein (g)	50	60	+20	Meat, fish, poultry, dairy
Calcium (mg)	800	1,200	+50	Dairy Products
Phosphorus (mg)	800	1,200	+50	Meats
Magnesium (mg)	280	320	+14.3	Seafood, legumes, grains
Iron (mg)	15	30	+100	Meats, eggs, grains
Zinc (mg)	12	15	+25	Meats, seafood, eggs
Iodine (µg)	150	175	+16.7	Iodized salt, seafood
Vitamin A (µg RE)	800	800	0	Dark green, yellow, or orange fruits and vegetables, liver
Vitamin D (IU)	200	400	+100	Fortified dairy products
Thiamin (mg)	1.1	1.5	+36.3	Enriched grains, pork
Riboflavin (mg)	1.3	1.6	+23	Meat, liver, enriched grains
Pyridoxine (mg)	1.6	2.2	+37.5	Meats, liver, enriched grains
Niacin (mg NE)	15	17	+13.3	Meats, nuts, legumes
Vitamin B_{12} (µg)	2.0	2.2	+10	Meats
Folic Acid (µg)	180	400	+122	Leafy vegetables, liver
Vitamin C (mg)	60	70	+16.7	Citrus fruits, tomatoes
Selenium (µg)	55	65	+18.2	Grains, extra-lean meats

Adapted with permission from RECOMMENDED ALLOWANCES: 10TH EDITION. Copyright 1989 by the National Academy of Sciences. Courtesy of the National Academy Press, Washington, D.C.

Chapter 3

DIAGNOSIS: It's Twins!

Reasons to Be Suspicious That You Might Be Carrying Twins

Maybe you've been going through assisted reproductive technology and you *know* that you are likely to be blessed with a multiple pregnancy. . . . Or, you've done your home pregnancy test and you're pretty sure you're pregnant, but have not the faintest idea that it's twins. . . . Or, you've had a first appointment with your practitioner who has confirmed that you are pregnant and you've raced home to share the great news. No matter which scenario applies to you, at some point fairly early on in your pregnancy, you are going to have certain symptoms that are going to make you, or your practitioner, suspicious that you are carrying twins.

Certainly, you and your doctor will be looking for any indications in your medical history that point to twins: family history, age, race, or the use of fertility drugs. But there are other indicators that may tip off your practitioner:

- **Rate of Weight Gain**

  The rate at which a pregnant woman gains weight can be the first tip-off to a twin pregnancy. A twin pregnancy is likely to show additional weight as early as the first trimester due to increased blood volume and uterine size. But sometimes a woman and her practitioner do not discover the twin pregnancy until the second trimester, when considerable weight gain raises their suspicions.

The average weight gain (and of course these are approximate) in a singleton pregnancy is as follows:

· five to seven pounds from week one to week twelve

· ten to twelve pounds from week twelve to week twenty-six

· ten to fifteen pounds from week twenty-six until delivery at forty weeks

The average total weight gain tends to be in the realm of twenty-five to thirty-five pounds. In a twin pregnancy, weight gain is increased as follows:

· five to ten pounds from week one to week twelve

· ten to fifteen pounds from week twelve to week twenty-six

· fifteen to twenty pounds from week twenty-six until delivery

The average total weight gain tends to be in the realm of thirty-five to forty-five pounds.

• Size of the Abdomen and Increased Itching on Its Surface

A uterus that seems exceedingly large based on the date of the last menstrual period is a very strong indicator of a multiple pregnancy. All women experience a sensation of itchiness as the skin of the abdomen stretches, but the feeling may occur earlier and be more pronounced for the twin mom.

- **A Feeling of Heaviness in the Pelvis or Vagina**

- **Greater Tendency to Retain Water**

    The woman pregnant with twins will retain more water than her singleton counterpart. "A feeling of unexpected kinship with Lake Superior," was the way one surprised Michigan mother of twins put it. The unwitting mom of twins may develop swelling in her lower extremities and hands earlier than would normally be expected.

- **Varicose Veins**

    There is a tendency for relaxation of the walls of the blood vessels during pregnancy and this may be increased in the event of a twin pregnancy. Oh, boy . . . support hose!

- **Increased Fatigue**

    This is sort of a dicey symptom, since fatigue is one of the early hallmarks of any pregnancy. But a woman who has been pregnant before and feels that her exhaustion in this pregnancy is excessive should mention it to her practitioner.

These indicators are pretty straightforward. But there is also a fair amount of discussion in the medical community about whether women carrying twins feel more movement in the early stages than a singleton mom. Even when a twin pregnancy has been diagnosed, it is hard to say in the early stages exactly *when* a mom is feeling the babies move and if she can distinguish *which* baby is moving. Both babies can be active or quiet at the same time. But a mom's sense that there seem to be several muffled drum solos going on at once in there may be a reason to call for a diagnostic ultrasound. Finally, many very experienced obstetricians agree that it is exceedingly difficult to confidently identify two separate heartbeats, even with the use of sophisticated listening devices. Using a Doppler tone, which is a device that utilizes ultrasound technology, the earliest opportunity to definitely hear a heartbeat is between ten and twelve weeks. By the sixteenth week, the heart can be heard with a specially designed stethoscope.

At Your Diagnostic Visit

The first thing that is likely to happen is that you will be asked to fill out an extensive medical profile, including details of your menstrual and obstetric history as well as what you may know about the reproductive history of your mother and sisters. Then you will undergo a thorough physical exam. In the case of a first pregnancy, this may be a woman's most thorough health evaluation since she began her reproductive years.

- The exam inevitably begins with recording of your height, weight and blood pressure.

- **Evaluation of Your Skin**

  Your practitioner will begin by looking at and touching your skin, noting its color, texture, and the presence of any varicosity due to high estrogen levels. (Pregnancy is an equal-opportunity condition, and it is possible for veins other than those in your legs to become swollen or dilated during pregnancy.) Your skin is a remarkable organ, offering insight into many facets of overall health. Very dry skin, for example, is indicative of hypothyroidism. Certain skin lesions on the skin can suggest the presence of infection. An increase in estrogen levels during pregnancy creates a distinct redness to the palm and heel of the hand. You may also develop a redness or an increased pigmentation on the bridge of your nose extending beneath your eyes as though you had developed a light tan. This is called "the mask of pregnancy" and is another hormonal reaction that can be expected to fade after delivery of your babies.

- **Examination of the Neck**

  The exam will include palpation of the neck to look for any thyroid enlargement or abnormal masses.

- **Breast Exam**

  The breast exam will include observation of the skin, nipple, areola, and palpation of the axilla (armpit) for any masses or nodularity.

- **Assessment of Your Lungs and Heart**

  If this is your first visit, your practitioner has not yet had an opportunity to get to know you or your body. This is an opportunity to hear how your lungs sound. Later on, you may have complaints about shortness of breath and this exam offers a sort of baseline assessment of your pulmonary function. It is also important to determine that the size, location, and rhythm of your heart is normal and to rule out the presence of any heart murmurs.

- **Evaluation of the Abdomen and Kidneys**

  This will help to determine the size of your uterus as well as assess the size of your liver and spleen. Palpation of the kidneys is key to determining the presence of any kidney infection.

- **Appraisement of Your Back**

  This will rule out or confirm the presence of scoliosis or any suggestion of arthritis of the back that would have an impact on how you might deliver your twins.

- **Pelvic Exam**

  The pelvic exam will include observation of your external genitalia as well as looking within the vagina to make sure the skin looks normal and is free of lesions. Then your practitioner will go on to palpate the uterus, checking for any enlargement of the ovaries, and go on to look at the cervix, making sure there are no areas of concern there.

- ## The Musculoskeletal System

  The rest of the exam is largely related to the extremities—making sure the musculoskeletal system appears normal and checking for any limited range of motion or history of trauma. Finally, checking your reflexes will give your practitioner insight into your nervous system.

Having completed the physical exam, you'll move on to the laboratory tests that are performed in the beginning of a pregnancy:

- ## Human Chorionic Gonadotropin (HCG)

  This is the pregnancy hormone and it can be measured in the blood or the urine to determine if a woman is pregnant. It is the presence of this hormone that is reliably detected in home pregnancy tests, whereas the blood test can help to gauge how far the pregnancy has advanced. A greater than anticipated level of HCG in a blood sample is sometimes a practitioner's first clue that a twin pregnancy is likely.

- ## Pap Smear

  This will check for any abnormal cell growth on the surface of the cervix.

- ## Vaginal Cultures

  These tests are obtained in order to rule out the presence of gonorrhea, chlamydia, or vaginitis.

- **Routine Blood Tests**

This will include a VDRL, which is a serologic test for syphilis; the rubella titer to determine if you are immune to rubella; a complete blood count (CBC) to check for normal levels of hemoglobin and to test for anemia; assessment of your blood type and Rh in the event of any Rh incompatibility with your fetus.

Early Use of Diagnostic Ultrasound

Use of the ultrasound can be very enlightening during every stage of pregnancy. If you have one or more indications of a multiple pregnancy, your practitioner may call upon ultrasound technology for confirmation of the diagnosis. Many obstetricians argue that all pregnant women would benefit from the use of such routine ultrasound screening, but unfortunately many health-insurance carriers object to the attendant costs. A recent article in the *American Journal of Obstetrics and Gynecology* supports wider use of routine ultrasound, but this debate—like so many others in the arena of health care—is likely to rage on without consensus from health-care providers and insurance companies.

In an initial evaluation during the first trimester, the ultrasound can be invaluable in documenting the number of gestational sacs present, and then looking for the number and size of embryos that inhabit them. The ultrasound can also be helpful in the first attempts at determining the form of twinning your pregnancy has taken. If, for example, there appears to be just one gestational sac containing two embryos, that is an indication of the presence of monozygotic (identical) twinning.

The ultrasound is also helpful in determining how far along the patient is. Of course, there is always some margin of error in the dating capabilities of ultrasound. In the first trimester, when we try to measure the size of an embryo to predict its gestational age, the margin of error ranges from five to seven days in either direction. It is also very useful to use ultrasound to confirm the length of the cervix and

Early diagnostic ultrasound image: two sacs with small poles.

the location of the placenta or placentas. That early diagnostic information helps to verify that the cervix is doing its job, the placenta is in
a good position, and there is no evidence of bleeding within the
uterus.

It is also possible to have an early diagnosis of twins and then, with
progressive observation of the pregnancy, discover that one of the
gestational sacs has failed to develop. This is a phenomenon known as
vanishing twin syndrome. While some women may experience bleeding,
cramping, or even some passage of tissue, frequently there are no
signs of miscarriage, and the patient will go on to have an uncomplicated pregnancy and deliver a perfectly healthy singleton baby. Of
course, miscarriage can be a matter of great emotional consequence to
parents, even if it occurs in the earliest weeks of pregnancy. But it is
sometimes helpful to consider that the failure of one of the twin
embryos to thrive may be nature's way of averting serious difficulties
further down the line. The parents who understandably grieve over
the loss of one of their unborn twins may find some comfort in recog-

nizing that the survival of the second embryo is an early indicator of the vitality of that baby.

The Miraculous Placenta

When we describe the development of the placenta we are talking about a miraculous system of blood vessels that are derived either from fetal cells or from the maternal uterine wall. These two separate sources come together as an integral part of the network of the placenta. In fact, sometimes the two sources are so close together that there is little more than a few cells separating the blood supplies of the mother and each baby. The nutrients carried by the mother's blood are transported across that cell layer and diffuse their important load of nutrients, oxygen, calories, and fluid into the baby's blood. At the same time, the baby's blood needs to have waste products removed. The baby's waste products will be transported out of its bloodstream and into the mom's to be disposed of as she would her own waste.

The placenta delivers nutrients to the fetus and carries waste away.

The development of this extraordinary organ, on temporary loan to every mother-to-be, will determine how well your twins are going to receive the nutrients that are so vital to their well being. If, as is the case in some monozygotic twinning, twins share a placenta, there is additional attention paid to whether there is equal sharing of the goodies. And there are occasional circumstances in which there is some vascular communication between the two placentas, so your practitioner will want to track those twins very carefully.

Are You Seeing the Right Practitioner?

OK. So you've got your diagnosis. And you've begun to make your transition from stunned to numb to overjoyed.

First of all, you can be sure that one time on the roller-coaster ride of these emotions is not going to be enough. Most couples report at least several weeks of riding these feelings up and down: eyes wide open, eyes shut tight; hands clutching each other, hands thrown sky high just for the thrill of the ride. But as the reality sinks in, the prospect of twin birth is overwhelmingly met with a deep and abiding impression of having been favored with a miracle.

Now it is time to begin thinking about assembling the team that will help you to make this miracle become real. Perhaps you have gone through fertility treatments or have been seeing a practitioner since your prenatal preparation. If that is the case, you may have been developing a relationship for years. But many couples get their initial diagnosis from a home pregnancy test and find themselves in the position of needing to choose a health-care provider. Whether you have a practitioner in place or are just beginning your search, ask yourself the following questions:

- Is this person accessible?

- Are they receptive to my thoughts about my own health care?

- Are we able to communicate effectively and with respect, even if there is a difference of opinion?

- Has this practitioner handled many multiple births?

- Does this person make it clear that they know my time is equally valuable to theirs?

If you can answer *yes* to these five questions then you have found an excellent provider, and you and your twins are off to the best possible start. Ease of communication is the engine that will drive your whole pregnancy. The more time you spend as a couple talking out your own attitudes toward pregnancy and childbirth, and discussing your joint expectations of a practitioner, the better off you'll be when it comes time to interview prospective candidates. It is important to trust your instincts. Behavioral scientists describe instinct as an unalterable tendency of an organism to make a complex and specific response to environmental stimuli without involving reason. Hey, if it has been good enough for the survival of the species, it is good enough for you to trust yourselves when it just feels right as you interview a potential member of your twin team. Conversely, some one may say all the right things in an interview but if you walk away with an uneasy feeling about the long-term survival of the alliance, keep on looking. The realities of health-insurance cost and availability, as well as geography, will play a big role in the process. The couple living in a large metropolitan area is going to have more options when it comes to choosing health care than the couple in a small town. But even an area with a limited number of doctors is likely to have access to the diagnostic capabilities available in urban medical centers. The more informed you are as a consumer of health care, the more effectively you will be able to advocate for your own pregnancy. And advocate you will!

If none of your friends or family members has experience with health-care practitioners in your community, start with a call or visit to the nursing staff in Labor and Delivery at your local hospital. Many obstetric nurses will have wonderfully informed opinions about providers in the area. Find out who they trust, who handles the greatest number of multiple pregnancies, and ask them who delivered their babies. These are dedicated professionals who are under no obligation to promote anyone's practice. The people who specialize in this area of nursing are concerned only with your health and the health of your unborn babies.

Finally, as you consider all the factors that go into choosing your practitioner, you need to make inquiries into the kind of practice in which they participate. The most common scenarios are as follows:

• **The Group Practice**

It is not unusual to find a practice comprised of four obstetricians who will divide their patients equally. This equates to your having a 25 percent chance of seeing any one of them for an appointment, emergency, or delivery of your babies. You can inquire as to the pos-sibility of your choosing to see one of them on a consistent basis, but be very specific in your questioning and don't assume that you will be able to choose which member of the practice will be on hand to deliver your twins.

• Shared Office Space

You may find a four-person obstetric practice where they share office space as well as nursing and clerical help, but where each has a specific list of patients and under most circumstances you will see them exclusively throughout your pregnancy. Again, it is important to ask about their commitment to delivering your babies, but in this type of practice each tries to deliver their own patients except in the case of an unexpected emergency.

• Private Practice

As health care in our country continues to change, the number of private practices is diminishing. But you can still find practitioners who work without benefit of partners or office mates. If you have done your homework and know that this is the practitioner for you, you have the advantage of knowing that, barring an emergency, this will be your exclusive provider from your first visit through your labor and delivery. Of course, if unforeseen circumstances prevent your practitioner from being available to deliver your babies, you run the risk of being delivered by a physician with whom you have no prior relationship.

Your decision-making process will be informed to some to degree by your health-insurance coverage. Read your policy carefully and don't hesitate to call your insurance provider or to speak with your obstetric office about how to most effectively take advantage of its benefits.

It is also important to note that a multiple pregnancy is considered "high risk" and should (whenever possible) be treated by an obstetrician with a track record of attending to multiple births. Certainly, there are many highly skilled nurse-midwives in practice throughout the country, but they have been trained to attend to low-risk pregnancies and uncomplicated births. If you are interested in enlisting the support of a certified nurse-midwife (CNM), look for an obstetric practice that has a midwife on staff. You then have the best of both possible worlds: a member of the team with a "natural" approach to childbirth, and an obstetrician with a lot of experience handling multiple births.

The proliferation of fertility enhancement throughout the country has made twinning a much more frequent occurrence throughout the general population. As a result, even obstetricians with smaller practices are growing increasingly familiar with the particular needs of women delivering twins. If you live in a smaller town, be sure to ask your obstetrician about her experience with multiple pregnancies and find out who she consults and what diagnostic resources will be available to you if something comes up that requires additional attention.

4 TO 8 WEEKS

Twins' development at four to eight weeks.

YOUR DEVELOPING TWINS

At four weeks, what shows up on ultrasound are two little gestational sacs. (Or in some rare cases of monozygotic twinning, only one.) The amniotic sac, the fluid, and the embryo reside within but are not visible at this time. Between four and eight weeks the brain, bladder, kidneys, liver, reproductive tracts, spine, heart, and extremities are

Ultrasound image of twins at four to eight weeks.

all in development. Twins are developing at the same rate as singletons at this point. By the sixth week, we can see some evidence of a fetal pole or embryo on an ultrasound. The first time your twins are visible, they are about two to three millimeters long, less than the size of a grain of rice. By the seventh or eighth week, each is about the length of two grains of rice and cardiac activity is visible by ultra-sound.

YOUR PREGNANT BODY

One of the first and most remarkable symptoms of pregnancy, whether singleton or multiple, is a *change in appetite*. Most women experience an increase in appetite between the fourth and sixth weeks. This increase is perfectly normal and may continue throughout the pregnancy. Many women report appetite swings. For the most part, this is your body indicating its increased caloric needs. The woman carrying twins has about one and a half times the caloric need of the singleton mom, and she should listen to what her body is telling her and eat accordingly.

You may have complained of feeling tired at times before pregnancy was a consideration, but a couple of nights of uninterrupted sleep or a weekend to take it easy had you back to normal. The *fatigue* associated with pregnancy is another thing entirely. You may just feel pooped–from the moment you haul yourself out of bed to the moment you hurl yourself back in. It's true of most pregnant women, and most of them are not carrying twins. This is the body as factory–and you're manufacturing twice the product with no extra personnel. You are working to produce two, brand-new life-support systems with the ultimate goal of their being independent of you. But for now you're the only game in town, and as such you need to take extra good care of yourself. Aim for extra sleep every night, and

Your pregnant body at four to eight weeks.

maybe you'll actually get it half the time. A good diet, consistent exercise, and managing stress will help, but be prepared to slow down. Traditionally, the fourth month of pregnancy begins a second trimester res-pite from fatigue, but twin moms may not experience it as dramatically as their singleton pals.

You may also notice an *increase or decrease in saliva formation* during pregnancy. A dry mouth is most likely a sign of inadequate hydration. Pregnancy increases blood volume, as well as creating additional fluids in the breast, uterus, and virtually everywhere in your body. Again, twin pregnancy calls for more hydration than singleton pregnancy, so you must be sure to drink water throughout the day. Increased saliva seems to be related to nausea and perhaps vomiting in the first trimester of pregnancy. The saliva production remains the same, but a woman with an irritated stomach will naturally refrain from swallowing as much as she otherwise would.

Almost all pregnant women report *increased frequency of urination* in the first trimester of pregnancy. The bladder is a little sac that fills and empties at a rate that corresponds to how large and how full it is. The enlarging uterus in the pelvis of a pregnant woman is adjacent to the bladder. When there is pressure from the uterus, the bladder can only fill to a certain size before it is compressed between the back of the uterus and the front of the pelvic bone, sending you the signal that you need to urinate. So, even in the early weeks of pregnancy, the uterus begins to take up extra space and the bladder does not have its usual capacity. If you have any burning sensation or pain associated with frequent urination, or if you notice any blood in your urine, you should alert your practitioner at once. Pain in the flank or lower back, or fever associated with any of these symptoms, is also reason enough to call your practitioner so that you can be screened for the presence of a urinary tract infection (UTI). An untreated urinary tract infection can quite quickly develop into a serious infection of the kidneys. Women with undiagnosed bladder infections are at increased risk of kidney infection during pregnancy. This may be due to the fact that the urethra, while an adequate barrier to vaginal bacteria in nonpregnant women, seems to relax during pregnancy, allowing bacteria to find its way up toward the kidneys.

The pregnant woman with an undiagnosed, or asymptomatic, urinary tract infection (UTI) needs to be treated as aggressively as the patient who has symptoms. This is one of the most important reasons for taking a urine sample at each of your obstetric office visits. Ampicillin (a penicillin derivative) is a frequently prescribed antibiotic for treatment of urinary tract infections during pregnancy. Macrodantin (a non-penicillin antibiotic) is also safe during pregnancy and is used for patients with an allergy to penicillin. The broader-spectrum antibiotics such as Cephalosporin are also safely used during pregnancy. It is very important to complete your antibiotic prescription. Don't be tempted to stop when your symptoms subside. *Ciprofloxacin and all floxin derivatives are to be scrupulously avoided during pregnancy, though they are frequently used to treat UTI's in the general adult population.*

The time-honored practice of drinking lots of water is extremely helpful because the increased volume of liquid does help to flush out bacteria. And yes—cranberry juice does help! It alters the pH or acidity of the urine, making it less hospitable to bacteria.

A UTI that develops into a kidney infection is a potentially serious illness and needs to be treated aggressively with intravenous antibiotics and occasionally may require hospitalization. The most common symptoms are fever with chills and low back pain.

The well-documented nausea and vomiting known as *morning sickness* is a common occurrence in pregnancy, and seldom leads to a seriously disturbed nutritional status for the mother-to-be. We know that the feeling of morning sickness is secondary to several physiological changes that take place early in pregnancy. A pregnant woman produces increased levels of progesterone. This progesterone has the effect of decreasing the muscle tone and motility (the ability to squeeze) of the stomach. During pregnancy, the volume of the stomach increases, and that contributes further to its diminished capacity to empty completely. So the stomach works overtime, but with limited success. And in case that is not enough good news, the "morning" part of this sickness can also be a bit misleading. Nausea or vomiting can happen at any point throughout the day. However, it would appear that the symptoms of nausea are worst when your stomach is empty, such as when you first wake up in the morning.

A *heightened sense of smell* is also common in pregnancy and can unfortunately contribute to a pregnant woman's complicated appetite. Many women find that frequent small meals are the best approach to combating morning sickness. Speak with your practitioner about the value of vitamin B_6 in combating nausea. The onset of morning sickness is usually between week four and week eight of pregnancy and may persist until week fourteen or sixteen, though in twin pregnancies it can tend to go on longer. In rare cases, nausea and vomiting is so severe and extended as to pose a threat to the health of the mother and her babies. This condition, called *hyperemesis gravidarum*, is associated with weight loss, significant dehydration, and electrolyte imbalance. Your practitioner will take this very seriously and may call for hospitalization to ensure adequate intravenous fluids to restore water and electrolyte balance as well as sufficient caloric intake. Once fluid balance has been restored, steps will be taken to develop a healthy diet that the mother can tolerate and her fluids will continue to be monitored throughout her pregnancy.

Adding to the panoply of gastrointestinal delights that occur in pregnancy are *heartburn* and *indigestion*. Again, these symptoms appear to be secondary to physiological changes. The sphincter (muscular ring), where the esophagus joins the stomach, is also affected by increased progesterone and is acting with less efficiency. So, as pressure is increased on the abdomen, some of the contents of the stomach—now mixed with digestive acids—tend to push back up into the esophagus; the presence of that acid causes heartburn.

A twin pregnancy causes relatively more heartburn, and does so earlier in the pregnancy, due to additional pressure from a larger uterus. Antacids are usually very effective in controlling the symptoms of heartburn. Some have the added benefit of containing calcium, which your body needs during pregnancy. And let gravity work for you in controlling heartburn. Don't lie down after eating; stay seated or, better still, take a little stroll.

The final affront in the triple crown of gastrointestinal threats is *constipation*. Just as the motility of the stomach is compromised, so is motility throughout your entire intestinal tract. Matter is moving more slowly through the colon, and your pregnant body, ever vigilant in its nurturing of its precious cargo, is more efficiently absorbing water from your stool. As a result, the stool will tend to become hard and difficult to eliminate. Your first weapon in this battle is obvious: drink more water! Next, increase your intake of fiber-rich foods such as vegetables, fruits, whole grains, and legumes. Keep your meals small and frequent and, unless your practitioner advises against it at this time, develop a safe, consistent exercise plan.

Moving on to your respiratory system, the first symptoms you are likely to notice are *stuffiness* or *nosebleeds*. Both these symptoms are very common in pregnancy and have a lot to do with the fact that every mucous membrane in your body is experiencing an increased supply of blood. This makes the mucous membranes in the nose become a bit swollen and secrete additional mucus. Many women may self-diagnose colds or allergies during their pregnancies that were, in fact, the pregnancy-induced swelling of their mucous membranes. It is important to avoid nasal inhalers to alleviate these symptoms, as they can alter the function of the tissues lining your nose if used on a long-term basis. Steam inhalers are a safe and soothing alternative treatment. A bloody nose may be the result of increased blood supply to the tiny capillaries in the nasal passage—but frequent bloody noses, yellowish discharge from the nose, or fever associated with either event should be brought to the attention of your practitioner.

It is not unusual for pregnant women to describe a sensation of *breathlessness* (called *dyspnea* in medical texts). It is a feeling that you cannot quite catch your breath, or that you seem to be breathing regularly and then feel the impulse to sigh deeply every so often. As many as 70 percent of pregnant women experience this in the first trimester of pregnancy, and it is most frequently attributed to a change

DR. AGNEW COMMENTS ON LISTENING TO YOUR BODY

"You should never ignore a substantial level of pain in the chest. If it is severe and unrelenting, you may have a hiatal hernia, a condition that occurs when the sphincter located at the base of the esophagus fails to function at all. Under this circumstance, your practitioner will want you to be evaluated by a gastroenterologist."

in the capacity of the rib cage. A pregnant woman has an increase in the size of her rib cage, with the result that she increases the amount of air moving in and out of her chest. It follows that you have to use more effort to completely fill your lungs. In a twin pregnancy the uterus takes up substantially more space during the second and third trimesters, so this symptom is more pronounced than in the singleton pregnancy. By the last weeks of a twin pregnancy, shortness of breath is further exacerbated by the simple mechanics of the large uterus pushing on the diaphragm. Certainly, this contributes to discomfort in the final weeks before delivery, and breathlessness accompanied by a cough or wheezing should be reported to your practitioner immediately.

It is perfectly normal for a pregnant woman to experience an *increased heart rate* and the sensation of feeling her pulse that she was not aware of detecting before. This is due to the combined effects of increased blood volume and decreased blood pressure. Your blood volume will increase by 50 percent during your pregnancy and many of the hormones of pregnancy have the effect of lowering your blood pressure. As a result, your heart has to increase its rate to maintain blood pressure.

Breast tenderness is frequently an early symptom of pregnancy. It is interesting to note that feelings of soreness or tenderness of the breasts seem to diminish in subsequent pregnancies. But if this is your first pregnancy, especially with twins, you are likely to experience considerable tenderness along with associated swelling, particularly in the first trimester. A woman's breasts may increase by as much as three cup sizes before she delivers. It is not unusual, especially for fair-skin women, to notice a new prominence to the veins in her breast. This too is normal and is attributable to increased blood volume. Your nipples and the areola (the pigmented area surrounding the nipples) may show increased pigmentation during pregnancy. These changes are completely normal as long as the rest of the breasts' skin coloration is also normal and the tenderness is uniform over the whole breast. However, if you should find a localized area of swelling, like a small nodule anywhere in the breast, bring that to the immediate attention of your practitioner. Some women report a *leakage of clear fluid from the nipple* during pregnancy. That is probably an early discharge and is no cause for alarm. If, however, there is ever blood or opaque liquid passed from the nipple, your practitioner will want to know about that.

It is very important to adequately support your breasts during pregnancy. Avoid underwire bras and choose bras with substantial straps across your back as well as over your shoulders. You don't have to make a special trip to a maternity store to find bras that are designed to accommodate your breasts during pregnancy. Most department, and even discount, stores carry reasonably priced pregnancy bras, some of which can be converted to use as nursing bras when the time comes. Sports bras are terrific at holding your breasts in a careful but nonbinding way. But, as your pregnancy advances, you may find these bras too confining.

THE CHECKUP

DISCUSSING YOUR PREGNANCY

Unless you are seeing a practitioner with whom you have a long established relationship, you are still in the early stages of establishing your relationship. Don't make assumptions about what may or may not be an important factor in your pregnancy. Ask about anything that you think might be important:

- How frequently will your practitioner wish to see you throughout your pregnancy?

- What is the procedure for handling your telephone calls?

- Who would you expect to see if your practitioner is unavailable?

- How soon can you expect your telephone calls to be answered?

- Is there a protocol for distinguishing between questions that might need an answer between visits and a genuine obstetric emergency?

- What constitutes an emergency, and how are you to handle it?

- Describe the nature of your employment, including stress, physical activity, and environmental factors that might be important to your pregnancy.

- Mention any travel plans you have and discuss your practitioner's attitudes toward travel during your pregnancy.

- What sort of exercise plan is appropriate for you?

- Discuss your diet and ask your practitioner about vitamin supplements if you plan to take them.

THE PHYSICAL EXAM

At this point, your physical exam will first entail evaluating your blood pressure and the rest of your vital signs. Your practitioner will be very interested in gauging your blood pressure throughout the course of your pregnancy, with special attention paid to women who appear to be at risk of hypertension, a condition we'll discuss in greater detail later in this book. There will be discussion as the exam progresses: Are you tired? Any unusual things going on in your family or at work? You are on far more intimate terms with your own body than your practitioner is, so offer any insights you can about your symptoms and concerns.

The physical exam will go on to assess heart, lungs, breasts, abdomen, extremities, skin, and a complete pelvic exam. The pelvic will include palpation of the cervix, uterus, and ovaries, and also a pap smear if it was not done at your diagnostic exam. Any vaginal cultures that we've described in chapter three that were not taken at the time of your diagnosis will be taken now. You will be asked to give a urine sample to measure glucose, protein, and screen for any evidence of a urinary tract infection.

TRANSITIONS

The undeniable excitement of knowing that you are pregnant with twins is tempered by some sobering realities, not the least of which is the possibility of miscarriage. In the general population of women of childbearing age, there are some who are identified as being at greater risk of miscarriage:

- women with multiple pregnancies
- women with a history of miscarriage
- women with uterine abnormalities such as double uterus, heart-shaped uterus, or uterine septum

While no one wants to unnecessarily alarm you, your practitioner will most likely discuss the most common symptoms of miscarriage in one of your early office visits:

- **Bleeding**

  Many women experience spotty bleeding during the first few months of pregnancy without any ill effect. However, it can be a symptom of miscarriage and should be taken seriously. Even a small amount of bleeding should be brought to the attention of your practitioner, particularly if it continues for several days. Bleeding at the level of your menstrual period—enough to warrant use of a sanitary napkin—warrants immediate attention.

- **Cramping and Pain**

  The sensation of menstrual type cramping or pain—whether mild or severe—may be associated with miscarriage.

- **Fever**

  If you have a fever associated with any of the symptoms already listed, this should also be considered a possible sign of miscarriage. If you have chills or feel feverish, take your temperature.

- **Passing of Grayish or Pink Tissue, or Blood Clots**

    The presence of these materials may mean you have begun to miscarry. If possible, try to save the matter for analysis as it may be products of conception.

If you experience any of these symptoms call your practitioner right away. If you reach an answering service, follow the instructions for how to proceed in the event of a medical emergency.

If you have these symptoms, and are advised to come into the office or to go to the hospital, this is what you can expect to happen:

- Your vital signs, including pulse and blood pressure, will be assessed.

- There will a physical examination of your uterus and an abdominal exam to check for any other abdominal mass.

- A pelvic exam will check for any evidence of tissue or blood clots.

- Your cervix will be evaluated to determine if it is open and if there appears to have been a miscarriage, or if the cervix is, in fact, closed.

- Your practitioner may schedule an ultrasound exam.

At this point, depending on the findings, there are several options to consider. Your practitioner may want to confirm rising hormone levels. If the ultrasound shows evidence of a blood clot in the uterus, that does not necessarily mean a miscarriage will ensue. But decreased activity and some degree of bed rest are likely to be advised. A follow-up ultrasound will be ordered to make sure that the blood clot is continuing to shrink. Some practitioners will recommend the use of a progesterone supplement to a patient who is threatening to miscarry. There is an ongoing dialogue in the obstetric community about this practice because of continued controversy about its effectiveness.

If the embryo or fetus is the right size for how far along you are in your pregnancy and the bleeding is what doctors call "acute and finite"–meaning you don't continue to spot for months afterwards–then you and your practitioner can be very optimistic about your pregnancy continuing. Miscarriage of a twin may put you at higher risk for preterm labor, but there are two very important factors to remember when you hear that news:

- Preterm labor can frequently be identified and managed with good results.

- The miscarriage of one fetus does not seem to have negative implications regarding the health or genetic integrity of the surviving fetus. In fact, there is evidence that its survival probably denotes a healthy fetus with a high likelihood of continued survival.

Many professionals in the obstetric community would agree that, given the opportunity to evaluate the pregnancy material from one hundred women who had miscarried, more than fifty of those tissue samples would be found to have some sort of defect–either a genetic or chromosomal abnormality, some structural problem, or an anomaly of the placenta. Few people find that an easy statistic to absorb. It makes sense that we would struggle with this eccentricity of nature. Why, in the grand scheme of things, would nature permit a pregnancy to require all this effort, and then not allow it to thrive? It seems oddly uneconomical for an evolutionary process that we think of as being so discreet and energy-efficient. Perhaps it is nature's way of nipping a problem in the bud. So even while you grieve over the loss of one life, a couple should be encouraged about the probability of carrying their second fetus successfully and delivering a healthy baby.

Exercise for Mom-to-Be

Exercise is beneficial to everyone. Our bodies function best when they are regularly exercised. Pregnancy need not be a time when exercise is to be avoided–but it is not the time begin a new sport. Learning a new sport can be challenging, even for skilled athletes. Your center of gravity is different when you're pregnant and you might injure yourself. If you are a swimmer, continue swimming. If you are involved in aerobics classes or dancing, look to tailor your program to your pregnancy.

The most important aspect of responsible exercising in pregnancy is not to get too hot. This stands from the first week of pregnancy to a week before you deliver. Our bodies dissipate heat fairly well through sweating, but it is possible to exercise to the point that you increase your body temperature. Your twins want to be in a 98.6-degree environment, so overheating your body is not in the best interest of the developing embryo or fetus. Be sure to stay adequately hydrated during exercise.

Your heart rate during exercise is another important consideration. If, for example, you are a highly trained athlete, it is important to decrease your maximum heart rate during exercise by 30 percent. The best exercises during pregnancy provide all the benefits of calorie use, increased blood supply to the skin, and increased heart rate but don't allow the body to overheat. That is why swimming is such a superb form of exercise for the pregnant woman. The length of time you might swim is proportional to what you are accustomed to: If you swim a mile each day, you might want to decrease that by one-third. If you are used to swimming a few laps each day, say for twenty minutes, it is safe to continue doing so.

The woman who is not used to exercise and determines that she wants to discover the benefits of exercise during her pregnancy has a wonderful opportunity to begin to take daily walks. Walking for fifteen to twenty minutes each day is of benefit to mother and babies. With guidance from your practitioner, you may want to develop a modest fitness program that will be a consistent part of your life even after the twins are born.

When developing a program of exercise, it is important to exercise to the point of benefit, but decrease any likelihood of injury. The pregnancy hormone progesterone has the effect of relaxing ligaments across every joint in your body. The benefit in pregnancy is that this helps the pelvis to be less rigid, allowing the process of birth to move forward with less resistance. The negative aspect is that pregnancy can predispose you to spraining an ankle or knee. You are more likely to injure yourself participating in exercise that requires sudden changes in direction, with tennis being the classic example. Even the trained athlete is wise to avoid tennis during pregnancy.

Any high-impact sport, such as running, is to be avoided, particularly after the twentieth week. There are so many forms of exercise, such as a Stairmaster, swimming, or low-impact aerobics, to provide the benefit without the pounding. Any exercise that offers the possibility of impact to the abdomen should be avoided during pregnancy. This includes snow skiing after the first trimester, horseback riding, basketball, scuba diving, or ice skating after the first trimester.

Exercises for Pregnant Women

These are a few examples of simple exercises that can be performed at home and are useful for toning muscles.

Always speak with your practitioner regarding the benefits or possible drawbacks of any particular exercise before beginning an exercise program. Remember to dress comfortably, drink plenty of water, and avoid becoming fatigued or overheated.

Modified Abdominal Crunch

Begin from seated upright position with feet slightly apart and back supported by pillows. With hands grasping lower thighs behind knees, tighten abdominal muscles and slowly lean back into supporting pillows. Continuing to use abdominal muscles, raise torso back to upright position. Repeat ten times.

Pelvic Tilt

On a padded surface (a carpet or exercise mat) carefully position yourself on hands and knees with arms and upper legs parallel to floor. Knees should be spaced slightly apart, and back should be straight. Tighten abdominal muscles and raise spine into curled "cat" position as the pelvis tilts downward. Repeat twenty times.

Incline Press

Using light weights (less than five pounds), lie down with back well supported at a 45° angle. Knees should be bent, with feet flat and shoulder-width apart. Press weights toward the midline–above the head–and then lower arms. Repeat ten times.

This exercise may not be suitable after the fourth month of pregnancy due to discomfort from lying on your back.

Abdominal Crunch

Lie down with back well supported by at least two pillows. Knees should be bent and feet flat on the ground and shoulder-width apart. Clasp hands behind head and tighten abdominal muscles as you raise your head, tucking chin in to touch chest. Repeat ten times.

This exercise is best done in the first few months of pregnancy as you may experience discomfort lying on your back in later months.

Biceps Curls

Using light weights (less than 5 pounds) sit upright with feet flat on ground. Raise weights from extended to flexed position. Repeat ten times.

Triceps Exercise

Using a straight-back chair for support, place right arm on chair for stability and lower head until resting lightly on right hand. Right leg should be positioned one long stride ahead of left. Holding a light weight (less than five pounds) in left hand and keeping right shoulder and right knee aligned, raise weight until upper arm is parallel to floor. Repeat five times on each side.

Chapter 5

8 TO 12 WEEKS

Twins' development at eight to twelve weeks.

YOUR DEVELOPING TWINS

From eight to twelve weeks, the last month of the embryonic period, your twins still have a remarkable amount of development ongoing within the kidneys, intestines, and extremities. At eight weeks they are about four centimeters long and by twelve weeks they will have more than doubled to be about nine centimeters long. Each weighs about one gram at eight weeks, but will have grown to twenty grams by the twelfth week. By the end of twelve, remarkable weeks, the embryological structure is completed.

Ultrasound image of twins at eight to twelve weeks.

YOUR PREGNANT BODY

You may continue to notice *changes in your appetite* that make all those pickles and ice cream jokes we've all heard seem to make a little more sense. A patient pregnant with twins who had been experiencing acute morning sickness since her pregnancy began woke up one morning during her twelfth week and announced to her husband that she felt great, but was starving . . . for a nice big bowl of spinach and a glass of root beer! Just like that—weeks of nausea became a thing of the past and she had entered the wonderful world of *food cravings*. Food cravings are probably your body's intuitive attempt to obtain some substance it is deficient in. It is a good bet that a woman craving spinach is hungry for the iron it will supply. As for the root beer, maybe it was the sugar, or maybe she just liked root beer.

Mild anemia is not uncommon during any pregnancy. The woman pregnant with twins is certainly at increased risk of anemia since her blood volume is way up while her red-cell production is down. Don't be surprised if, along with the spinach salad, you find yourself ordering up a steak or some other iron-rich food.

Change in sexual desire is a variable response to pregnancy. More women than not report a decrease in libido during the first trimester, and that may be a secondary response to nausea, breast discomfort, and the increased pressure on the bladder at this time. But once the first trimester passes, that may all change. If you were to survey one hundred women it would be reasonable to find a third for whom desire is increased, a third for whom it has diminished, and a third with no noticeable change. Many practitioners report great concern from their patient's husbands about causing their wives discomfort or "hurting the babies" during sex. Men should be reassured that sex is perfectly safe during a twin or any pregnancy. Time of day may play a role in a woman's desire, and there may be a need for increased lubrication

Your pregnant body at eight to twelve weeks.

because of the tendency for pregnant women to be somewhat dehydrated. Sexual activity should be guided by both partner's comfort. This is a time to really communicate and get creative.

Changes to the complexion during pregnancy can be very obvious. The *glow of pregnancy* is a very real phenomenon. This time, that increase in blood volume has a lovely cosmetic payoff. Additional blood pumped nearer the surface of the skin creates a real look of radiance. Pay attention to caring for your skin. Pregnant women are *more sensitive to sunburn*, so do apply a moisturizing sunscreen to your face each morning, and use common sense along with a sunscreen when exposed to the sun at the beach, pool, or during any recreational time. This increased blood flow to the skin is likely to make you particularly sensitive to skin products, so go with what has worked for you in the past. This is not the time to try a new line of skin-care products or makeup.

All pregnant women have an increase in their blood volume during pregnancy and some *swelling of the gums* is a natural consequence of the increased volume of blood. *Bleeding gums*, particularly after a trip to the dentist for a cleaning, should not alarm you. Be extra gentle when brushing and flossing your teeth.

Stretch marks are a natural and sometimes unavoidable consequence of skin that is doing its job to capacity. They are simply the telltale evidence of the collagen in your skin separating as your uterus expands or as your breasts enlarge. Good lifelong nutrition may be a factor in limiting a tendency toward stretch marks. We also know that the more pigment in your skin, the less obvious your stretch marks will be. It is best to develop an accepting philosophy toward stretch marks because while they will fade, sometimes becoming barely noticeable after pregnancy, no amount of oil, vitamin-E cream, massage, or exotic lotion is going to make them disappear.

SYMPTOMS THAT MAY BE ONGOING

breast tenderness
breathlessness
constipation

fatigue

frequent urination

increase or decrease in saliva

increased heart rate

leakage from nipples

morning sickness

nasal stuffiness

THE CHECKUP

DISCUSSING YOUR PREGNANCY

If you have any questions that you forgot to ask at your last checkup, or that have come up in the interim, now is a perfect time to bring them up. Your successful participation in this partnership depends upon your being well-informed every step of the way. We are used to hearing a twin pregnancy described as "high risk," but much of the time twin pregnancies are almost more about a high level of alertness and involvement. Practitioners nationwide concur that consistent participation from husbands who join their wives at most, if not all, office visits seems to have a wonderfully bonding effect on couples who are about to become the parents of twins. A twin pregnancy can be a very humbling experience to the husband or wife who is a take charge kind of person. Suddenly, there are two tiny beings whose needs take precedence over pretty much everything else, and the couple who thought they had it all figured out may find themselves back at square one.

This is the time to review with your practitioner your family's genetic history, include inherited disorders such as:

- hemophilia
- muscular dystrophy
- cystic fibrosis
- sickle-cell anemia
- Tay-Sachs/Gaucher's disease

- Huntington's chorea
- thalassemia
- other devastating genetic illnesses

These are known inheritable disorders that you might choose to investigate if they are known to be a part of your family history. In the absence of any history, they are unlikely to affect your twins or any other pregnancy you may have in the future. There is one very important question expectant parents must ask themselves about screening for genetic defects in their twins: Is this information that they care to know about their pregnancy? It is important to recognize that the question is not only about whether or not you would terminate the pregnancy based on the results. Some couples are certain from the outset that termination of a pregnancy is not an option they are willing to consider. Nevertheless, they feel that screening information will help them to be better prepared psychologically, mentally, and practically for the birth of their babies. Others make the considered decision that screening information is nothing that they will find useful in preparing for the birth of their children. Couples, and indeed individuals within each couple, have very personal responses to results that indicate the likelihood of a genetic disorder. This is a very private decision and is not to be made by your practitioner, health-insurance company, or anyone else but you.

THE PHYSICAL EXAM

- assessment of weight gain
- check blood pressure, pulse, and respiratory rate
- check heart and lungs
- breast exam
- external palpation of the uterus
- measure height of fundus
- check for fetal heartbeats
- urine screens for blood, sugar, and bacteria
- ultrasound assessment

An appointment for chorionic villus sampling (CVS) can be arranged at this checkup. CVS is a screening procedure used to detect fetal genetic abnormalities including chromosome disorders such as Down's syndrome, and single-gene defects such as sickle-cell anemia. This screening is offered earlier than amniocentesis, which we'll discuss in a later chapter. It is accomplished by inserting a catheter through the cervix (or rarely, through the abdominal wall) and into the placenta between the lining of the uterus and the chorion (which is destined to become the fetal side of the placenta).

A sample of the villi (the tiny projections lining the chorion) are retrieved, and cultured at the laboratory; the sample is considered a reliable source in evaluating the chromosomes of the fetus. The test is repeated for each fetus. In the case of a single placenta you cannot assume the results are accurate for both fetuses. If there are separate gestational sacs, amniocentesis can be performed on both sacs to provide more definitive results. The procedure is frequently done in the tenth to eleventh week of pregnancy and the results are usually available in less than seven days. The risk of miscarriage from CVS is thought to be about one in 100, whereas the risk of miscarriage from amniocentesis appears to be between one in 200 or 300.

TRANSITIONS

Don't Be a Heroine

One of the first things you will need to think about is decreasing your expectations of yourself. Forget about your coworker who came into the office until the day her water broke, took two months off (but continued to work at home), and returned to post third-quarter sales that were higher than anyone else's. That is not going to be you. Get in the habit of delegating more and more physical activity to other people who really *will* be eager to help. Your fatigue from being pregnant with twins may very well be twice that of the singleton mom, especially in the first and last trimesters of your pregnancy. There is a certain simple logic to a twin pregnancy. You're going to have two

Chorionic villus sampling.

babies. It follows that you're going to need to eat more, rest more, gain more weight, and spend more money. But with proper care, and a medical team you're confident in, you shouldn't really have to worry more. Your practitioner has most likely "been there, done that" when it comes to guiding couples through multiple pregnancies. Take advantage of all that wonderful experience. Be sure to talk with you practitioner about the term "high risk." Yes, it is true that multiple pregnancy has a greater risk of developing complications, but overall, women pregnant with twins deliver healthy, beautiful babies. They may deliver a few weeks earlier than their singleton pals, but the odds are in their favor that they will be fine. Ask questions; communicate with your practitioner.

The impact of ultrasound technology on twin pregnancy is considerable. You will have the extraordinary opportunity to look at two little people and watch their two little hearts beat as you carry them until their delivery. That relatively new privilege of actually *seeing* the babies seems to have the effect of making the notion of twin birth very real and very vital. Many twin moms who have struggled with symptoms of preterm labor say that the opportunity to see the irrefutable evidence of two babies gave them the strength they needed to move ever closer to a term delivery.

It is not too early to start talking to each other about practical matters:

- Can you cut down on your work load or stop working if necessary?

- What are the financial implications of cutting back on your work time?

- Before one of you drops your insurance coverage to cut down on expenses, are you really sure that is a wise idea?

- Is there someone in your extended family who would be just the right person to help out for the first few months?

You'll generate your own list once you start talking, but even though your babies are just a little bulge in your belly right now, twin pregnancy has a way of catching people by surprise. Start planning early!

Making It Work for the Whole Family

If you were to speak with teachers of elementary-school age children about what factors outside the classroom seem to have an impact on students' attitudes and behavior in the classroom, the impending birth and the appearance of a sibling would be right up there in the top five. We will discuss this at some length in the second half of this book, but it warrants some attention well before your twins are born.

The way you'll discuss the impending birth of your twins will have much to do with the age of your children at home. For the toddler, an announcement that there are going to be two new babies, especially before there is any visual evidence of their arrival–is likely to be confusing. To tell a two-year-old in January that the babies will come when it is summertime, or when it is hot outside, or when he gets to go in the pool is not meaningful. Your two-year-old will not understand "next month" or "next year." They are just beginning to comprehend, "Snack time is right after *Sesame Street*." What they will understand is that the mommy who was taking them to the park every afternoon, playing chase, and tumbling around on the living room floor is not as available for those activities. You can tell them you just know you'll feel more energetic after your first trimester ends, but we all know that won't mean a thing to a pouting two-year-old. This is the time to call upon the resources you've developed or to begin to look for people to help out. The mothers in your play group may be happy to scoop up your daughter for an outing while you get off your feet for a couple of hours. Your usual family outing to the park on Saturday can be just the father and kids while you sleep in. The fact that you can manage to drag yourself out to the birthday party or that you usually make Thanksgiving dinner for twenty-five doesn't mean you should be doing it when your body is working so hard to accommodate your rapidly developing twins.

Your children from ages four through nine are going to be more tuned in to changes in your body and are better equipped to begin to deal with the time element involved in your pregnancy. They, too, would benefit by having some extra support as far as managing their play and recreational time. But if you are just not up to taking your seven-year-old Rollerblading, look for a less physically taxing alternative. How would he like to make his own Play-Doh, or help you to make dinner, or illustrate a book for Grandma's birthday? Your own sense of guilt at not performing up to speed can be your worst enemy. As you ponder the impact these two new babies will have on the lives of your other children, you are particularly vulnerable. Many mothers say they feel pressured to work doubly hard to make certain their other children don't feel displaced by the birth of the twins. The management of your time and limited energy are important reality checks, and can set the standard for how you choose to cope with many of the difficult decisions that will arise after your twins are born.

Once children hit the double digits, their social lives can be vitally important to them. They are more likely to be concerned with your availability as a chauffeur than your skill at in-line skating. But don't be fooled by a seemingly laissez-faire attitude about the impending births. Your teenagers also have a range of issues to deal with. One mom of twins said of her fourteen-year-old son, "He was so mortified by the very obvious evidence that my husband and I were doing it that the double consequence of our actions assumed a secondary role. He was actually very relieved, and became super active as a big brother, after they were born." Encourage your older children to talk to you about what they may be thinking. Putting aside the bluster and independence that are completely appropriate to the teenage years, your children still need to know that you continue to see them as being vital participants in the life of the family. Their needs may have changed, but you are as much their parents as you've always been.

ROUNDTABLE TALK

PRESENT AT THE DISCUSSION ARE:

Dr. Connie Agnew
Jill Ganon
Tom & Sarah
Nick & Laura
Joan & David
Robert & Grace
Kate & Matt

TOPICS FOR DISCUSSION ARE:

Choosing a Doctor
Dad's Reaction

JILL: Let's talk about choosing your doctors.

LAURA: I was moving from Pasadena over to the West Side and asked my gynecologist to recommend somebody. I wasn't pregnant; in fact I was just married, but I got pregnant pretty soon. So it turned out that for my very first visit with this new doctor, I was pregnant. He asked me to come back in ten days so he could tell me how far along I was. He did a second ultrasound and said, "It looks like there's two in there." I said, "Two what?" It's a good thing I was lying down. I think you really need to start researching right away what questions to ask. When you are pregnant with twins they ask you to do a lot of tests and it doesn't matter if you're twenty-five or fifty. And you need to do a lot of reading and generate questions because if you're informed you have more of a say in your own care.

JOAN: Our first big decision came when I had to choose a different obstetrician [OB] because the doctor I'd always seen for checkups had just decided not to deliver babies anymore. And I also had some pre-existing medical conditions that we knew would make my pregnancy and delivery high risk. So we had to find a doctor who was affiliated with a hospital that had the right level of intensive care unit [ICU] for the babies. We ended up going with a doctor who came highly recommended for his capabilities in dealing with high risk. That was at Cedars Sinai [in Los Angeles], a definite commute from our home in Ventura County. But our local hospital would not have been able to deal with potential complications either in my pregnancy or the babies' birth.

DR. AGNEW: You were fortunate to have that opportunity because in many rural or suburban areas it might not be an option. When I have patients who are moving to a new area I usually tell them to call the Labor/Delivery Unit of the local hospital and ask the nurses who they use. That seems to work out well. Generally, if there was a twin pregnancy and everything seemed to be going well from the obstetrician's point of view, everyone may sort of cross their fingers and hope their local hospital can handle things . . . and usually, nature does it just right and things are fine. Twins do have a tendency to come early but under lots of circumstances it is not early enough to cause a significant problem. Sometimes if the OB has a concern, she'll call in a consultant . . . or maybe send the patient to an urban center for a diagnostic ultrasound. Here in Los Angeles we have the luxury of being close to many

Level III Nurseries. But the truth is that, while you hope it isn't neces-sary, many smaller hospitals have excellent emergency medical air transport.

TOM: Our situation as regards choosing a pediatrician was kind of crazy since Sarah gave birth [to triplets, one of whom did not survive] at one hospital and when it was time to really decide about a doctor for the babies we found that the doctor we wanted had no affiliation there. By the time we committed to him, it felt a little crazy because he had a very different approach than what we'd grown used to even in those first weeks. We started to have second thoughts because we were pretty green and felt concerned that no two doctors seemed to have the same approach. Our kids were born at twenty-eight weeks and were in the hospital for several months. There were a lot of complications. . . . We felt very much at the mercy of whatever we were told. Pretty soon, we realized that the truth was that there were frequently several ways to achieve the same result and just because two doctors don't have the same approach, doesn't mean that one of them is wrong. But it wasn't easy.

JILL: I have a question for the dads. Can you talk a little about your reac-tion to the news that you were having twins?

NICK: Laura called me at work. I work in television and I was in a screen-ing room with a number of colleagues. I was stunned. I said, "I have twins." Everybody thought I was talking about some idea for a sitcom or something. But as it sunk in I got really excited.

TOM: When I found out we were pregnant with three, Sarah says my face just drained of all color. We had an idea that it was possible. . . . Five weeks after confirmation of the pregnancy we had an ultrasound and there they were—three heartbeats. It was just incredible. I tried to imag-ine how you'd love three babies. It seemed so overwhelming. After we lost one I still loved him and it seems odd that I ever thought there was a question.

SARAH: But I was thrilled right away. I knew I wanted all three. I really didn't even want to consider having a reduction [a procedure to reduce the number of fetuses] so we decided to take our chances.

MATT: I thought it was great, especially with Kate being a twin. We had kind of put off having children, and now we were having two. I figured, you're already getting up in the middle of the night anyway. . . . And now we are at a time in our lives when we can afford it. We both knew we wanted to work and that good help would be very expensive. . . . O.K., incredibly overpriced.

DAVID: I found out by walking into the doctor's consultation room and Joan was just sort of sitting there. . . . The doctor walked in after me and said, "Have you told him?" I knew she was pregnant, so what else was there to know? I was shocked because for so long we were not going to have children, and suddenly we were having twins. Neither of us had twins in the family. At our first ultrasound they showed up as little, black dots and the doctor said, "One of these may disappear, but it looks like you have twins now." My shock wore off and I got really excited and didn't want that second dot to disappear. After they were born I'd walk around the hospital and I felt kind of sorry for the couples with only one baby.

NICK: I think our reaction mirrors that. But then there are those times that you wish you could give all your attention to one of them. But I kind of figure they'll balance things out and they will have a lot of things that singletons won't experience. I think they'll be really good at sharing.

Chapter 6

12 TO 16 WEEKS

Twins' development at twelve to sixteen weeks.

YOUR DEVELOPING TWINS

At twelve weeks, each embryo is now considered a fetus. The average weight for the fetus at twelve weeks is about twenty grams. By the beginning of the thirteenth week, each of your twins is perhaps an inch-and-a-half long and appears like the familiar tadpole image we have grown accustomed to seeing. Their embryological structural devel-

Ultrasound image of twins at twelve to sixteen weeks (the babies heads are clearly visible in profile).

opment is pretty much complete. They don't appear to have any obvious organization of movement, but if you see them through an ultrasound, they will show reflexive motions and move around in the amniotic sac. Between twelve and sixteen weeks, the size of each fetus goes from twenty grams to 120 grams, and they will reach a length of about four inches. At sixteen weeks we can observe water in the stomach, as well as urine in the bladder. This indicates that the fetus is swallowing and the kidneys are beginning to operate. Gastrointestinal function has begun. The production of urine by the fetus contributes to the amniotic fluid, and the fetus—no longer a passive passenger—is beginning to assert some control over its environment.

YOUR PREGNANT BODY

In the majority of pregnancies, nausea has dissipated completely and the pregnant mom will enjoy a *hearty appetite*. It is not unusual for moms of twins to describe their appetites as "ravenous," and that is fine. Follow the dietary rules that you and your practitioner have discussed and enjoy knowing that you are providing for your growing babies. You may continue to crave certain foods and that, too, is fine. But discuss extreme cravings with your practitioner, who might wish to prescribe particular vitamin or mineral supplements as needed.

Vaginal discharge that is white and creamy in texture is very common and is usually a function of estrogen production. Any discharge that is a color other than white, or is associated with any symptom such as itching or burning discomfort should be brought to the immediate attention of your practitioner.

It is not too much of a stretch to imagine that a pregnant woman's need to urinate frequently during the night is

Your pregnant body at twelve to sixteen weeks.

another example of Mother Nature's droll humor–putting you in training for your new arrivals. But the end of your first trimester may provide a *decrease in your frequency of urination*. You still may not sleep through the night, but you won't need to stop several times on the hour-long drive to your in-laws' house.

In addition to waking less, there may be other sleep changes. Some women report *increased dreaming*, and more vividness to their dreams. *Restlessness* is the predictable result of a woman who is learning to find comfortable positions for her changing body.

There is an increased likelihood of *constipation*. Adequate exercise and hydration, along with fiber in the diet, are very important now. Your practitioner may recommend a fiber supplement. At least one bowel movement a day is optimum.

Some women report an *increase in headaches*. There are several types of headaches, and if you experience severe and/or frequent pain you need to report it to your practitioner. It is probably wise to discuss headaches of every type with your practitioner since you should not be taking any over-the-counter pain reliever without the consent of your practitioner. Migraine headaches are particularly debilitating and there is speculation that they may be related to hormone production. Some women consistently have migraine headaches at a particular point in their menstrual cycle. A migraine headache is caused by a spasming blood vessel within the brain. It can be preceded by a condition called an aura for thirty to sixty minutes. The aura may be as mild as a slight change in vision, or it can be associated with nausea, vomiting, and neuromuscular problems such as numbness on one side of the face, tingling, or loss of sensation. Some migraine sufferers report either expressive or receptive aphasia, meaning they are unable either to articulate or comprehend what they wish to say or what is being said to them. The migraine pain itself can be localized to one side of the head or it can spread across the skull.

Among women who have had migraines prior to pregnancy, a third have them less frequently while pregnant, a third have no change, and a third have increased incidents. If you have been diagnosed and have some insight into what may cause your migraines, such as stress, overwork, or a reaction to a particular food, be vigilant about caring for yourself. There are several medications that are very effective and are safe to use during pregnancy.

By this point in your pregnancy, your waistline is something to commit to memory as *your abdomen expands* quite dramatically. This period of expansion comes early to the mom of twins. Loose, comfortable clothing will be your fashion statement for the duration of your pregnancy. Borrow your husband's shirts and maybe even his sweatpants for casual wear. The goofy, tentlike maternity clothes worn by our mothers have been relegated to museums and memory. Manufacturers of maternity wear are designing lovely, tailored, flattering clothing for every imaginable use. The price range in women's apparel is reflected in maternity clothes: You can spend a week's salary or find great outfits that are very sensibly priced. Keep in mind that as the mom of multiples, your waist is going to expand much more rapidly than that of the singleton mommy. Before you spend a fortune on a dress for your cousin's wedding, call friends and relatives to see what they might have in the closet.

It may also be time to let Victoria tell her secrets to somebody else for awhile. Maternity bras are very important to the twin mom. Though your breast tenderness may have subsided, you're already likely to have noticed a *significant increase in breast size.* Now is the time to buy the bras that will see you through your pregnancy; wide straps around shoulders and back are very important. Some maternity bras are even usable as nursing bras after the twins are born. Whether or not you are showing any sign of varicose veins in your legs, support hose can be very helpful in keeping up your energy, for walking, or for any exercise program.

Swelling of your feet over the course of a day is natural at this point in your pregnancy. The increase of weight in your abdomen has the effect of *increasing the curve of the spine.* High heels exacerbate that curve and the result is not good for the long-term health of your back. Fortunately, between the popularity of athletic shoes and increased awareness on the part of shoe manufacturers, it is possible to buy great-looking, nonbinding, low-heel shoes with adequate support.

SYMPTOMS THAT MAY BE ONGOING:

increase or decrease in saliva	nasal stuffiness
food cravings	bleeding gums
constipation	anemia
breathlessness	increased heart rate
change in sexual desire	leakage from nipples
change in appetite	glow of pregnancy
breast tenderness	fatigue
heartburn	stretch marks
sensitivity to sun	

THE CHECKUP

DISCUSSING YOUR PREGNANCY

Any unusual symptoms should be discussed at this time. Weight gain in a twin pregnancy may really take off at this point. If you have concerns about weight–whether too much or too little–bring it up with your practitioner. It is important to remember that it is never appropriate to attempt to lose weight during your pregnancy. Many practitioners encourage their patients carrying twins to pay extra attention to their exercise at this point in pregnancy. Having your abdominal muscles in good shape throughout your pregnancy will go a long way toward regaining your waistline after the twins are born. If you are not used to exercising regularly, discuss it now and work with your practitioner to develop some moderate exercise goals. Mood swings consistent with PMS are not unusual at this point. A woman pregnant with triplets told her practitioner that her mood seemed to change according to what aisle of the supermarket she was in. A walk down the baby needs aisle had her in tears, just looking at the pictures of babies on the diaper boxes. By the time she got to the pasta, she was overcome with resentment that she had to cook dinner for her in-laws that night. Dads are also likely to have questions at checkups. Any questions are better asked than wondered about.

The Physical Exam

- assessment of weight gain
- check blood pressure, pulse, and respiratory rate
- check heart and lungs
- breast exam
- external palpation of the uterus
- measure height of fundus
- check for fetal heartbeats
- urine screens for blood, sugar, and bacteria
- ultrasound assessment

Along with your standard physical exam, you may also have an ultrasound assessment of the babies at this time. A blood test for hemoglobin may be performed if there is a suspicion of anemia.

The triple marker test is a screening test that tells us if a baby may be at risk of chromosomal abnormality. It can be done as early as fifteen weeks (one week before amniocentesis is likely to be considered) and poses no danger to your babies as it only requires a mother's blood sample. It has limitations as far as its reliability, and is not a substitute for amniocentesis. But it is an inexpensive way to take a first look at women (those with no family history and/or are under thirty-five) who would not otherwise undergo genetic evaluation. The triple marker measures certain proteins in the mother's blood:

- human chorionic gonadotropin (HCG)
- estriol
- alpha-fetoprotein (AFP)

Elevated levels of AFP may indicate an increased risk for neural tube defects such as anencephaly or spina bifida. We know what normal values are for singleton, twin, or even triplet pregnancies, and many times the elevated triple marker is a practitioner's first sign of a multiple pregnancy that is perfectly healthy. A lower than anticipated AFP can alert a practitioner to increased risk for chromosomal defects such as Down's syndrome. An initial high reading can be a false positive, or it may be telling you that you are further along than you thought you were. Don't hesitate to talk with your practitioner about a follow-up session with a genetic counselor to help you understand how to assess the results you have in hand and how to proceed with additional testing if appropriate.

TRANSITIONS

Spreading the Good News

There is a moment in the life of each couple who is diagnosed with a twin pregnancy when they receive their diagnosis for the first time. Whether it comes as a complete surprise or is the confirmed result of fertility treatments, the time will come that your practitioner will tell you that you are carrying twins, or maybe even more. It is a moment you are not likely to forget, whether Mom and Dad hear it together, or Mom brings the news home to share with an unsuspecting father-to-be. These moments frequently become part of the family lore to be told again and again to delighted twins, their siblings, and happy grandparents. But it is important to consider carefully when to take that precious information and share it for the first time with anyone outside your exclusive circle of two.

For couples who have experienced the sorrow of miscarrying one or both of their unborn twins, this can be a hard-learned lesson—especially for couples who have endured months, or sometimes years, of in-vitro fertilization! The confirmation of a pregnancy seems like a victory of overwhelming proportions. They may feel almost guilty about not sharing the thrilling news with parents, siblings, or close friends who have supported them in their struggle with infertility. But those who have faced the loss of one or both of those embryos to miscarriage will tell you that making that call to tell Grandma to stop knitting, or telling a best friend that you won't be having your babies at the same time, has been terribly difficult. The pain of the loss is unavoidable. The need to relive it and even feel obliged to comfort your loved ones is compelling. There is something to be said for play-ing close to the chest when it comes to spreading the word of your joyous event. Wait until *at least* your twelfth week to share your news. Most practitioners agree that in a twin pregnancy that's more than twelve weeks, that has two normally growing embryos with nor-mal heart activity, the likelihood of either one miscarrying is less than 5 percent. Remember that the mom of twins will most likely begin to show early—so you can begin to spread the fantastic news just as the world is beginning to suspect you might have something to share!

ROUNDTABLE TALK

PRESENT AT THE DISCUSSION ARE:

Dr. Connie Agnew
Jill Ganon
Tom & Sarah
Nick & Laura
Joan & David
Robert & Grace
Kate & Matt

TOPICS FOR DISCUSSION ARE:

Parents' Ages
Traveling with the Twins

JILL: Was your age a significant factor in your decision to get pregnant?

JOAN: It was a real issue for us. I'll be forty in July. I was thirty-nine when the boys were born and I really feel that my energy level, or the lack of it sometimes, has been a factor in handling the twins. And just maintain-ing your overall health as you get older. It is almost more important than when I was in my twenties. It's not as if we'd been trying for a long time. It was a fairly recent decision, and we'd decided that if I didn't get pregnant the old-fashioned way, we would not take any other measures.

We'd been married for twelve years and I'd been a career woman for a long time. Now, as we look at our friends, they either have older kids or no kids at all. It has not been easy to develop a support system.

LAURA: I was twenty-five when the babies were born. We're lucky in that my mom is our primary baby-sitter right now and she is very understanding even when we have to go out on short notice.

NICK: But it took a little educating. At first, they would want to come and see the babies and do this or that. . . . But they saw that with two babies, we both always had a baby in our arms and it was impossible to accomplish anything unless they were both sleeping.

TOM: I'm glad we waited actually. Because I feel like I know more about myself. I wouldn't want to be twenty years old, raising twins, and not even know who I am.

JOAN: Even though the energy isn't there, I hope I have more wisdom and I think I do. I think I'm more patient with just letting them be kids than I would have been when I was younger. If I'd have had children earlier, I'd have been a little more pushy. Now I can let them learn at their own pace. I might have had more energy when I was younger but I think I'd have been worn out from my own frustration.

NICK: Laura was twenty-five when our boys were born, but she is great. People say to us, "I don't know how you do it with twins," but *I* wonder how people with triplets survive.

JILL: Dare I ask you about traveling with the twins?

MATT: I fly a lot for my business and I used to think when people brought babies on planes about when it would be my turn. We had to make a trip with the whole family and treated ourselves to first-class seats. So here we come into first class with all these people who have paid for premium seating and our guys are yelling at each other. . . . It was funny.

I thought, this is it ... this is my revenge. Right after that a couple boarded with triplets! [laughter] Our kids were six months old and they pretty much slept the whole time, and so did the triplets.

KATE: The biggest challenge is finding enough room. You really learn to pack light. My carry-on was the diaper bag. Red-eye flights are good because the babies will hopefully sleep. We each held a baby and switched off every once in a while.

MATT: You learn to book aisle seating. We were finally all seated in a row and they made us move because there are only three oxygen masks. It was ridiculous. Everyone around us offering us seats so we could sit together ...

JOAN: We discovered the same thing. This was on the trip from hell. A series of canceled flights. Our boys were screaming ... it was a two hour flight.

DAVID: When we got back, the airline lost one of the car seats. Here we are at 2 A.M. ... and we couldn't go anywhere because we didn't have a car seat. Luckily the airline loaned us this dilapidated seat. I'm sure it was unsafe—but it was a car seat. Eventually they found ours.

Chapter 7

16 TO 20 WEEKS

Twins' development at sixteen to twenty weeks.

YOUR DEVELOPING TWINS

From week sixteen to week twenty, your twins grow from sixteen to twenty-five centimeters. At twenty weeks, each of your passengers is a little, seven-and-a-half–inch person. There is an increase in movement, and it is usually in this magical month that the mother may begin to feel that movement. Now each fetus is almost solely responsi-

Ultrasound image of twins at sixteen to twenty weeks (the babies' heads are again visible in profile).

Your pregnant body at sixteen to twenty weeks.

ble for producing its own amniotic fluid. Prior to this point, the placenta had been doing most of the job. Ultrasound can now clearly detect the membrane between the two babies. It is very thin, but very resilient, as the babies can be observed kicking each other through the membrane with great regularity. It seems logical to conclude that they have knowledge of each other at this time. They cannot yet see or hear, but each fetus has the very typical appearance of a tiny baby. By eighteen weeks, their movements appear very deliberate and far more coordinated. They seem to yawn, and then move their little hands after yawning just the way they will as newborns. With much of the development complete, now is the time that everything really needs to grow. The one structure that will continue its development throughout the pregnancy is the brain. It is this continuing development of the brain that makes it so important for the mother to avoid harmful substances throughout the second and third trimesters of pregnancy.

YOUR PREGNANT BODY

There is no longer any doubt in the mind of anyone who looks at you. You are *definitely* pregnant. The singleton mom might be able to squeeze into her loosest jeans, but you have absolutely made the move to your husband's closet and maternity clothes. Your *uterus is substantially larger* to accommodate your extra passenger. The singleton mom feels the top of her uterus right at the level of her belly button, but the top of your uterus is at least two or three inches higher because you have that additional amniotic swimming pool to account for.

Congratulations! You have entered the honeymoon period of pregnancy. Nausea and vomiting are a thing of the past, your appetite is probably great, and you are likely to have more energy than you've felt in months. This is at least in part because your uterus is no longer expanding downwards toward your bladder, so you are sleeping a lot better.

The only new symptom likely to be troubling you is *round ligament pain*. It feels like a sharp pain in a very precise location on one side of your abdomen or the other. It is typically midway between the hip and belly button. It may be brought on by movement, or just appear out of the blue. It is due to the stretching of the uterus and the ligaments that support it. The pain usually resolves within a matter of minutes and requires no additional attention. However, any recurring abdominal pain should be brought to the attention of your practitioner. Unfortunately, pregnant women are not immune from appendicitis or kidney stones, so always play it safe.

SYMPTOMS THAT MAY BE ONGOING:

fatigue	nasal stuffiness
sensitivity to sun	bleeding gums
constipation	anemia
breathlessness	increased heart rate
change in sexual desire	leakage from nipples
hearty appetite	glow of pregnancy
sleep changes	abdomen larger
heartburn	headaches
swelling feet	stretch marks
vaginal discharge	decrease in urination
spine curving in response to heavier abdomen	

THE CHECKUP

DISCUSSING YOUR PREGNANCY

As always, discuss any new symptoms that you've noticed. This is the time to talk about the results of any screening tests that you have had to date. You will be discussing your ultrasound examination, and your practitioner will describe the amniocentesis if it is going to take place at this visit.

THE PHYSICAL EXAM

DR. AGNEW COMMENTS
ON "THE LITTLE
WHITE LIE"

"It is not unrealistic to suggest that at the halfway point in your pregnancy, you look to be about six months along. If you get tired of explaining this to friendly strangers in the supermarket, or even other women in your doctor's waiting room, tell them you are six months pregnant! There is no harm in a little white lie if it can save you a conversation you would rather not have for the third time in one day."

- assessment of weight gain
- check blood pressure, pulse, and respiratory rate
- check heart and lungs
- breast exam
- external palpation of the uterus
- measure height of fundus
- check for fetal heart beats
- urine screens for blood, sugar, and bacteria
- ultrasound assessment

Your practitioner may perform a pelvic exam at this visit. This is an important time to make sure that the size of your uterus is increasing as it should. If you have a history of premature delivery in other pregnancies, it is important to assess the length, size, and dilation of your cervix. This can be very important in determining if you are at risk for premature delivery of your twins.

The ultrasound exam that takes place at twenty weeks is probably the most important and visually extraordinary ultrasound of your entire pregnancy. This is the time that the anatomy of the babies can best be established. Each fetus is suspended in a relatively large amount of fluid. They are not overlapping each other as they will in later weeks. Your practitioner will locate each placenta, making sure there is sufficient amniotic fluid available to each baby. The ultrasound image offers a tremendous amount of information about the structural integrity of each twin. Since it shows the length of the cervix, it can also help to predict prematurity.

You will have already discussed many of the implications of genetic evaluation, and had time to think about how you wish to approach it. It is very important to keep in mind that nature has a remarkable record of success when it comes to pregnancy. So how do we assess when, in the absence of family history, genetic evaluation should be used? If we consider Down's syndrome, we know that it occurs with increasing frequency as mothers get older. A twenty-year-old woman has a one in 2,000 chance that her pregnancy will be complicated by a chromosomal abnormality. At thirty-five, the incidence is one in 200. By the time a woman is forty, there is a one in forty chance and that increases to one in twelve for the forty-five-year-old mother-to-be. Clearly the odds increase as a woman ages. But what do those numbers actually mean? Let's consider the thirty-five year old with the one in 200 chance: That means out of 100 women, she has a one-half percent chance of her baby having the chromosomal abnormality that would cause Down's syndrome. So the odds are 99½ percent in her favor for a healthy baby. (See appendix C, "Midtrimester Risk for Chromosome Abnormalities.")

Genetic amniocentesis is typically performed between sixteen and twenty weeks on patients for whom it is recommended due to their age (thirty-five or older), family history,

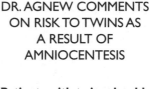

DR. AGNEW COMMENTS ON RISK TO TWINS AS A RESULT OF AMNIOCENTESIS

"Patients with twins should be reassured that the incidence of miscarriage has nothing to do with the number of times a needle is placed into the gestational sac, therefore there is no increased rate of miscarriage for a multiple amniocentesis procedure."

Amniocentesis

"In a twin pregnancy that occupies only one gestational sac (this is the rarest form of monozygotic or identical twinning), the babies have a higher-than-average risk of birth defect. These defects can range from mild to very serious.

Twins (whether they are identical or fraternal) who occupy separate sacs are at no higher risk than any singleton birth. Twins in separate gestational sacs can be at risk of a lack of concordance, or an uneven distribution of nutrition from the placenta. The structural evaluation at twenty weeks is a vital tool in making sure the babies are tracking normally as regards their size. Most of these twins are fraternal, and though one may take after the 6'4" father and the other one, the 5'2" mother, that genetic aspect of growth has not yet entered the picture and both kids should be around the same size. When I estimate the weight of the twins, I look for them to be within 20 percent of each other's weight."

or an abnormal triple marker test. The procedure is guided by an ultrasound image that locates each fetus and placenta before a thin, hollow needle is inserted through the abdomen and uterus, and amniotic fluid is withdrawn from the sac. The fetal cells floating in that fluid are cultured and chromosomal results are available within seven to fourteen days.

The risk of miscarriage from amniocentesis is less than one-half percent. Reactions to the procedure can include mild, menstrual-like cramping, and in some cases there may be a little vaginal bleeding or leaking of amniotic fluid. Report all symptoms to your practitioner.

TRANSITIONS

Now You're (At Least) Halfway There

As you cross the threshold of the first half of your pregnancy, the undeniable physical implications grow very real. Singleton parents have the luxury of time on their side, but the likelihood of a somewhat early delivery is high for you. You will find it reassuring to discuss your various birthing options with your practitioner earlier than might be necessary for the couple expecting one baby. You'll want to discuss each of the scenarios that might apply to your birth. Find out about the labor and delivery capabilities in the facility you and your practitioner anticipate will be the likely place for the birth of your babies. What if your practitioner anticipates complications? Is there a different facility that would better suit your needs? Is it possible to arrange for you to deliver there? What is the protocol if your obstetrician (OB) is not available to attend your birth? Can you arrange to meet the OB who would be attending?

This is a good time to look into prepared childbirth classes. Certainly it is not prudent for the couple expecting twins to wait for the twenty-fourth week that is frequently recommended to parents expecting a singleton birth. The number of classes in a complete program can range from four to ten. Try to schedule around the twentieth week, just in case you need to be on bed rest some weeks before you deliver.

If you find a great program, these classes are terrific for Moms, Dads, and anyone who is acting as a birth coach. Even mothers for whom the twins are not their first babies will benefit. There is always more to learn and these classes can provide their own little support groups for pregnant couples. If you have the opportunity to attend a class that provides a lot of information to parents of multiples, so much the better. Typically, whether they are Bradley, International Childbirth Education Method, Lamaze, or some other method, these classes have three basic premises:

- **Educate the Family**

  An understanding of the basic anatomy of mother and babies is a very important part of becoming comfortable with pregnancy, the mechanics of labor, and the process of delivery, whether it is vaginal or by cesarean section.

- **Offer Useful Techniques for Relaxing and Focusing**

  Relaxation techniques help a laboring woman to focus her efforts on the birthing process. Establishing a pattern of calm, direct breathing is an effective way to manage pain and have a positive impact on muscular control. The techniques learned in this class carry through to stressful situations throughout life and can provide insight into lifelong stress management.

- **Foster the Relationship Between Mother and Birth Coach**

  Whether the birth coach is your husband, another family member, or a close friend, you are entering into an agreement to share

DR. AGNEW COMMENTS
ON TRAVEL DURING
PREGNANCY

"As far as flying during pregnancy is concerned, I think it is wise to stay off airplanes after twenty weeks. There are several concerns about airplane travel. It can be stressful due to business or time constraints. The best laid plans can go awry and you can find yourself needing to haul around heavy luggage. Don't do it! Leave plenty of extra time for connecting flights and be certain that there is someone to handle your bags from beginning to end—that includes lugging them out of the trunk! Take bottled water with you, and once you're on the flight, be sure to drink plenty of it. There is no question that one gets dehydrated on a plane, most likely due to the air filtration

one of the most significant experiences either of you is likely to have. The remarkable spirit of cooperation and tolerance that develops can reveal to both partners aspects of themselves and each other that they had never before recognized. The process itself helps to decrease anxiety about the impending birth.

Speak with friends about the classes they have attended. Make a call to the local twins club for references or call Labor and Delivery at your hospital and ask for recommendations on childbirth preparation classes. Make sure the teacher is somewhat comfortable talking about aspects of twin birth, and will not find your questions a diversion from what she is used to teaching. If you don't find a class that has other multiple-birth parents currently enrolled, you may still want to take the class and save some of your questions for your practitioner or the nurses at Labor and Delivery who are specially trained to handle twin births.

If you find that two weeks into your ten-week class you are placed on bed rest, inquire about private instructors who may be available to come to your home. Many hospitals have videos that offer excellent instruction in labor, childbirth, and newborn care as well.

ROUNDTABLE DISCUSSION

PRESENT AT THE DISCUSSION ARE:

Dr. Connie Agnew
Dr. Alan Klein
Jill Ganon
Tom & Sarah
Joan & David
Robert & Grace
Kate

TOPICS FOR DISCUSSION ARE:

The Impact on the Family of Having Twins
Selective Reduction

ALAN: We haven't yet really touched on things like how and what and when you tell your extended family about your pregnancy, or relating to the babies after they are born. Many people have preconceived ideas about family. For women, these ideas may start as early as puberty. I don't really know how or when men start to really feel the import of the babies' births.

DAVID: I didn't do much visualizing about family life until it was upon me.

JOAN: When I look back on it, I think I always had a sense that children were an option for me. When we got married we talked about it but it was very noncommittal for both of us. Sort of maybe, maybe not... We were married for twelve years before the babies were born. And on a very personal note, my father was ill for nine years after cardiac arrest... very brain damaged. This was right before we married and for several years after. It was like caring for a very needy child. After he died I was not capable of caring for anyone else for some time. But after the earthquake [the Northridge, California, quake of 1994] I began to feel that life was short. I had very demanding work that I enjoyed. I'd gotten my master's degree, but something was missing. So I sort of started a time of transition.

DAVID: I didn't feel any transition time. It was sort of, wham ... I'm the father of twins. And Joan's pregnancy was pretty rough on both of us. I don't feel like I did a lot of thinking. . . .

system. On long flights, get up and walk around at least every two hours to enhance the circulation in your lower extremities. It is also a good idea to carry a copy of your medical records with you. Chances are good that you won't need them, but for the woman who has a medical emergency away from home, those records will be invaluable. Try to get the name of a practitioner wherever it is that you'll be. Just because you can't see your own doctor doesn't mean you should wait if you have any symptoms that worry you.

I tell my patients, especially those with multiple pregnancies, that after twenty weeks I don't like them to be more than sixty miles from home."

ROBERT: We tried for a long time to get pregnant. So we were very, very excited about the babies.

GRACE: We had a miscarriage a year and a half before the babies were born. We were using fertility drugs but it took us three and a half years to get pregnant again.

ROBERT: We were very cautious about telling people. It was very intense. First our amnio came back saying they were girls and then we saw penises on the ultrasound. It was terrifying, but it turned out after another amnio that it was fine . . . that we had boys. We were bursting with excitement but we kept quiet because the hardest thing we'd ever done was telling everybody after the miscarriage.

CONNIE: It must have been that your blood cells were present in overwhelming numbers in the amniotic fluid and when they were cultured, you got a false reading of females.

ROBERT: I think that's probably what did happen, and at the time our doctor did his best to calm us, but he was very thorough about explaining all the possibilities.

GRACE: He was wonderful. He answered all our questions patiently and completely. Robert always asks for the worst-case scenario, and our doctor was used to it. He couldn't have done more. Through every stage, we were just terrified. Happy, but very nervous. Robert was with me every step of the way. At every appointment . . . he had his list of questions. We'd jot things down whenever we thought of it.

ROBERT: We felt constant fear mixed with excitement. We were kind of superstitious and had a sense that multiple pregnancy carried its own set of risks. We really talked about our marriage. We did not want to lose what we had. So we kind of said, "this is what we'll do and this is how we'll handle things." But what looks good on paper is a lot of work to stick to in reality.

JOAN: I didn't say anything at work until I was starting to show. When I started to tell people I began to feel more excited. I had a great relationship with my OB and that really helped.

KATE: I don't know if Matt would agree with this [Matt missed this discussion] but we were married for twelve years before the babies and I think Matt wanted children way before I was ready. I was kind of selfish. I liked my life the way it was. I didn't want to get fat and dumpy and the whole bit . . . but it reached a point where you realize you have all this stuff. A great job, lots of freedom, and so what? It's boring. So Matt was very gung ho when we found out it was twins. And being a twin, I really wanted twins and really wanted boys and sure enough . . . two boys. And Matt also had long lists of questions.

TOM: I always wanted kids but I never dreamed about twins. We were married seven years before the babies were born though we'd started trying right away.

SARAH: I knew there was a problem so we started fertility counseling. We tried for years and years but we gave up and decided to adopt. But we ended up trying one other fertility clinic and were pregnant within a month. I am very superstitious so we didn't tell anyone until I was over three months. I was terrified we'd lose them because they were multiples.

TOM: And we were encouraged to consider reduction because we had three.

JILL: What exactly is a reduction?

CONNIE: Selective reduction is used to decrease a pregnancy number. Usually the circumstances are such that a patient has a multiple-order pregnancy and wants to reduce risk in that pregnancy. In an age where there are magnificent advances in infertility, multiples in the orders of three, four, and five are more common than they used to be. If, after counseling about the risks of prematurity, a patient desires to decrease that risk, it is thought that if one stops the heart of a fetus, depending on the stage, the remaining fetuses will be less prone to prematurity and other problems. It is clearly something that should be the patients' decision.

ALAN: There may also be an element of personal ethics here in what a physician is or is not comfortable doing.

JILL: Might a reduction go from four to two?

CONNIE: No, usually a reduction is done to accomplish either a twin or triplet pregnancy. And that is a gray area because the data shows the risk of a triplet compared to a twin pregnancy is not much greater. But sometimes the reduction is not about risk of prematurity, it is simply that the patient does not want twins. Maybe she has five kids at home. Certainly, the expanded size and other side effects of a higher-multiple pregnancy put the mother at greater risk than twin pregnancy.

TOM: What's done is done. We made the decision not to have a reduction and didn't second-guess it. Though from what we saw on the screen we thought the third one might vanish on its own. It was smaller. Intellectually at least, we know we did what we thought was right. It does come up between us, but less and less. We did it for the two who are still with us. Sometimes words aren't necessary. It's going to sound crazy but sometimes when I'm holding one or the other of the babies I see them sort of looking over my shoulder and I swear that the spirit of their brother is around.

ALAN: Do you still discuss your decision?

TOM: Even though we lost our boy, even with all the pain, there is some-thing very spiritual about it. We feel that though he was only with us for eleven days, we have all gained by having him.

Chapter 8

20 TO 24 WEEKS

Twins' development at twenty to twenty-four weeks.

YOUR DEVELOPING TWINS

By the twentieth week, each baby weighs at least one pound, and by the twenty-fourth week they'll weigh up to a pound and a half and be approximately one foot long. Your twins are continuing to grow and there is now a little bit of fat under the skin. They are developing the soft, furry growth of hair (lanugo) over their skin that we tend

Ultrasound image of twins at twenty to twenty-four weeks (the placenta and membrane are visible).

to see still covering the bodies of twins (and singletons) born prematurely. Your twins are also starting to be covered with a cheesy substance called the vernix caseosa coating that appears to be produced by the cells of the skin and helps the twins to maintain properly balanced levels of hydration. Now they are in constant contact, kicking and jostling each other for space. Amazingly, the membrane that separates them continues to exhibit great elasticity. Every joint in their little bodies is now flexed. The chin is on the chest, the elbows are tucked at the sides, and the babies' hands are frequently up at their face—like boxers with their guard up. The hips are flexed, bringing the knees up to the chest. Their feet, with ankles crossed, are frequently tucked up under their little rears. This is the classic fetal position. During their periods of wakeful activity (they won't always coincide), their extremities will extend and move around, and then they will resume their fetal positions.

YOUR PREGNANT BODY

You should be *feeling your twins moving* every day. Whether you can tell which baby is which is hard to say. Don't be overly concerned if you only feel movement on one side, because it could be that both sets of legs are stretching out in that direction.

It isn't unusual for pregnancy to cause *edema*, which is an excessive accumulation of fluid in the connective tissue of your body. This fluid retention, which is exacerbated during twin pregnancy, sometimes results in *carpel tunnel syndrome*. This is a tingling or numbness in part of the palm and fingers due to excessive compression of the ulnar, and sometimes the median, nerve within the wrist. Symptoms almost always retreat after delivery. The first course of action is to reduce the underlying edema, through rest and,

Your pregnant body at twenty to twenty-four weeks.

paradoxically, by drinking lots of water. You can also purchase carpel-tunnel wrist guards at any pharmacy and they will provide some relief. In order to decrease swelling in the hands and wrists, try to find a sleep position in which your hands are higher than your heart.

You are more and more likely to notice that you feel warmer than everyone else in the room. Your resting metabolic rate is increased during pregnancy and as a result, you may *feel overheated*. This is not a fever due to illness, it is just the sensation that you want to take off your sweater when everyone else is putting theirs on. If you are perspiring excessively, be sure to drink lots of water to replace the fluids you are losing.

Anyone who has ever been wakened from a sound sleep by a sudden *cramping in the calf of the leg* knows it can be terribly painful. Anyone, man or woman, can experience leg cramps, but the woman pregnant with twins is once again at increased risk. Your two little passengers are very greedy when it comes to getting the minerals that they need for sound nutrition. You may be suffering from a shortage of calcium. You and your practitioner should assess your diet and vitamin supplements to see if there are appropriate changes to make.

Treat the cramp by straightening your leg and flexing your ankle to put your foot at a right angle to your leg. You are likely to have awakened your sleeping husband by jerking to attention from the pain. Enlist his help in very gently stroking the long muscle of the calf. You may need to walk it off for the first hour or two of the next day.

SYMPTOMS THAT MAY BE ONGOING:

nasal stuffiness	sensitivity to sun
bleeding gums	constipation
anemia	change in sexual desire
leakage from nipples	hearty appetite
glow of pregnancy	sleep changes
abdomen larger	uterus expanding
honeymoon of pregnancy	fatigue

heartburn	headaches
swelling feet	round ligament pain
stretch marks	vaginal discharge
spine curving in response to heavier abdomen	decrease in urination

THE CHECKUP

DISCUSSING YOUR PREGNANCY

Along with discussing any new symptoms you may be experiencing, take the time to review your nutrition and describe your exercise program. Your practitioner may want to see some element of your workout to make sure that it is indeed safe for you to be doing. Make sure you describe any changes to your lifestyle: Are you starting a new job? Have you decided to stop working? Maybe you are moving out of your apartment and into a house. Talk about how much activity is right for you at this time. It is vital that you get enough rest now. You may be feeling great and tend to overdo the physical aspect of your life. Any test results that have not yet been reviewed should be discussed now. Talk at length about the movement of your babies and the areas in which you feel them move. Any unusual change in the patterns of the twins' sleep and wakefulness should be described and discussed. At this time your practitioner will also review the results of any tests you have not yet discussed.

THE PHYSICAL EXAM

- assessment of weight gain
- check blood pressure, pulse, and respiratory rate
- check heart and lungs
- breast exam
- external palpation of the uterus
- measure height of fundus
- check for fetal heart beats

- urine screens for blood, sugar, and bacteria
- ultrasound assessment

Additional elements of the physical examination will depend on whether or not you have any symptoms that require further assessment. Particular attention will be paid to any edema or swelling that is present in your extremities. The results of the ultrasound of the twentieth week will be discussed at this time.

TRANSITIONS

Preterm Labor and Early Delivery

The definition of preterm labor is delivery before thirty-seven weeks' gestation. So theoretically, many twins are delivered preterm. The majority of twins are delivered at thirty-six weeks or more and do just fine. And many twins who deliver preterm between thirty-four and thirty-six weeks are a little immature, but after several days or several weeks in the neonatal intensive care unit (NICU) they mature sufficiently to go home without any lasting deleterious effects of their early arrival. We'll discuss early delivery in much greater detail in the pediatric second section of this book. But it is an undeniable fact that twin births occur early with greater frequency than singletons. And since early birth is preceded by preterm labor, it follows that couples preparing for the birth of twins should familiarize themselves with its symptoms:

- **Obstetric History**

  If you have had preterm labor in the past, your risk of having it again is high.

- **Multiple Gestation**

  The fact that you are carrying more than one baby puts you in a higher risk category.

- **Early Symptoms of Preterm Labor**

  Any early symptoms will mean that your practitioner will watch you very closely.

- **Incompetent Cervix**

  This is a term that the medical community should banish! It means a cervix that is structurally different than most. Or it can be a cervix that is weakened as a result of a surgical procedure.

- **Vaginal Infections**

- **Placenta Previa**

  A scenario in which the placenta completely covers the cervix.

fundal placenta (the most common placement for placental implantation)

- **Placental Abruption**

  The placenta separates from the wall of the uterus, causing bleeding.

- **Polyhydramnios or Oligohydramnios**

  The presence of too much (poly) or too little (oligo) amniotic fluid.

- **Poor Growth of Either Fetus**

  A structural malformation or failure to thrive is associated with preterm labor.

- **Medical Conditions of the Mother**

  These can include hypertension, lupus SLE, long-standing diabetes (as opposed to gestational or mild diabetes)

placenta previa (the edge of the placenta covers the cervix) central placenta previa (the bulk of the placenta completely covers the cervix)

- **Inadequate Nutrition of the Mother**

- **Exposure to Alcohol, Cigarettes, or Recreational Drugs**

Having identified the things that may contribute to preterm labor, how can you tell if you're experiencing it? The medical texts tell us that preterm labor is the progressive change of cervical effacement and dilation. But these are the symptoms you are likely to recognize:

- a sense of pelvic fullness
- recurrent contractions
- vaginal discharge
- bleeding
- ruptured membranes (you'll feel a rush or a trickle of fluid from your vagina)
- cramping

The fact that you are experiencing symptoms of preterm labor does not necessarily mean you are about to have your babies. First of all, *call your practitioner no matter what time of day or night if you are concerned that you are experiencing signs of early labor.* Next, you will be evaluated as to your general health. A physical exam will be done, and uterine contraction monitoring and fetal heart rate monitoring (the non-stress test) will also be evaluated.

An ultrasound evaluation may be performed to evaluate the growth and well-being of the fetuses. A urine sample will rule out or confirm the presence of a urinary tract infection. A vaginal culture will be assessed for the presence of bacteria associated with preterm labor. After making sure that you are alright, and treating any underlying medical problems, the first line of treatment is usually to administer fluids. Women who are dehydrated have significantly more contractions and are at higher risk of preterm labor. As you receive intravenous (IV) fluid, your medical team will observe how your contraction pattern responds to rehydration. If, after several hours, there is no dilation of the cervix and contractions decrease or stop, the patient may be sent home, though the mother may be admitted to the hospital just to err on the side of caution.

If you've gone home, your activity level is likely to be drastically reduced by your practitioner. This may be the first time you hear the term "bed rest." And it means exactly that: remaining horizontal. No cleaning out the closet, no hauling out the boxes of pictures to orga-nize, no rolling a ball on the floor with your toddler. If you are directed to take bed rest, you will get instructions on how it is to be accomplished and you will probably be highly motivated to follow those instructions to the letter.

If symptoms recur, the IV fluids, monitoring, and observation begin once more. If the cervix shows progressive change and the contrac-tion pattern remains high in spite of hydration and bed rest, you are going to be admitted and there are several medications, called tocolytic drugs, that may be used:

- Magnesium sulfate delivered intravenously is considered safe during pregnancy and has the effect of relaxing the uterine muscle, thereby decreasing contractions. Unfortunately, it relaxes your other mus-cles as well, leaving you feeling kind of tired and limp. There is also a sensation of flushing and overheatedness. If this treatment is suc-cessful, some practitioners follow up with a form of oral magnesium.

- Ritodrine and terbutaline can also be used to decrease the frequency of uterine contractions. These have the effect of making a patient jit-tery, and some experience nausea. This is contraindicated for a patient with heart problems and, although it makes a woman feel peculiarly fidgety, it can be used for several hours or several weeks as needed.

- If preterm labor is threatening, a steroid called betamethasone is likely to be administered to the mother. This has the effect of enhancing the babies' pulmonary maturity. It stimulates the fetal

lungs to start producing the proteins that are critical to lung operation after birth. (We'll discuss this later in the book as we examine
fetal development.)

What is the prognosis as far as stopping preterm labor in the
mother of twins? Our success is directly proportional to how dilated
the mother's cervix is when attempts to stop labor are made:

- The woman whose cervix is more than three centimeters dilated, no
  matter the gestational age, has about a 20 percent chance of holding off
  delivery for up to forty-eight hours.

- The patient who is easily treated in less than twenty-four hours has a
  better than 50 percent chance of achieving a respite of up to several
  weeks.

- The woman whose membranes rupture early stands a 90 percent
  chance of delivering within the week.

Your Very Public Pregnancy

There is something remarkable about the way people respond to
very pregnant women: They want to touch them—and frequently they
do! Whether an unassuming young woman in the grocery store or a
high-powered executive at a board meeting, people seem to see an
invisible "please touch" sign on the protruding belly of a pregnant
woman. Complete strangers are liable to come up to you and put their
hands right on your abdomen. It is a fascinating aspect of our culture.
Think about how we tend to walk up to children, even those we
don't know, and touch their faces or stroke their hair. It is as though
the pregnant belly has broken through the usually inviolate barrier of
personal space we each carry with us. Somehow, because you are carrying a child—or in your case, two children—inside you, it is suddenly
OK to touch you, too.

Women express a whole range of reactions to this phenomenon,
everything from amusement to anger to distaste. It is perfectly appro-

priate to affect whatever attitude best works for you at this time. If you wish to insulate yourself from unwanted attention, a well-timed remark can do wonders. If another person's fascination with your condition does not feel like a burden, then by all means, let them experience the thrill of touching your belly–maybe even getting to feel the babies move.

Unfortunately, this interest in your pregnancy, particularly a twin pregnancy, can bring every weird tale of pregnancy, childbirth, and misinformation out of the woodwork. It is difficult to comprehend why someone would feel the need to burden you with the usually exaggerated and frequently inaccurate saga of her hairdresser's sister's niece who endured some horrifying ordeal giving birth to her babies (twenty years ago). Again, this is the time to excuse yourself, thank her for her interest, and go home to your loving husband and a good comedy on the VCR.

ROUNDTABLE TALK

PRESENT AT THE DISCUSSION ARE:

Dr. Connie Agnew
Dr. Alan Klein
Jill Ganon
Tom & Sarah
Joan & David
Robert & Grace
Kate & Matt
Laura & Nick

TOPIC FOR DISCUSSION IS:

Twin Clubs

DR. AGNEW COMMENTS ON TAKING BED REST SERIOUSLY

"To the casual reader, the idea of bed rest might sound great. . . . Write a few letters, plow through the teetering pile of books next to your bed, watch a bunch of movies. But it is actually very hard. Most of us are highly functioning individuals, used to accomplishing a lot each day. And bed rest can go on for anywhere from several days to several months. So recognize that you are making a huge investment in your babies. Every day you gain is another day they might not have to be in the neonatal intensive care unit at your hospital."

DR. AGNEW COMMENTS ON GOOD INTENTIONS GONE BAD

"I usually tell my patients not to share the details of their pregnancy with casual acquaintances. It just seems to create problems when you mention that you are having this diagnostic test or that genetic screening. . . . I don't know why it happens, but people tell pregnant women scary things. I can't tell you how many times I've heard, 'My secretary told me they had to do her test eight times!' And I say, 'Not in my office.' I constantly reassure women who have been unnecessarily frightened with inaccurate information. Why is it that people don't share stories about nice, easy births? And strange and potentially bad advice is another problem. The one thing I tell all my patients is to remember that everyone's intentions, however misguided, are usually good. So just try to be patient, listen to what they say, and then be prepared to disregard it."

JILL: Have any of you found it helpful to get involved with a twins club?

LAURA: We came into this knowing nothing. I read everything I could find about babies in general. But I was the baby of my family and I just didn't know about handling babies. I thought the twins club was great. The one I belong to has about ninety members, and there is a once-a-month support meeting. I was twelve weeks pregnant when I went to my first meeting and I think it's especially helpful to pregnant women. It is really nice to talk to women who have been through a twin pregnancy . . . hearing about all their different experiences.

MATT: Neither Kate or I have ever been to a twins meeting. My concerns were more general . . . here's a baby and I don't know what to do with it. Twin . . . single . . . it didn't matter. This little guy is looking at me and he wants something and I don't have any idea what it is. We relied on my brother and his wife for information. Kate's sister and her husband have two kids, so we had a lot of "part-time doctors" to tell us what to do.

JOAN: Ours isn't really a couples sort of group. It is more mom's night out or something. Sometimes there are meetings that are sort of getting together and doing crafts or something and they lose me there. . . . Actually, when I first went I didn't feel as welcomed as I'd hoped. I still looked pregnant, my boys were very young, and I was pretty overwhelmed. It would have meant a lot for someone to talk to me . . . ask how old my twins were . . . something like that. So I actually stayed away for a couple of months. But then I thought, no, I need support from people who are also dealing with twins. So, now I go most of the time and I have bonded with some women in that group. And sometimes there are good speakers on particular issues.

SARAH: I'm involved with three different twins groups. In the first one I just didn't really feel like I belonged. So I joined another one at my temple. The groups are small . . . maybe six families at a time. Most of the people I hook up with have small babies that were born at a pound or two. They are going through the same things we've gone through.

LAURA: Where we live, the original twins club started in 1955 so those moms have kids who might have kids themselves. It is more like a social club. They don't have that immediate need of, "my twins were just born–help me!" So the younger women split off. Originally it was moms with kids under six, but they finally became the twins club they are now and it is great. Most of the kids are between two and four and there is the sense that they have just been where you are.

SARAH: I'm also a member of The Most [Mothers of Super Twins]. So I'm in contact with people all over the United States who have been in my situation . . . have had triplets and lost a baby the same way. I feel like I've made friends all over the country. I stay connected through Internet, letters, pictures. . . . I feel very involved.

TOM: It's great. People pose a lot of questions. I pose my share of questions, too. But it can seem to end up on a little more negative note. When it's informative it can be great. But to be frank with you, by the end of a meeting I was worn out. It really helps for someone like myself to keep it on a more positive note because the information is wonderful–it's really valuable.

DR. KLEIN: I'm sure that as parents of twins, and Tom and Sarah having had triplets, you feel you are in a unique situation that singleton parents don't relate to. Certainly the twin-specific things like feeding two babies at the same time won't interest them. But parents with one baby can also get a lot out of support groups.

LAURA: I think it's a great resource. You find out that you're not alone and that there are common difficulties and common joys. You meet with people who have "been there, done that" and they offer great perspective.

LAURA (cont): The speakers are really good and there are other resources. I found out about the "Mothers & Twins Notebook" newsletter. There are lots of interesting research studies, articles about development, and other resources. You can find out about cribs, car seats, and things like that. And that helps because you really have to economize with twins. I would tell people never to give up on twins clubs. Continue to go to meetings and take from it what you need.

Chapter 9

24 TO 28 WEEKS

YOUR DEVELOPING TWINS

It is at the magic gestational point of twenty-four weeks that your twins enter the stage of viability. By twenty-eight weeks, with the extraordinary advances that have been made in caring for preterm babies, they have a miraculous 90 percent rate of survival. Your twins are going to double their weight in these four weeks. By twenty-eight weeks, they may be fifteen inches long and will weigh as much as three pounds. The babies are starting to accumulate a more substantial layer of fat and get more pigment in their skin. The hair continues to grow and their facial features grow ever more distinct. It is during this time that your babies' eyelids will become unfused and we can observe them opening and closing their eyes, though the lack of light makes it very unlikely that they are seeing anything. Ultrasound observation shows that their little eyes move just like yours during rapid eye movement (REM) sleep, the stage of sleep associated with dreaming. We know that their brain waves register the four stages of sleep. Your twins are already very individual with their own cycles of sleep and wakefulness. It is fun to speculate that the baby

Twins' development at twenty-four to twenty-eight weeks.

who is more active in utero will turn out to be the more physically active child, but there is not a lot of great observational data on intrauterine/extrauterine behavior. During this month, they begin to respond to sound. Up until now, they may have responded to some vibration in music, for example, but after the twenty-sixth week we believe they are hearing, as we can use sound to wake them. Now is the time to put on the Mozart.

YOUR PREGNANT BODY

By twenty-eight weeks, you are likely to feel that the honeymoon is over. You are feeling pretty heavy, and the *weight of your pregnancy* is starting to really affect your back and your legs. As one mother of twins put it, "The hits just keep on coming." The pressure of your growing uterus can cause backaches. In some cases, the pain or pressure may be relieved when the babies shift position.

As the babies move down into your pelvis you'll experience *pelvic pressure* and may also feel *increased pressure on your rectum*. And your old friend *frequent urination* is back to stay for the duration of your pregnancy. While you no doubt enjoyed the brief respite, as the twins move a little lower in your pelvis they are back to crowding the bladder.

The frequency of the babies' movement should be about the same, but the *intensity of their movement* may be perceived differently. Your twins are a little more confined in there, so they can't quite wind up and sock you like they used to.

Women carrying twins can expect to experience a lot more *Braxton-Hicks contractions* than singleton moms. A Braxton-Hicks contraction is a contraction of the muscle of the uterus. It feels like a menstrual cramp, and is usually not painful. It feels like a tightening in the uterus that some women have described as the baby "balling up." If you feel

Your pregnant body at twenty-four to twenty-eight weeks.

your belly at this time, it not pliable or soft but feels hard, like a basketball.

You may notice that a change in position triggers Braxton-Hicks contractions. Many women experience Braxton-Hicks contractions after sex. That is a typical response to orgasm and is perfectly normal, as long as it doesn't continue in a pattern.

This is also a time to be particularly aware of any *changes in vaginal discharge*. You have probably become accustomed to more white discharge then you experienced pre-pregnancy. Any change in that discharge, especially if it grows more abundant and is associated with mild itching or burning, should be reported to your practitioner. There is a great deal of research to suggest that preterm labor is associated with an ascending infection from the vagina. They are easily diagnosed and treated. The three bacterial infections most commonly associated with increased risk of preterm labor are:

• bacterial vaginosis or *Gardnerella vaginalis*
• *Trichomonas vaginalis*
• group B beta streptococcus

DR. AGNEW COMMENTS ON BRAXTON-HICKS CONTRACTIONS

"The thing that distinguishes Braxton-Hicks contractions from early labor contractions is that there is no pattern to them. A woman may have three in one hour and then have none for four hours. Braxton-Hicks contractions are perfectly normal and the woman pregnant with twins can have as many as three of them in an hour. But if you have four Braxton-Hicks contractions in an hour's time, you need to call your doctor. Pain is not an indicator here. Even if the contractions are pain-free, four in one hour is the magic number."

SYMPTOMS THAT MAY BE ONGOING:

nasal stuffiness	sensitivity to sun
bleeding gums	constipation
anemia	increased heart rate
change in sexual desire	leakage from nipples
change in appetite	glow of pregnancy
leg cramps	increase in fetal movement
fatigue	heartburn
overheating	stretch marks
carpel tunnel syndrome	edema

THE CHECKUP

DISCUSSING YOUR PREGNANCY

At this point the frequency of your office visits is likely to be increased from every four weeks to every two weeks. Your practitioner is likely to want to talk about scaling way back on your physical activity. The first thing to look at is your energy level. If you are overly tired, or the growth of the babies is less than what your practitioner wants to see, get ready to drastically modify your workout, give up your evening walk, or stopping work if it entails being on your feet. It is time to start delegating, big time. Remember the friends who keep asking if they can do anything? The answer is an emphatic, "Yes, thank you!" You can keep your brain going at top performance speed, but it is time to invest some energy into taking it easy. And be assured, it sounds a lot easier than it is. In an uncomplicated twin pregnancy, sex can continue to the degree a woman's changing body and a couple's imagination permits. You'll likely be advised that bleeding or contractions following intercourse are serious warning signs of preterm labor. If you've already been admitted to the hospital because of preterm labor, your practitioner is not likely to be enthusiastic about your resuming your sex life until after the babies are born.

THE PHYSICAL EXAM

- assessment of weight gain
- check blood pressure, pulse, and respiratory rate
- check heart and lungs
- breast exam
- external palpation of the uterus
- measure height of fundus
- check for fetal heartbeats
- urine screens for blood, sugar, and bacteria
- ultrasound assessment

You will be screened for group B streptococcus; if it is present, your delivery team can treat you when labor begins so as to prevent infection of the babies. This checkup may or may not call for a pelvic exam. Even if you are feeling great, your practitioner may want to gauge just where you are as far as the length and feel of your cervix at twenty-four weeks. Then, if you start to develop symptoms of preterm labor, there is a baseline established. If you have any signs of preterm labor, your practitioner may place you on a uterine contraction monitor at this checkup. You may even be required to use a home monitoring unit. Twice each day, you will lay down and place on your abdomen a pressure transducer attached to a wide belt. The device is strapped around your belly and is connected to the telephone. The nurse at the other end of the phone will measure the frequency and intensity of the contractions and forward the pertinent information to your practitioner. You can also have daily contact with the nurse to discuss your symptoms.

TRANSITIONS

Gestational Diabetes

If a pregnant woman is going to develop gestational diabetes, it will most likely be identified in the second trimester of pregnancy. The rate is increased with multiples. It occurs when a woman's body fails to respond adequately to insulin to match the increase in blood sugar brought on by the demands of pregnancy. Fortunately, it is a condition that responds very well to a carefully monitored diet, though in some cases insulin is also needed. Gestational diabetes will abate after the babies are delivered, but there is a likelihood that it can recur in subsequent pregnancies, particularly if there is a genetic tendency toward diabetes in the family. If you do develop gestational diabetes, your best hedge against developing diabetes in the years to come, or in subsequent pregnancies, is to maintain a healthy weight through exercise and excellent nutrition.

- **Who is most likely to get gestational diabetes?**

  Any woman who is pregnant is at risk for developing gestational diabetes. Known risk factors include:

  - obesity
  - previous history of gestational diabetes
  - previous infant weighing nine pounds or more
  - previous unexplained fetal death
  - previous infant with congenital anomaly
  - one or more family members with diabetes
  - mother is over age twenty-five

- **How is it diagnosed?**

  Every pregnant woman not already known to have diabetes should have a glucose challenge test between the twenty-fourth and twenty-sixth week of pregnancy. A urine test for glucose is inadequate to test for gestational diabetes, so you'll be asked to drink a solution containing fifty grams of glucose (and you thought Coca-Cola was sweet). One hour later your blood will be tested for its glucose level. A level of 140 ng/dl or less is considered normal. If the level is higher than that, it does not conclusively mean you have diabetes, but you will need a glucose tolerance test. This involves a three-day, specially designed diet that includes a lot of sugar and carbohydrates. Then, after having had no breakfast the day of the test, blood is drawn. Then you consume 100 grams of a very sweet drink and follow up with three more blood tests after one, two, and three hours. The results of these four blood tests will indicate whether a patient has developed gestational diabetes.

- **Are there symptoms that you should be aware of?**

  You may show elevated glucose in your standard urine test, and that would prompt your practitioner to administer the glucose challenge test. But inordinate thirst and frequent and excessive urination are classic symptoms of this condition and should be brought to your practitioner's immediate attention.

- **Will your babies be affected?**

Identification of the condition, followed by close monitoring and careful treatment, will minimize risk to your babies. Timing is on your side here. Gestational diabetes is not associated with increased risk for birth defects. However, diabetes that has been diagnosed prior to pregnancy is associated with an increased risk of birth defects. Your twins will not be born with diabetes, though children born into a family with a history of diabetes are at risk for developing the condition later in life. There is, however, a likelihood of high birth weight due to the babies having been "overfed" on their mom's glucose. Your medical team will monitor you and the babies closely to determine if increased size will be a factor in deciding how your babies should be delivered.

Low blood glucose in either baby can occur as a result of that baby's increased production of insulin in response to its mother's high blood glucose. This can have the effect of excessive insulin production after birth. Again, your medical team will need to be alert to prolonged low blood glucose in the newborn twins and take appropriate steps to control it.

- **Is a weight-loss diet an appropriate response to a diagnosis of gestational diabetes?**

Weight loss is never recommended during pregnancy, but we have identified gestational diabetes as putting a woman at risk of developing diabetes within five to ten years of her pregnancy, particularly if she is overweight. Weight control, exercise, and a carefully developed diet are very important in helping a woman to postpone or completely avoid diabetes in future pregnancies as well as in the rest of her life.

- **Does gestational diabetes affect labor and delivery?**

Happily, many women with gestational diabetes are able to carry their babies to term and begin labor naturally. If you have been able to treat your condition during pregnancy without the use of insulin, you will not need to take insulin during labor or delivery.

Gestational diabetes is not necessarily a mandate to perform a cesarean delivery but, if your doctor feels one or both of the babies is too large to labor through the birth canal for a vaginal delivery, a cesarean delivery may be appropriate. If you are diagnosed with gestational diabetes it is important to discuss each of the possible birthing scenarios with your doctor so as to minimize your stress over the unknown.

Treating Gestational Diabetes

The goal of treatment is to maintain blood glucose levels equal to those of a pregnant woman without this condition. Careful attention to diet may keep blood sugar levels in the normal range, effectively managing the problem without resorting to insulin injections. Your doctor may enlist the help of an experienced nutrition specialist who will no doubt pay careful attention to your caloric intake, the avoidance of foods which increase blood sugar, and emphasize the use of foods that enhance the body's ability to sustain normal blood sugar levels. Your blood glucose will be carefully managed through the use of meal plans and, where possible, a moderate schedule of regular exercise. An accurate food journal will help you and your medical team to assess your progress.

- Avoid going longer than four to five hours without eating. Eat three meals and three snacks each day.

- Choose water over fruit juices as juice contains high levels of naturally occurring sugar.

- Fruit sweetened foods, as well as dried fruits, are to be avoided.

- For breakfast, choose high-fiber, whole-grain cereals or bread with no more than half a cup of milk. Avoid most commercial breakfast cereals.

- Eat a high-protein breakfast that includes eggs, hard cheese, cottage cheese, or lean meats.

Sweets, such as cakes, candies, pastries, pies, and frozen desserts are obviously high in sugar and should be avoided. But it is important to read labels on all foods and condiments. If sugar, corn syrup, corn sweeteners, honey, molasses, dextrose, fructose, and glucose occur as one of the first four ingredients, it should be off your meal plan. The following foods may contain hidden sugars, so be scrupulous in your label reading:

- jams and jellies
- ketchup
- spaghetti sauce
- granola
- baked beans
- teriyaki sauce
- honey mustard
- canned fruits
- nondairy creamer

Remember, weight loss is not an appropriate response to a diagnosis of gestational diabetes. If you are overweight, it is absolutely advisable to limit your intake of fats such as oil, butter, margarine, and mayonnaise. Select nonfat or low-fat dairy products and lean meats; skinless poultry; and broiled or poached fish.

ROUNDTABLE TALK

PRESENT AT THE DISCUSSION ARE:

Dr. Alan Klein
Tom
David
Robert
Matt

TOPICS FOR DISCUSSION ARE:

Fathers on Fathering
Would You Have Another Baby?

ALAN: Do you all love being dads?

ROBERT: People ask what is fatherhood like, and I say I don't know yet, I know more what mothering is like. My kids aren't old enough for me to be a father . . . or my idea of a father. You know . . . I can't throw a football to them yet. I am more like a second mother. Because of my idea of what a father should be as opposed to a mother, I tend to handle the one that is easier to handle and my wife will deal with the difficulty, whatever it is. I get the one that is doing more, is looking around more. . . . It is sort of more having a relationship and not just nurturing.

MATT: I travel a lot and now I'll do anything to get out of going. Generally speaking, it's not that I didn't love spending time with my wife, but if there was a meeting that had to happen I was there and I just didn't think about it. Now . . . if it can possibly be done without my being there that is what I'll do. I just want to get home and see the guys.

TOM: I've really worked to be ready to be a father. If you don't know who you are how can you instill values in a child? I had to look at myself. I'd like to talk to someone who was just thrust into fatherhood to see how they cope.

MATT: I was always more ready to have children than my wife was. And what is really amazing to me was how she has changed. I don't think she could imagine life without the boys.

ALAN: How have your twins affected your couple relationship?

ROBERT: We try, but it is very hard. In the back of my mind I wasn't sure if she wanted them as much as I did. We talked about how it would affect our relationship. But you don't really know until they are born.

MATT: We were married eleven years before the babies so we'd gotten a lot out of our systems. Travel and freedom is not a loss. I think it is more traumatic to people who haven't been married so long. I'd rather talk about the babies than discuss our work.

DAVID: Our relationship is totally different but I think it is better now. We're closer. It was like we were living parallel lives. I had my life and she had hers. Having the boys brought us together.

TOM: After you have your kids there is no such thing as "no shop talk." Our kids are us. Everything we imagined about child rearing went right out the window as soon as the kids were born. Certain things that I'd always thought were important have changed; career goals and such. It is interesting, since the kids were born, that she is Jewish and I am Christian and we never really examined that together, but now with all the problems our babies have had, we pray together and some spiritual element has drawn us closer. And I remember that before the kids were born we always said we'd never fight in front of our children. Well, that went right out the window. It is new territory. We are not the same people we were.

ALAN: Do you think it is different having twins than if you'd had a singleton?

ROBERT: I remember before people knew we were expecting twins they said, "Get your sleep now before the baby is born." Now, when it is some ridiculous hour and we are each holding a baby, we think one would have been so easy. You can take turns. Just feed it, burp, and throw it in the crib . . . no big deal.

TOM: It is kind of abstract because these are the first babies for all of us.

MATT: I don't think it would have been that different.

TOM: There are so many factors for us. What if we'd had all three and what if they had all been healthy? I mean we had three. Two survived but were in the hospital for three months. I remember they told us at the

ICU [intensive care unit] to try and relax and maybe even go away for a weekend. That seemed irresponsible . . . impossible to me.

ALAN: How about more kids?

ROBERT: I'd love to have more but I'd like them to be twins. It is the only way I know to be a parent. . . . There is so much work at this stage of the game and it all feels worth it for the five minutes of peaceful time with the babies. . . . And the quiet times get longer and the intensity of the work diminishes. I feel like I could do it again. We'd both love it.

DAVID: We were not home a week, when Joan said to me, "You know, I could maybe do this again." You have to understand that she did not have a well day throughout her entire pregnancy. She'd gone through delivering one vaginally and one by C-section. . . . She could barely get up to go to the bathroom. I was astonished.

TOM: If we stop here, that's fine; but if we had more that would be great, too. Either way.

Chapter 10
28 TO 32 WEEKS

YOUR DEVELOPING TWINS

Your babies will weigh four pounds each by the end of their thirty-second week. Twins are still tracking along quite similarly to singletons at this point. They are thirty-five to forty centimeters in length, and mom is likely to be very familiar with their patterns of movement. They are putting on a lot of fat now. There is continued growth and the vernix and lanugo are still present. It is during this month that the size of the body begins to grow a little larger in relation to the size of the head, which up until now had been disproportionately large. The organs are operational with the exception of the lungs.

Twins' development at twenty-eight to thirty-two weeks.

YOUR PREGNANT BODY

You will probably notice a somewhat more *reliable pattern in the babies' activity* now. And it will surely be more difficult to determine who is who. You may notice a new type of movement from the babies that could be described as repetitive or jerky. Your babies may have the *hiccups*. This is quite normal and will come and go.

Your pregnant body at twenty-eight to thirty-two weeks.

Fatigue grows ever more pronounced and it is important to listen to what your body is telling you and take naps, or at least get off your feet at regular intervals throughout the day. Try to be conscientious about putting your feet up to minimize swelling in your lower extremities.

Breathlessness may be more pronounced and has to do with your diaphragm accommodating a very large uterus at this point. It is harder to take a deep breath because your diaphragm can't expand downward as effectively as it should. Sitting upright may be your most comfortable position.

You may have *difficulty sleeping* and will have to struggle to find a comfortable position in your bed. By now, you may have your bed filled with pillows, or you may want to buy a full body-size pillow to get you through the night.

Certainly, you may have *more conspicuous backache*. Pay attention to any new or unusual pain or aching in your back. It could be a sign of preterm labor. Alert your practitioner if you have any questions. For backache that is not associated with labor, try a nice, warm bath. There is nothing wrong with taking the strain off your abdomen and lower back by sitting in the tub for a long, soothing soak. Several baths a day are not unusual for a woman seeking relief from a constantly aching back. But stay out of the Jacuzzi, which is too hot for you and your babies at this point.

An increase in *hemorrhoids* is likely to be noticed if you spend long periods of time standing or even sitting upright. Continue to maintain a healthy diet and drink lots of water to alleviate any constipation that could be contributing to hemorrhoids. You may find relief in cold packs that are shaped like sanitary napkins and can be applied to soothe the rectal area. Taking a sitz bath for fifteen or twenty minutes a few times a day is likely to make you more comfortable.

SYMPTOMS THAT MAY BE ONGOING:

nasal stuffiness	sensitivity to sun
bleeding gums	constipation
anemia	increased heart rate
change in sexual desire	leakage from nipples
change in appetite	glow of pregnancy
leg cramps	increase in fetal movement
fatigue	heartburn
overheating	stretch marks
carpel tunnel syndrome	edema

THE CHECKUP

DISCUSSING YOUR PREGNANCY

You may have some questions at this time about the positions of your babies and the implications as far as your delivery. This is the time to discuss a frequency in Braxton-Hicks contractions, if you're experiencing them. If you are not on bed rest, your practitioner will want an accurate accounting of how you spend your day so as to assess any need for additional rest. Your practitioner may recommend Kegel exercises, which help to firm the pelvic muscles, if you are experiencing any stress incontinence as a result of pressure on your bladder from your increasingly large uterus. If your childbirth preparation classes have raised any unanswered questions, you may find it helpful to bring them up. As always, it is important to discuss any new symptom at your checkup.

THE PHYSICAL EXAM

- assessment of weight gain
- check blood pressure, pulse, and respiratory rate

DOCTOR AGNEW COMMENTS ON PREECLAMPSIA

"During weeks 28 to 32 of your pregnancy, you can expect your practitioner to discuss the warning signs of preeclampsia. Preeclampsia affects nearly 25 percent of all pregnancies, and is more common in first pregnancies, multiple pregnancies, and patients with prior hypertension. This uniquely human pregnancy disorder is characterized by hypertension (elevated blood pressure), edema (swelling of the face, hands, and feet), and proteinuria (the presence of protein in your urine). The symptoms to be aware of are:

- changes in your visual field, such as blurriness or dark spots
- headaches
- abdominal pain
- increased swelling of face, hands, or feet.

When preeclampsia is diagnosed prior to term, some prolongation of the pregnancy is possible. For mild forms, bedrest (accompanied by frequent monitoring of the mother's blood

(continued)

pressure and biophysical profiles of both fetuses) is the mainstay of treatment.

I really want to stress that bedrest means exactly that! While it may seem like the perfect time to organize your closet or assemble the crib you've bought for the nursery, your job is to plant yourself in that bed and follow your practitioner's instructions to the letter. If you have young children at home, you may be placed in the hospital in order to take every precaution that you'll stay off your feet. This is something that only you (with more than a little help from your friends and family) can do for your babies, and the benefits are very significant. In more severe cases, early delivery may be necessary.

You and your practitioner will discuss the specifics of your case in order to determine the safest, most appropriate course of action for you and your babies."

- check heart and lungs
- breast exam
- external palpation of the uterus
- measure height of fundus
- check for fetal heartbeats
- urine screens for blood, sugar, and bacteria
- ultrasound assessment

Your physical exam may include a pelvic examination to determine if there has been any dilation of the cervix. The ultrasound will confirm fetal well-being and make sure that the level of amniotic fluid is normal for both babies. This exam may also include a biophysical profile, which is uses the following components to assess fetal well-being:

- the volume of amniotic fluid
- fetal breathing
- the non-stress test
- the rate of fetal movement
- fetal tone

TRANSITIONS

Banked Blood—Will You Need It?

It is very rare that a woman will require any banked blood after vaginal or cesarean delivery, though the risk is a little higher for twins. The uterus may be so stretched from its need to accommodate two babies, their placentas, and amniotic fluid that it takes a little longer to contract. The mother of twins will continue to lose blood until contraction of the uterus is completed.

Our concerns about contaminated blood products have had the effect of making our blood banking systems very sophisticated in their abilities to screen blood, but many mothers still prefer to make an autologous donation of their own blood so that it can be at the hospital waiting for them if it is needed. This may not be possible if you are severely ane-mic, but you can discuss it with your practitioner and with the local blood bank. *You can never accept your husband's blood because there is the possibility that mixing your husband's blood with yours could create complica-tions during future pregnancies.*

ROUNDTABLE TALK

PRESENT AT THE DISCUSSION ARE:

Dr. Connie Agnew
Jill Ganon
Tom & Sarah
Nick & Laura
Joan & David
Robert & Grace
Kate & Matt

TOPICS FOR DISCUSSION ARE:

Some Pregnancy and Birth Experiences

LAURA: All through the pregnancy we were concerned with what to expect at any given point. I would really advise you to think about things early. We were just starting to look for a pediatrician when I was put on bed rest. So there I was, totally restricted–no driving, no going to interview doctors–when the twins were born on the first day of my thirty-fourth week.

ROBERT: The day the babies were born, after calling to tell family about the birth, I had to call three pediatricians to cancel our interviews. Our babies were born the thirty-fourth week, too. We asked our obstetrician who he took his kids to. We figured if it was good enough for him, it would probably be good enough for us. But I would say that as far as the obstetrician is concerned, find out what the backup plan is, because when the primary isn't there, you can suddenly find yourself in the hands of someone you don't know at all.

JOAN: The doctor I had been seeing for checkups and things had just decided to stop delivering babies. I had some pre-existing conditions that made me high risk apart from the twin aspect. We needed to think about the hospital the doctor was affiliated with—making sure it had the right level of NICU [neonatal intensive care unit] in case there were problems with the babies. We live outside Los Angeles but we chose our doctor here [in Los Angeles] because we didn't know if a local doctor and hospital could handle potential complications. I think it is really important to feel confident in your information. I'm a nurse and I would say that one thing that disturbed me was that in a lot of the books I read during pregnancy, there seemed to be a real bias about "just say no to drugs during labor and just say no to a C-section." That can be very misleading and even scary for women to read.

JILL: What is the recommendation for women with higher risk pregnancies if they are in small towns seeing their local OB?

DR. AGNEW: If there is a twin pregnancy that is going along just fine in the obstetrician's view, they might bring in a consultant for a particular issue or maybe some diagnostic ultrasound. Usually the patient will need to travel to the urban area. Most of the time, nature does it just right and the babies are healthy and mom is fine. Twins have a tendency to come early, but many times it is not early enough to cause significant problems. When a patient tells me they are moving to a new town and want to know how to find a doctor, I tell them to call the labor/delivery unit of the local hospital and ask the nurses who they see. You can get terrific information that way.

JILL: Did you feel ready by the time the babies were born?

KATE: I'm a twin and my mom came the day we got out of the hospital. They were able to come home right away and we had nothing done.

Through the hospital, we hired one person to come and do house cleaning so I could try to get organized.

TOM: Ours were in the hospital for a long time. They were born at the end of June and first it was, "They'll be home by Christmas." That seemed so far away. A few months later they said, "Maybe Thanksgiving . . ." A few weeks later we took the CPR classes because they said the babies might be coming home in a few weeks. The *next day* they told us the babies would be going home tomorrow! So after all that waiting, suddenly we were running around, getting cribs and everything. It just got frantic.

LAURA: Even though it was early, my mom suggested that I pack a bag, and the next day my water broke.

NICK: And I was really glad we'd taken those childbirth classes. I didn't want to go but I'm glad I did.

LAURA: We ended up having classes at home because all the classes were booked and by the time they were available I was on bed rest. Our instructor was great and actually ended up attending the birth. She wanted to be with us.

KATE: I figured they would tell me what I needed to know at the hospital. I was going to have an epidural. . . . I thought, "Drugs are wonderful. Why should I have to learn how to breathe?" I didn't even have a tour of the hospital. I figured, "Don't worry. You walk in the front door, you go to the emergency room, and they send you up to labor and delivery."

MATT: I didn't have any intention of going into the delivery room but our doctor, who I thought was sick of me by now because I asked so many questions, convinced me. I told him that if he could find a surgical outfit that fit, I'd go in. He did, so I did. I was really thinking my presence might be counterproductive in there. I hadn't really thought about those classes. I figured it was the doctor who needed an education and he had gotten it. I just tried to stay out of everyone's way. There were wires everywhere and no escape route. Thank God my wife cooperated and five minutes later one was being born. They introduced me to my son and three or four minutes later the other one was coming out.

LAURA: I'll say one thing for the classes—our instructor would fully describe a process and then I'd ask, "But how does that work for twins?" I was afraid it would bore everyone else but our instructor was great about it.

JILL: Did you realize you needed to look for a class early because you were pregnant with twins?

LAURA: I was neurotic enough that as soon as I got the paperwork from the hospital I started thinking I should get it all ready right away. It wasn't like I was worrying because it was twins, I'm just neurotic. . . . When I tried to book a tour they told me they could do it in December. They said wait till you're five months to call. I was at four months and they were already booked. They found a spot for me.

MATT: At thirty-two weeks Kate started exhibiting signs of premature labor and we got the forty-eight-hour speech. . . . Our OB was always saying the same thing: "Try to get to thirty-six weeks. If you can make it through March I'll be thrilled; I'll take you out to dinner." We didn't expect to make it past thirty-six weeks. Psychologically speaking we were set for somewhere between thirty-two and thirty-six. She lasted until week thirty-four. The concern was for the babies. We never questioned Kate's safety.

GRACE: Our OB always said twins could deliver at thirty-six weeks as opposed to forty.

Chapter 11

32 TO 36 WEEKS

YOUR DEVELOPING TWINS

For twins, this is an especially remarkable period of development. Weight gain is now a little bit slower than for a singleton. This is the time they are relying on their mother's nutrition to help them put on the final layer of fat that is so important to the early weeks following birth. They will grow from 1,800 to 2,500 grams. Usually, a baby must attain a weight of 2,000 grams before it is discharged from the hospital, so the twins born closer to thirty-two weeks may need to spend some time in the intensive care nursery. They will grow in length from forty to forty-five centimeters. Their motor development is far more sophisticated and less reflexive. This is the point that the lung development surges ahead. The alveolar cells of the lungs begin to produce surfactant and phospholipids. These substances will help the babies' lungs to expand for their first breath. They will also help the babies to exchange gases with the air—dissolving oxygen into the blood and extruding carbon dioxide back into the lungs. The placenta is continuing to function remarkably well, but the twins are having to share a little bit. They are truly cramped now

Twins' development at thirty-two to thirty-six weeks.

and are molded against each other. Your practitioner will be carefully monitoring the twins' positions to see if their heads are down. The positions they assume now are not likely to change.

YOUR PREGNANT BODY

Your pregnant body at thirty-two to thirty-six weeks.

You may feel as though your hips are actually spreading and the *diameter of the pelvis* probably does increase somewhat by this time. The ligaments supporting the pelvis are really stretching now to accommodate the babies as they move ever lower into the pelvic area.

The babies' movement is still as frequent but does not feel as intense because the cramped quarters restrict their movement.

Braxton-Hicks contractions may be very frequent now. Continue to use the same rule of thumb: Anything more than four contractions in an hour means you should call your practitioner.

Sleep is difficult due to increased urination and difficulty finding a comfortable position. The babies still need a lot of fluid so it is important to keep up your own fluid intake.

Appetite may decrease as a result of your stomach having limited space due to the increasing size of your uterus.

Swelling of your lower extremities may grow more pronounced, so try to get your feet up as much as possible.

You may experience very *vivid dreams* or find yourself daydreaming with greater frequency about the impact the babies will have on your life.

SYMPTOMS THAT MAY BE ONGOING:

backache	nasal stuffiness
sensitivity to sun	bleeding gums
constipation	anemia
breathlessness	increased heart rate

change in sexual desire	leakage from nipples
change in appetite	glow of pregnancy
leg cramps	fatigue
heartburn	overheating
stretch marks	hemorrhoids
carpel tunnel syndrome	edema

TRANSITIONS

OK, Enough Is Enough

This is the point at which many practitioners report that their patients are starting to beg them to induce labor. No doubt about it, the woman carrying twins is ready to move on to a new role–from temporary shelter to dairy bar! No matter how frequently you've fretted as a couple that you just aren't ready, your body is telling you it has had enough. This is the time to summon all your resources to prepare for birth. That may mean being absolutely faithful to your practitioner's instructions if you are on bed rest, or finishing your research with the local twins club on which is the safest car seat.

ROUNDTABLE TALK

PRESENT AT THE DISCUSSION ARE:

Dr. Connie Agnew
Jill Ganon
Tom & Sarah
Nick & Laura
Joan & David
Robert & Grace
Kate & Matt

TOPICS FOR DISCUSSION ARE:

Surviving as a Couple
More Kids?

JILL: How is your intimate relationship now that you have the babies?

NICK: When we do end up with both babies in the bed—everyone sprawled out—we have found a way that I can be here, and Laura can be here [he gestures, creating a diagonal with his hands] and our feet are touching each other. Sometimes that is our intimacy. But these two little guys are the most joyous thing in the world. It's triple the work but it's quadruple the fun. I don't think our relationship has suffered.

LAURA: We joke ... saying we're on the nine-month plan. We knew each other for nine months before we got engaged, we were engaged for nine months, then we were married for nine months when I got pregnant with twins. They should have been born nine months later but they were born at seven months. Sometimes you just have to carve out some space to be together. Just say, "The babies are going to the sitter for an hour or two. . . . Let's watch a movie or just rediscover the couple."

NICK: As far as our intimate relationship goes, it's less than before and you don't have as long. It's sort of whenever you have the opportunity, like when they're napping or late at night, if you can keep your eyes open.

JOAN: At the end of a day we just sort of pass out together and say, "Look what we've done. . . ." There's a lot more cuddling [now].

LAURA: I think the key is patience and knowing the twins are going to take a lot of time. You need to understand that you are redefining your relationship. You're a family of four and not a couple of two. You just work with it.

NICK: You can get bogged down on a day-to-day basis, but when we are away from it all or if we're overnight somewhere alone, it's just like old times. It's the most fantastic thing in the world.

ROBERT: It doesn't sound very romantic but I think in a good marriage, you have to make appointments with each other and keep them. If the marriage is strong, it is good for the kids. It's easy to say, but it's much harder to do. Sometimes one says, "I don't want to keep this appointment. I'd rather go to sleep." But if you force yourself to stay with it, you get your second wind. . . . Whatever it takes, its crucial to the marriage and the children.

GRACE: Every two months we try to take off for four days together.

ROBERT: At least we try. In everyday life, everything seems to center around the children. I wonder about the divorce rate for parents of twins. I'm not sure it's separated out from the rate of parents of premature babies. The stress of dealing with prematurity must create a higher divorce rate. My question is, would they have ended up divorcing anyway? Maybe the relationship was too tenuous in the first place.

DR. AGNEW: Coping with prematurity brings out who you are as an individual and as a couple. It is a defining experience. The pressure is so great that you have to see yourself as a unit battling together against a struggle, rather than succumbing to the frustration and inconvenience it causes in the couple relationship. You really have to go into it as a couple and face it together.

JILL: Speaking of together, anyone thinking about more babies?

LAURA: As long as we work it around my ten-year high school reunion. . . . I want to be skinny when I go [laughter].

TOM: Well, kids are great. Our situation is somewhat unique because Sarah is working and I'm home with the kids. I'm a musician and when you're not playing, you're not really yourself. So I am trying to get out a little more now to work at night after Sarah gets home. That means we see less of each other. But you just have to have faith. On some level, you need to get yourself back before you can get back together as a couple. I feel complete with what we have, but if the Lord blessed us with another baby, that would be fine too. My kids have been through so much, and they are so strong.

SARAH: We're moving next week and we have all their bassinets and stuff. Do we get rid of them? It's up in the air, but I would not do fertility treatment again. If it's meant to happen, it will.

DAVID: I understand what Tom said. When our boys came we both lost ourselves. A hundred percent of everything went into taking care of our boys. We are now dealing with rediscovering who we are, and finally realizing that as a couple you have to make a very conscious effort to make time together. I think there was a time that Joan felt I didn't care about us as a couple . . . that I was more interested in the boys.

JOAN: It's like Nick said . . . He missed the boys so much, when he came home he just seemed to want to be with them. Now maybe every other week we get out to dinner together and it has been wonderful. Ultimately, I think we've grown closer. But there was a time that I felt we were living parallel lives, not really connecting. We were married twelve years when the babies were born and though we loved each other very much, we both had big jobs that seemed to take us away from each other. But it's funny–there was a time that I didn't think I would have children. Now we have the two boys, two cocker spaniels, not a clear space to put your foot on the floor, and I think, "How much difference would it be with one more?"

DR. AGNEW: At one point I had three kids in three different-size diapers. I'd push my cart up to the cash register and the guy would say, "Oh great–your own little landfill." I had a three year old, a toddler, and an infant. I agree with Joan–I didn't see much change going from two to three. Three to four was not planned, and that kind of threw a stick of dynamite into the house. If you do it while the kids are still little I think it's easier than waiting . . . and then heaven forbid you have another set of twins. That would be wild.

Chapter 12

LABOR AND DELIVERY TO POSTPARTUM

YOUR DEVELOPING TWINS

In twins, the average term weight is a little lower than that of a singleton, 3,200 grams as opposed to 3,400. Twins that get to thirty-seven weeks are considered term. They may attain as much as fifty centimeters in length. During these weeks the lanugo start to disappear. Your babies use this time to continue storing the vital body fat that will help them to maintain their body temperature after birth. Ultrasound assessment of the twins grows increasingly difficult because they are packed so tightly into the uterus.

LABOR

In the majority of twin pregnancies labor will begin before thirty-seven weeks. Nature is telling you that the babies are ready and your uterus has reached its maximum capacity. Over a period of several days there are several signs that may alert you of your impending labor:

- **Increase in Braxton-Hicks Contractions**

You may be lying on the sofa watching David Letterman and conscientiously timing your contractions, only to find that you've fallen asleep and the contractions have stopped. This makes perfect sense. Labor rarely starts out of the blue. It likes to have a few little test runs before beginning in earnest. Don't be surprised if you have several evenings of increasing contractions, only to fall asleep. Remember, practice makes perfect.

- **Definite Sensation of Fullness in the Pelvis**

    This may include pressure on the pelvic bone and even feeling like your hips are stretching wider.

- **Change in Vaginal Discharge**

    You may notice that vaginal secretions are thicker and may be present in increased amounts.

- **Spotting or Bleeding**

    There may be some appearance of blood as the cervix begins to become effaced or dilated.

- **Leaking of Amniotic Fluid**

A woman who is consistently having four contractions in an hour could be going into labor. With twin pregnancies, there is no doubt that your practitioner needs to hear from you under those circumstances. If you notice anything unusual about the way the babies are moving, you should share that information with your practitioner as well. At your examination you will be assessed in much the same way you have been at every exam of your pregnancy. Your vitals will be checked. If everything is fine, you will also have a pelvic exam at this point. If you are in fact in labor, there are three terms used by your medical team to note the progress of your labor:

- **The Station**

The station describes how far the head (or other presenting part) of the baby has progressed through the birth canal. A negative station (−3 or −4) is above the ischial spines on either side of the pelvis. The fully engaged baby is at zero station in the pelvis and the final descent continues, from +1 station until the baby crowns at +4 (the appearance of the baby's head at the vaginal opening).

- **Effacement**

This is the thinning out and shortening in length of the cervix.

- **Dilation**

In labor, the cervix will need to dilate from zero to ten centimeters in order to accommodate the vaginal delivery of your babies.

THE THREE STAGES OF LABOR

Stage One: Latent Labor

Latent labor describes the period of time that your contractions are beginning: The cervix is not particularly dilated, but rhythmic, active

The cervix has begun to efface (get thinner), but there is no dilation.

contractions are persistent for a matter of hours. This stage of labor can last from twelve to twenty-four hours. The cervix is continuing to efface and dilation will reach three centimeters. Women who are pregnant with twins can expect their practitioners to follow them closely, even in this earliest phase of labor. Contractions may last up to forty-five seconds and may or may not be painful. Your symptoms may include:

- leaking fluid from rupture of the membranes
- diarrhea
- a mucous discharge (mucus plug) which may be tinged with blood

Stage Two: Active Labor through Delivery

In a twin pregnancy there is evidence that your babies may benefit by being followed very closely through labor. At this point it is almost certain that you will be in the hospital and that both babies will be monitored with external fetal monitors. These are the same instruments used to measure the babies' heartbeats in your practitioner's office. The monitors are placed on your abdomen in a belt form, one for each baby. The use of fetal monitoring in high-risk pregnancies has greatly improved the outcome of these births. A third belt will be used to monitor the frequency of uterine contractions.

There is a tremendous amount of physical effort involved in labor, and you still need adequate nutrition during this time. But eating, even in little amounts, is likely to result in vomiting, which is unpleasant at any time and terribly uncomfortable during labor. Intravenous fluid and glucose is usually in the mother's best interest, keeping her from becoming dehydrated and allowing her to have some fuel for her extraordinary effort. It is not unreasonable to expect your practitioner to order an intravenous line.

As labor is progressing, the couple can call on all the skills they learned in prepared childbirth classes to decrease anxiety, relieve pain, and work together through this remarkable process. But contractions can be painful and unrelenting. (Neither member of the couple will ever have more respect for their own mothers than they do during this period of labor.)

Your labor nurse will be working with you throughout, helping you with tips about relaxation and offering expert guidance. Long before you go into labor you will have spoken with your practitioner about the opportunities available to you for pain relief. The most prudent approach takes into consideration the risks and benefits of each option before going into labor. Once you are in labor, your nurse will be able to help you to evaluate your options for pain relief and the impact they will have on you and your babies.

After a woman has dilated to between three and four centimeters, an intravenous or intramuscular pain reliever can be offered. Meperidine hydrochloride (Demerol) is safe and effective but can induce drowsiness. The effects wear off in about ninety minutes, but it will not be offered if you are too far along because it could interfere with your ability to push the babies out when the time comes. Demerol is a powerful analgesic but it does cross the placenta and will also have an effect on the babies. Your practitioner will not want the babies to have their respiration depressed at delivery. Therefore, it is not recommended for use if delivery is expected in sooner than two hours.

The cervix has dilated to 5 centimeters, and the first baby's head begins its descent through the birth canal.

DR. AGNEW COMMENTS ON THE VALUE OF EPIDURAL ANESTHESIA

"I am a tremendous advocate of the use of epidural anesthesia because I've seen how much more pleasant the birthing experience can be for a woman who is not overwhelmed by pain. I had delivered hundreds and hundreds of babies and when it came time for me to give birth to my first child, I wasn't sure I'd need anesthesia. Well, when I was dilated to two centimeters I thought I was going to die but I wanted to just handle it. I was rigid as a board—I couldn't even unflex my fist. That was the way I was dealing with my pain. I agreed to an epidural when I was at three to four centimeters. Once I was relaxed, I stopped fighting the labor and in an hour I was fully dilated. In my second pregnancy, it took forever to dilate to four to five centimeters. At that point I had an epidural and once again, in an hour I was fully dilated. I am convinced that, at least for me, the epidural had a relaxing and positive effect on my labor."

Keep in mind that everything you learned in your prepared childbirth classes will continue to be of tremendous benefit to you in labor. Another option for pain relief is epidural anesthesia. This is a regional anesthetic placed by an anesthesiologist by injection into the space outside the spinal column. First, a numbing medicine is administered. Depending on the levels of anesthesia to be used, a catheter may be placed in the area so that the anesthesia can be administered on a continuous basis. This epidural anesthesia can significantly alter your perception of pain from the umbilicus down. But it does not impede the progress of labor. And since it does not enter the bloodstream, it does not effect the babies and is considered very safe.

Epidural anesthesia can be administered at different levels. The level needed for surgical delivery such as a cesarean section can cause a patient to be numb from the waist down, having very little control over her extremities. A lower level can be administered in such a way as to block the pain of contractions, while allowing the mother to remain aware of the sensation. She can feel the pressure, but it doesn't hurt. This enables her to be a very active participant, perfectly capable of pushing when the time is right.

It very important for the doctor delivering the babies to be an active participant in the decision-making process of pain management. The presentation of the babies is of paramount importance here. In particular, the position of the second baby is very meaningful when pain management is discussed. Epidural anesthesia can be very effective during complex deliveries. If, for example, the second baby is to be delivered in the breech presentation or by total breech extraction, the relaxing effects of the epidural will make the birth canal less rigid.

Another advantage of epidural anesthesia is that once it

is in place, it can be administered in a matter of seconds. This can be vital in the event of cesarean section, particularly if there are signs of fetal distress and the practitioner wants to deliver one or both babies very quickly.

If the frequency of your contractions should decrease during your active labor, your practitioner may feel it is necessary to administer a hormone called oxytocin to help the uterus contract more efficiently. The rationale behind a decision to augment labor is clear: It is not in a baby's best interest to remain in the birth canal for an extended period of time.

Now that you are completely dilated to ten centimeters, your first baby's head descends down into the pelvis and through the birth canal to be delivered through the vagina. Your contractions are continuing and now you are being encouraged to push. This process can last anywhere from five minutes to several hours. As baby number one nears delivery, your practitioner will determine if an episiotomy is needed. This is a small incision in the perineum to temporarily enlarge the vaginal opening to accommodate the passage of the baby's head. The thinking is that a clean incision is preferable to the ragged tear that could result if a good-size baby is allowed to deliver, forcing the tissue of the perineum to lacerate spontaneously.

The head, which is typically the broadest circumference on a newborn baby, has passed through the vagina. Delivery of the rest of the baby's body can be expected to follow soon.

This is often a time of increased communication between mother and her birth coach—frequently, but not always, the father of the twins. The dose of epidural anesthetic may be reduced at this time and mothers report feelings from elation to fear to steely determination at this point. There are numerous positions that may feel right to the woman at this stage of her labor. Some women feel pushing in a supported but upright squatted position offers them the benefit of gravity. For others, that requires too much energy and they prefer to be in a birthing bed or seat. It is now that you truly understand why they call it labor: You are working very hard.

You are being guided by your medical team. The urge to push may feel uncontrollable at times. You are attuned to the laboring out of this baby and your body will assert its tremendous will to expel its first passenger. Again, everything you worked on in your birthing classes is coming into play. Many women describe an extraordinary sense of being connected to the voice of the practitioner who is directing the delivery of the babies. You'll rely on breathing techniques you've learned to help you to refrain from pushing when your practitioner tells you to hold off. As the first baby's head crowns and is then delivered completely, the rest of the body follows very quickly.

Labor of the second baby will continue and baby number two will slowly move lower in the birth canal. After delivery of the first baby there is a brief opportunity to enjoy the overwhelming sense of relief. The first baby's cord is double clamped, and the father can cut the cord if he likes. Then it may seem as though your baby is swept away to be quickly dried off and swaddled. The baby may then be handed to the mother, who may already be involved with pushing out baby number two. The father may hold the first baby while the mother continues her hard work of delivering the second of the twins.

These are three of the positions in which twins might present for delivery. If the first baby is vertex, and your labor is proceeding well, your practitioner is likely to recommend that a vaginal delivery be attempted. If the first baby is breech or transverse your practitioner will discuss the possibility of a cesarean delivery for both babies.

1. Babies in vertex/vertex positions.

The interim between delivery of baby number one and baby number two is seventeen minutes on average. But your time may be much shorter or longer by several hours. Your obstetrician will quickly evaluate the position of baby number two by pelvic exam. Second babies can appear in many different positions so frequently an ultrasound is performed to get the most accurate view of how the baby is lying.

If the baby is transverse or breech, the obstetrician might try to externally palpate your abdomen, gently guiding the baby into a vertex position. Sometimes the baby is not cooperative and will remain in breech position. At this point, your obstetrician will quickly decide whether or not to do a total breech extraction. Breech extraction is accomplished by the obstetrician reaching through the vaginal opening to where the baby's feet can be felt, grabbing the feet, and directing the second baby through the birth canal for complete delivery. The time factor is very important because your obstetrician (OB) wants to complete the delivery before the cervix begins to close down. If the cervix has closed down to eight centimeters, the OB is likely to wait for the mother to labor out the second baby, a process that can take another two hours. If the baby is presenting in a position known as a frank breech–hips flexed, knees extended, and the heels near the ears–the obstetrician may allow a breech delivery. There are several mitigating factors when considering cesarean delivery for the second baby:

· What is the size of the second baby? Is it smaller than the first, so that it will negotiate the birth canal without undue stress? The doctor may not permit a vaginal delivery if the second baby is larger than the first.

· What does the monitor tell us about how well the baby is tolerating labor? If the heartbeat monitor and ultra-

2. Babies in the vertex/breech positions.

3. Babies in back-down-transverse-lie/breech positions.

sound indicate that the baby is in a precarious position–lying trans-verse with its shoulder first, or the umbilical cord is ahead of the baby–a cesarean section may be indicated for the safety of the baby.

Cesarean Section

We can see how a decision might be made to deliver the second baby by cesarean section. There is also the possibility that a woman will enter labor with an ultrasound showing both babies in breech positions. There might be significant risks in labor with both or either baby entangled in the cords. Or there is the concern that the first baby will not be able to complete its journey through the birth canal without its head being obstructed by the other baby's feet. In twin delivery it may be the obstetrician's best call that a cesarean is needed because of the possibility of the two babies interfering with each other. If a mother has an active herpes virus there is risk that the babies will be exposed to the virus through contact with the vagina. Newborn babies do not have tremendous resistance to infection so cesarean delivery is an option that will be discussed. Other maternal medical scenarios–such as diabetes, or preeclampsia that has not ade-quately responded to treatment–may call for a cesarean section to be performed. Placenta previa will always require a cesarean section due to the risk of life-threatening bleeding during labor.

If a woman knows that she will be delivering by cesarean, there are several options for anesthesia:

· Epidural anesthesia, the process we've already discussed.

· Spinal anesthesia, in which the anesthesia is placed directly in the spinal canal without the use of a catheter. This allows numbness, no sensation, and adequate anesthesia for a finite period in order to accomplish the surgery.

· General anesthesia of the type used on most surgical procedures in this country will put a woman to sleep and is not considered optimal for a normal cesarean section. General anesthesia is used only where epidural or spinal anesthesia are contraindicated, such as in the case of prior back surgery or other medical problems. In most cases, the mother is awake and will feel pressure, but not pain.

The personnel will include:

- the anesthesiologist, who places the anesthesia and sits at the head of the bed

- the obstetrician/surgeon, who will deliver the babies

- the scrub nurse, who hands instruments to the obstetrician

- a pediatrician for each baby

- a pediatric nurse

- a respiratory therapist (particularly for premature delivery)

- a circulating nurse, who is not scrubbed and circulates through the room acting as a coordinator

If you were not about to deliver two babies you could probably field a softball team with the personnel present.

First, the mother's abdomen will be swabbed with iodine soap. An incision, popularly known as the a "bikini cut" will be made low down on the skin of the abdomen. The uterine incision—whether transverse or vertical—is made in the uterus depending on the obstetrician's best judgment for the safest delivery of the babies. The first baby will be delivered out of the uterus and the cord will be clamped and cut. That baby will be handed off to the pediatrician or nurse in attendance while the second baby is delivered and the same procedure follows. In most circumstances, the first baby will be shown to mother and father very quickly and the parents will meet their second baby shortly after that.

The birth of the twins is an experience in which the father can actively participate. Dads should not avoid cesarean delivery for fear of being queasy or uncomfortable with the surgical procedure. Whether vaginal or cesarean, the birth of your babies is nothing less than magical and every father should have the opportunity to share in the experience. Whether or not you wish to include any other family members is something you should discuss with each other and with your obstetrician. Find out what the hospital policy is regarding spectators *before* you approach the subject with your family. There are many ways in which you can arrange for your family's participation that does not include being present at the birth itself. Your older children might be able to visit you in labor and visit the babies while you are in recovery. They might want to be the ones to call the grandparents or others in the extended family.

Stage Three: Delivery of the Placenta

With a twin pregnancy, the placenta is likely to weigh about a pound and a half. That is a substantial amount of material to be expelled from the uterus so there is likely to be continued cramping. Your obstetrician will hold the umbilical cords and help to guide the placenta in conjunction with your contractions. Within thirty minutes you will deliver the placenta, which will be placed in a container. Then your uterus will be massaged somewhat vigorously to enhance the contraction process so as to limit any additional blood loss. You may receive intravenous oxytocin to further stimulate your uterine contractions, or a shot of prostaglandin to expedite uterine contraction. Your obstetrician will carefully examine the inside of your vagina for any tears that may have occurred. A rectal exam will make sure that your rectal sphincters are intact and that there is no tear from the vagina into the rectum. If you had an episiotomy, that will be repaired with absorbable suture.

Following this, the obstetrician may examine the placenta to look for any unusual shape or membranes that might indicate unrecognized communication of blood vessels. The umbilical cords will be examined to make sure they appear normal and that there are three blood vessels within each cord. The presence of only two blood vessels can be a sign of kidney problems or other structural abnormalities.

The Apgar Test

Within the first minutes of each baby's life, he or she will be evaluated by the pediatrician and given an Apgar score. The Apgar evaluation is a method of assessing well-being in a newborn term baby using five criteria:

- heart rate
- respiratory rate
- skin color

- muscle tone
- reflex irritability

The baby can obtain up to two points for each category. The Apgar is performed at one minute, five minutes, and occasionally there is a third measure at ten minutes. While accepted as a standard for term babies, it is of limited value in assessing premature infants.

Following Delivery

Depending on what type of delivery you had, your hospital stay will be from two to five days. It is very important to understand that your body will need time, at least six weeks, to begin to feel "normal" again. If you have had a cesarean birth, be alert for any redness or swelling in the vicinity of your incision. Your practitioner will discuss the need to remove any staples from your incision. Your checkup visit will be scheduled for about two weeks postpartum. Your diet should stay about the same–don't think about a reducing diet at this point. The nursing mother will need a lot of energy to produce milk for two hungry babies and every mother of twins has extraordinary demands made upon her body in the early months of her twins' lives. Fluid shifts in your body will begin right after delivery. In the first few days you will notice a significant and very welcome decrease in edema as your body begins to flush out its excess fluids. Your urination will increase and you are likely to notice increased thirst. Be sure to stay very well-hydrated. Immediately postpartum your bleeding can be heavier than what you'd experience in a heavy period. The lochia (bloody vaginal discharge) may require you to change your sanitary napkin at least every few hours. Vaginal bleeding may continue for several weeks. If you had a vaginal delivery, your nurse is likely to offer you cold packs that fit right on your sanitary napkin and provide excellent relief for the soreness present in the vaginal and rectal areas. As your uterus contracts you may continue to feel contractions and they can be painful. Your medical team will help you to figure out how to best manage any pain.

Feeding Your Twins

Now—with some guidance from nurses and possibly a breast-feeding coach on staff at the hospital—you will attempt to nurse your babies if you are going to breast-feed, or to feed them their bottles if you will be using formula. The second, pediatric section of this book discusses in detail the pediatric implications of premature delivery and the feeding options you may face. For purposes of examining the parents' role in nourishing newborns we will assume that your babies are prepared to begin nursing from the breast or bottle. Every mom should be reassured that it takes time to get comfortable holding a newborn and finding just the right position for the baby to begin to latch on to the nipple to begin nursing. The new mother of twins needs extra encouragement from her husband and the nursing staff. Perhaps most important, she needs to be patient with herself. Term babies have a terrific suck reflex and babies born a little early will catch up pretty quickly. The babies' first nutrition from the mother's breast is called colostrum. It is a clear liquid that is produced in the first forty-eight hours after delivery and has considerable immunologic proteins within it that can help to support the twins' immature immune systems. Follow the instruction from the nursing staff, who will probably explain that frequent nursing stimulates milk production.

As your milk begins to come in you may notice a very obvious increase in the size of your breasts and they may be somewhat painful. Let your twins feed every few hours for up to fifteen minutes on each breast. The response of your breasts to your hungry babies is remarkable. These organs that you may have perceived as being rather decorative or cosmetic are suddenly pressed into service as the functional source of your babies' complete nutritional needs. Amazing! Mothers will find that their breasts anticipate feeding time by tingling or sometimes "letting down" their milk in response to the cry of their hungry babies–or any hungry babies, for that matter. The pressure can be slight or extreme enough to make you race for your babies just to relieve the urgency of an overabundance of milk.

You will want to take great care not to let your breasts become engorged, a term that describes breasts that are filled beyond their capacity. An engorged breast will feel almost rock hard and be terribly painful. You may need to pump some milk if your babies are not interested in nursing. You can use a breast pump or simply express some milk by hand as you shower. The second section of the book will address the use of breast pumps, storing milk, and the health implications for your twins. But there are important concerns about careful hygienic care of your breasts for *your* health as well. Your nipples contain numerous tiny openings from which the milk is released. These openings are more dilated now than they are at any other time. If bacteria enters a milk duct and infection ensues, you can get mastitis. Mastitis can be very painful and be accompanied by fever, chills, and overall malaise. If mastitis is suspected, alert your practitioner and examine the color of your breast milk. Your babies should not drink any milk if it is not white in color. A yellow cast to the milk is a sign of infection. You will be administered an oral antibiotic and will need to pump and discard the milk from the affected breast. Your practitioner may administer an antibiotic that is compatible with breastfeeding so you can continue to nurse from the unaffected breast.

Your nipples will take some time to adjust to the demands of two hungry babies. Some moms say that childbirth was a snap, but getting their nipples accustomed to nursing was really the hard part. Lanolin cream is a must for the bedside table of every new nursing mother. Between feedings, remember to rinse your breasts with warm soapy water. Be sure to rinse with clear water afterward as the babies will taste the soap.

If you are not going to nurse your twins, your best course of action is to wear a somewhat binding bra and avoid any stimulation of your breasts. Some practitioners may use medication to inhibit the production of milk.

Postpartum Depression

There is a wide range of emotional reactions that follow birth. Most of us have heard about "postpartum depression," or "baby blues." It is possible to break down this range of reaction into three categories that may help a mother to self-appraise and begin to address her own emotional condition:

· The first is a sort of mild and transient depression that we call "baby blues" or "maternity blues." It is very common and is probably present in 50 to 70 percent of mothers delivering twins. There can be teariness, anxiety, irritability, and restlessness. It usually manifests within ten days postpartum and will subside within a matter of days. It is tempting for the medical community to associate this blue period with shifting hormones but we don't really know if there is a clear connection. There is the suspicion that it is related to altering levels of the hormone tryptophan, which is present in the neurotransmitters of the brain. On the other hand, many experienced mothers will tell you they believe it is associated with sleep deprivation in the early weeks following the birth of the twins.

· The second category is classic postpartum depression, and it appears in 10 to 15 percent of mothers of twins. It seems to occur more commonly in women who were previously diagnosed with depression at some point prior to pregnancy. It also seems to be more present in women who had some degree of complication in the pregnancy, who are taken by surprise on the day of the twins' birth with a complicated delivery, or even an unrelated problem, such as the death or severe illness of a member of the extended family.

· The third category is an overt psychosis that is exceedingly rare.

So how do you know if you have some degree of depression or if you are just more exhausted than any book, friend, or doctor could possibly have prepared you to be? Symptoms such as weight loss and fatigue may very well be just a part of the postpartum package. Low thyroid function (hypothyroidism) can occur after pregnancy and some practitioners will be inclined to check their patient's thyroid function. Replacing thyroid hormones can cause a dramatic improvement in mood. But add to these signs feelings of ambivalence toward your children and husband, and most practitioners will be inclined to see this as a red flag and want to look further into the need to treat you for postpartum depression.

It can be very uncomfortable for a new mother to acknowledge these symptoms. The first course of action is unlimited support from the family and understanding from her practitioner. A new mother's ability to acknowledge her feelings of guilt, fear, or uncertainty are the first steps back to sound emotional health. Continued follow-ups in the form of support groups, a therapeutic environment, and the possible use of medication are vital to the well-being of the mother and her whole family.

When Postpartum Depression Is Beyond the "Baby Blues"
One Family's Success Story

Joan and her husband David had been married for twelve years when they got pregnant with twins. Joan, a psychiatric nurse, considered herself to be an extremely focused, competent, and independent woman. Her pregnancy was not without complications and she describes feeling anxious, ". . . but I still don't feel like it was inappropriate . . . I was having twins, I was on bed rest. . . . It provoked some understandable anxiety." After the babies were born, she began to feel far more distressed.

I felt constantly overwhelmed and terribly sleep-deprived those first few months. But the depression really hit about four months postpartum and coincided with my first postpartum menstrual period, though I don't think I made that connection at the time. I cried all the time. I didn't have any interest in doing the things I normally loved to do. I remember thinking how odd it was when I did not want my closest friend to come and see us for New Year's Eve. I did not feel suicidal, but I remember feeling I wanted to make sure the babies were fine; call my husband or my mother and say, "The boys are safe, but you have to come and take care of them," and walk out the front door. I wanted desperately to get away. Remarkably, I never had any thoughts about harming the children, though many women in the throes of depression do.

No matter how capable I'd been in my professional life, and no matter how well I'd cared for my father when he was ill, I did not really feel confident about caring for a baby—let alone two. My friends either had grown children or had decided not to have children, so I did not have a natural circle of peer support. My husband had stayed home for three weeks and my mom helped during that time, but now it was pretty much me and the babies. I was extremely anxious. I worried all the time that something would happen to them: that they would get sick, or I'd drop them . . . something horrible would happen. Now I understand that excessive worry is a classic symptom of postpartum depression. But at the time, all I knew was that I just didn't feel good. I didn't feel happy. I mean, I had a deep feeling of happiness at having these two beautiful babies, but I felt sad all the time. If you were to look at me, you would have seen a very sad person. And the feeling that was with me constantly was that I was not a good mother: I saw all these other mothers who looked great and seemed to have lots of energy.

Right about that time, the babies started sleeping through the night a little bit more—but I didn't. It was a horrible irony. I could not turn off my mind. I have always had very high expectations of myself, and I felt I was failing to live up to my own standard of "being a good mother"— though what that meant, I couldn't have really said. The one exception to all of this was my experience in nursing the boys. I loved nursing and it seemed to go well for us. It was also the only time I got to devote to one baby at a time. Sometimes

I nursed them at the same time but I preferred to nurse them one at a time. When I complained about being tired and generally overwhelmed, my pediatrician tried to guide me to nurse them at the same time, and I was able to, but that took much of the joy away. I must say that he was very supportive of my desire to nurse the boys. And it meant a great deal to me to feel that he really heard me and my commitment to nursing and didn't waiver in his support of my decision.

My mother finally came to me and told me she thought I was experiencing postpartum depression. She had found a book called Mothering the New Mother, *and as I looked at the book I came to agree with her. I called Jane Honikman, the author of the book, who, it happened, was the leader of a support group in Santa Barbara. That was the beginning of my identifying my depression and actively seeking help. Jane told me to write down several statements: "I will get better"; "This is not my fault"; and there was a third, but those were the ones that were most important to me. I read them over and over. I began going to a support group where there was a room full of women who shared my experience. I was the only mother with twins, but I know that there is a significant incidence of depression in mother's of multiples that can go undiagnosed because they may have the expectation that they are going to feel overwhelmed and that is just the way it is. . . . I know that for the first four months of the boys' lives I constantly compared myself to the mothers I saw and assumed my problem was just that I had two, so naturally it was tougher. It was so impor-*

tant for me to finally have a diagnosis: This was postpartum depression and I would get over it. In addition to the support of the group, I saw a therapist who was familiar with postpartum depression and that was important, because the therapist I'd seen earlier suggested my depression had nothing to do with the birth of the babies . . . that I was unhappy about the loss of autonomy and career. . . . This second therapist recommended that I see a psychiatrist to be evaluated for medication. I was unwilling to do so at that point because of my belief that I could not nurse and be on medication. I started to feel a little better and resolved to take really good care of myself. In retrospect it was kind of ridiculous. I joined a gym and went one time! But I was determined to "handle this myself." I went to the group and saw my therapist weekly. My symptoms continued but they were no longer constant. I felt I was improving.

Then, at nine months, Robert weaned himself and I was devastated. I got my second postpartum menstrual period and entered another cycle of depression that I can only describe as being in hell. There were mornings I couldn't get out of bed. At that point I agreed to be evaluated for medication. I saw a psychiatrist who was very familiar with this type of depression. I think the most important thing I can share with moms of twins who might be experiencing this awful dilemma is that I came to understand that what my boys really needed was me. More than they needed my breast milk, they needed me to be their mother. They had a person who nursed

(continued)

them, but couldn't sing them a nursery rhyme, or even play with them. My psychiatrist explained to me that the type of antidepressants that would enable me to continue nursing would also have more side effects,. The ones that were most effective in treating my kind of depression had not been adequately assessed as regards [to] their effects on nursing babies.

Once I'd decided to begin medication, my pediatrician guided me in how to manage weaning. On my fortieth birthday, I nursed Paul for the last time and Robert had pumped milk in a bottle and it was really extraordinary—all of a sudden it just felt OK to stop nursing.

My understanding of the protocol for handling medication in postpartum depression is that the most significant relapse of symptoms is most likely to occur twelve months from the time of remission of symptoms. So they like to keep you on antidepressants for up to eighteen months. This is for those who, like me, don't have a prior history of depression. So I continue with my therapist every other week and my husband and I sometimes see her to discuss the impact of all of this on our marriage. I really want to stress the importance of support groups for any woman dealing with postpartum depression. I feel I lost a significant part of my boys' first year because I was sort of lost in this sense that it was just the "baby blues" and took so long to recognize my condition as treatable. I now have every expectation that I am going to come through this to feel better than ever.

A Few Parting Words

You have taken the extraordinary first steps in your journey with your twins. And the substance of this book is about to shift into the next epic segment of your travels: the first year of life with your two, new babies. Your regular visits to your practitioner will change to regular visits to the babies' pediatrician. And you will begin to take the postpartum pulse of your family:

· First of all, how is the new mother? Are you able to sleep at all? How is your appetite? Are you feeling increasingly competent about nourishing your babies? Have you begun to establish a list of resource people to help you through these early months with twins? Do you have some sort of routine going in the house?

·   How about the couple relationship? Are you finding a little time to communicate each day? Do you each feel supported and recognized for your extraordinary efforts?

·   Are your other children finding their place in the newly redesigned family? Are the young ones acting out? Do they have a little of your time each day that they can count on to be just for them?

You will find that there is some natural crossover in the discussions that follow. Just as there is no discussion of Mom's pregnancy without looking at her two passengers, there can be no reflection on the twins' first year without placing them in the context of the family. As we shift from a maternal to a pediatric focus, we wish you and your beautiful babies continued safe travels.

THE FIRST YEAR OF LIFE

Chapter 13

READY . . . SET . . . TWINS!

Preparing for Your Twins' Arrival

The first section of this book looked at multiple pregnancy from the parents' point of view, taking us through prenatal counseling to the birth of your twins. Now we need to back up a little bit in order to examine your babies' impending birth from the *pediatric* angle. In one of nature's exquisite ironies, parents of twins have *less* time to prepare than their singleton counterparts. On the average, gestation for twins is two to three weeks shorter than it is for singletons– thirty-seven weeks rather than forty–so forget any ideas you may have about last-minute preparation: By the time you get close to deliv-ery, everything will feel like it ought to have been completed yester-day! Once you've entered your third trimester, you have limited time to think about some very basic questions:

- Will we get two cribs or co-bed our twins?
- What is the best twin stroller for us?
- Will we dress the babies differently from the start?
- How do we want to name our twins?
- Should we try to hire help or would it be better to ask our extended families to pitch in for the first month?

And this is just the short list, the specialized questions that you, as expectant parents of twins, need to resolve. You also need to make the basic preparations common to all prospective parents. The list goes on and on, easily outpacing the last weeks of your pregnancy. So let's take a look at what you need to do, keeping in mind that your schedule is likely to be a few weeks shorter than that of parents expecting a singleton delivery.

Choosing Your Pediatrician

Among the many important decisions you'll be making, your choice of a pediatrician is right up there at the top of the list. While parents of singletons often wait until thirty-five weeks gestation to start looking for a pediatrician, families expecting twins should start early, around thirty weeks or even earlier if recommended by your obstetrician. Sometimes this process has to go on from the mother's hospital room by telephone while she is on bed rest, or the father can start this process and ask the prospective pediatrician to visit the mother in the hospital.

Talking to your obstetrician, or friends who are parents of young children, is a good way to develop a short list of pediatricians who might be right for you and your twins. Of course, where friends are concerned, you must consider the degree to which their child-rearing philosophy mirrors your own. You can have a great pal with exactly the same taste in movies and books, yet you may think she is nuts when it comes to raising her children. Her taste in pediatricians is not likely to work for you. Your obstetrician or members of a local twins club may be able to supply you with a list of pediatricians whose practices have a high percentage of multiples. Call the pediatric practice and find out if they offer prospective parents an opportunity to interview the doctor.

Many pediatricians with substantial "high risk" practices have had a lot of experience in dealing with premature infants and twins. In the case of premature twins who may need to spend some time in the hospital before being discharged, it is best if the general pediatrician who will care for them after they go home is involved in their care as much as possible while they are still hospitalized.

Should you be preparing to start your family in an unfamiliar city, call the neonatal unit in the local hospital, explain that you are pregnant with twins, and ask the head nurse to recommend several pediatric practices for your consideration. If the person you speak with has children, ask them who they see. This gives you a good jumping-off point for interviewing pediatricians. Of course, insurance and financial considerations may play a big role in which doctors are available to you and in what capacity.

As new parents, it makes perfect sense for you to look to an expert for an endorsement of your emerging parenting skills. Many parents, reflecting on long-term relationships with their pediatricians, have acknowledged that there was an element of their desire early on to do well, noting the importance of receiving their doctor's approval for good parenting. Frequently, the most successful doctor/parent relationships acknowledge that phase and then go beyond it. Even at the outset of your association with your pediatrician, it is important to voice any questions you may have about specific recommendations, or even a general approach to child care. Open communication will often clear up any misunderstandings that you may have and will also serve to enhance your trust in your children's doctor. This relationship usually works out best when parents and doctor are on the same path, even though they may not be in complete agreement on everything. For example, it will be frustrating for you *and* your pediatrician if you continue to ask that your child be put on medication when your pediatrician doesn't think it is necessary. So it's a good idea to find out from the beginning if you are all in agreement about his general approach to medication, or any other aspects of care that you feel strongly about.

The pediatrician is an important source of information for your family. Some of the information he gives you is absolute: Your children's health and sometimes their very lives are at stake. Your pediatrician's directions on subjects such as the use of car seats or fevers must be followed to the letter. Other information, however, is more like guidance and may need modification to work for your family. Issues like feeding schedules or sleeping arrangements need to be flexible. With this type of information, you should do what feels right for you. If you are in doubt about whether a particular recommendation from your pediatrician is doctrine or simply a suggestion, you should always feel comfortable enough to ask.

Questions to Ask At the Pediatric Interview

A pediatric interview can be conducted in several ways. Some parents schedule an interview, start out by asking the pediatrician to describe his practice, and follow up with questions that have either been generated from comments or prepared earlier. Other parents prepare a detailed list and begin the interview by asking their own questions. The goal here is to get practical information about this doctor's approach to pediatrics, and to assess your gut reaction to the practitioner who will be caring for your twins.

These are some of the questions you might want to pose to a pediatrician you are considering. You may not be interested in all of them, but they will give you an idea of the range of subjects that you should be able to discuss comfortably with a prospective pediatrician. It's a good idea to discuss these questions with your mate beforehand so that you have some idea about what answers you both are looking for before the interview takes place.

- How soon after our twins are born will you see them?

- Do you see a lot of twins in your practice?

- What is your schedule for well-baby visits?

- What happens at a well-baby visit? How do you handle the visit with twins?

- How much time do you spend with a patient at a well-baby visit?

- Do you have a different schedule for premature babies?

- Who will answer my questions if I call the office?

- What are your office hours?

- What happens if we call after office hours?

- Is this your own practice or are there other pediatricians we might see in this office?

- If it is a group practice, can we request to see you exclusively?

- What is your philosophy about immunizations?

- Can you talk to us about feeding our twins?

- Can you speak with us about your philosophy regarding medication and the use of alternative approaches to health care?

- Where did you take your training?

- Do you have children of your own?

- What do you think about circumcision?

- What hospitals are you associated with?

- Are you board certified?

DR. KLEIN COMMENTS ON HIS WELL-BABY VISIT SCHEDULE

"For babies who are released from the hospital in less than forty-eight hours, I usually see them as recommended by the Academy [The American Academy of Pediatrics] in two to three days; then at two weeks of age; one, two, three, four, five, and six months of age; then at nine months and one year. We give immunizations beginning with the one-month visit and continue with immunizations at the two-, three-, four-, six-, nine-, and twelve-month visits. For premature babies, I often see them every week until they reach their actual due date, and then they go onto the same schedule that I use for term babies."

A Word About the Team Approach

As you move toward a due date, there are questions about your babies that will be on the minds of your physicians (obstetrician and pediatrician), yourselves, and anyone else you have brought into the twin loop. This is a good time for parents to make sure that they are talking with each other and attempting to have consensus about just who *is* in that intimate circle that makes up "the team." Successful communication with each other and with your physicians is all important now as your due date gets closer and you can no longer put off any important decisions.

The practice of medicine in the United States does not exist in a vacuum. Like theories in education or techniques in child rearing, medicine exists within the framework of popular culture and the broad scope of its influences. There might be several protocols for treating a particular symptom of your pregnancy, or even your child's illness. Medical practice can range from instruction in relaxation techniques to use of the newest drugs. Patients are becoming educated consumers of health care, and are far more likely to question their practitioners today than they were thirty years ago. The Internet is one of the few places a pregnant woman can go for information. There she can communicate with everyone from internationally recognized obstetricians to other moms whose twins are old enough to be asking for the car keys. All may offer valuable advice. But what do you do when you have conflicting information and the stakes are so high?

This is what the team approach is all about. Has a friend recommended an herbal tea to treat sleeplessness? Perhaps you are anticipating raising your twins as vegetarians. You need to discuss these things with your doctors. Just as it is imprudent to make an assumption about the tea ("Well, it's only an herb"), it is equally unwise to make presumptions about your doctor's attitude. Is he willing to look into a vegetarian diet for your seven-month-old twins? If not, does he have a colleague he can consult or recommend that you see?

It is interesting to note that we live in an age that seems to support extreme views of the medical community in general, and birth and delivery in particular. Certainly it is true that women were experiencing "natural childbirth" long before medical schools entered the picture. But along with advances in medicine have come enhanced diagnostic capabilities for both mother and fetus. The result has been a dramatically reduced rate of infant mortality. The medical team delivering twins is as delighted as the expectant parents when both deliveries take place without complications. But they are understandably pleased to have the very latest in technological support when it is needed.

People who flee the mainstream of medicine may embrace a natural philosophy that can be somewhat reactionary. For example, there are vocal critics of the medical establishment who feel that doctors are out of step with the needs of today's parents of twins: They maintain, for example, that medical intervention is frequently introduced to satisfy the comfort level of the physician and has no proven benefit to the outcome of the birth of the twins. But the truth is that in the case of high-risk pregnancies of twins or higher order multiples, there has been a significant decrease in infant morbidity with the practice of monitoring both twins during labor. Medical intervention may very well be the only responsible alternative if the natural approach is not the safest possible one for mother or babies.

Before Your Twins Arrive

Again, parents expecting twins need to be a few weeks ahead of the singleton parents' schedule when it comes to getting ready for their babies' arrival. Later on in this book we will discuss the specifics of baby-proofing your home and we'll talk about the safety concerns of those products you'll be needing for your growing babies. For now, let's limit our discussion to what needs to be in place for bringing your newborn twins home after delivery.

You may find it helpful to make a list of the material objects you'll want to have on hand once you bring your babies home. Heading this list, of course, will be your two car seats.

Car Seats

Every state in the U.S. requires the use of child car seats. All car seats manufactured today must meet a Federal standard established in 1981. Never use a car seat manufactured before that time, *and never use an infant carrier for a car seat!* When purchasing your car seats, make sure that they both fit correctly into your vehicle. If you have two cars, even if one will be used more frequently for transporting your babies, make certain that the car seats fit correctly into both.

The safest place in your vehicle for your car seats is the back seat. The car seats of babies weighing less than twenty pounds should be secured into the back seat, *facing backwards.* One car seat should be anchored in the center of the back seat, and the other should be behind the front right-passenger seat, allowing you optimum visual access to both babies in their car seats. Follow the precise instructions of the car seat manufacturer, and call the manufacturer if you have any questions regarding safe installation of the car seats in your vehicle. *Never use a car seat in a seating location that has an activated airbag, and never travel in a vehicle with your babies without having them securely strapped into their car seats.*

Cribs and Bedding

First you will need to decide whether or not you want to put your twins in two cribs, or co-sleep them in one. Crib slats should be no more than $2^3/8$" apart. End posts should be no higher than $1/16$" above the crib's end panel, as older babies can strangle if their clothing gets caught on a corner post. Apply these guidelines to cribs offered by friends or family, or that you might wish to purchase secondhand.

The crib mattress should fit snugly, and bumper pads should fit securely around the entire crib. Snap or tie bumpers into place, trimming any excess length from ties to prevent your twins from strangling or becoming entangled. *Remember, when you put your babies down to sleep, place them on their backs on a firm mattress without any pillows.*

Strollers and Carriers

One of your biggest challenges will be getting out and about with your very young twins. Most parents of twins get many hours of use from their strollers, so you want to buy the right one. If you already have one pram or carriage, both your newborn twins are likely to fit in it comfortably, so you may have a brief reprieve from purchasing your two-seater stroller. You will have some choices to make: there are limousine strollers with seats facing each other, side-by-side strollers, and even three-seaters if you already have a toddler at home. If you have not yet made contact with a local twins club, this is the time to seek opinions from parents who have been there.

The baby carrier, a soft, shoulder-slung "front pack" for holding your baby while freeing your hands, can also be very helpful. Some manufacturers make baby carriers designed for twins (see the resource guide at the end of this book), though not all parents choose to use them. Any soft carrier you choose should be washable, sturdy, and have adjustable straps. Your baby's head should be supported and her weight evenly distributed. *A soft carrier is for walking with your babies and should never be used to transport your twins on a bicycle or in a car.*

Basic Supplies

BATH TIME

Two soft, hooded, cotton baby towels for each baby will get plenty of use. You may want a portable bathtub or bath seat to hold your baby securely in the bath. Since you're likely to be bathing your young twins one at a time, one tub or seat will do. Several soft, cotton baby washcloths for each baby will come in handy at feeding time as well as in the bath. *Placing the bath seat in the sink or on a counter may save on back strain. Of course, never leave your babies unattended, even for a moment, at bath time.*

DIAPERS

Anticipate an *average* of ten a day for each of your newborn twins. You may choose cloth, disposable, or a combination of the two. Should you decide to use disposable diapers, don't load up on them until your babies are born and you see which brand and which size will work best for you.

If you do plan to try cloth diapers for your twins, a year's worth of diaper service would be a significant gift from a group of friends, co-workers, or family members. Don't be shy about making such a request of people who are hoping to give you a gift. *Cotton diapers make perfect shoulder protectors for keeping spit-up away from your shirts or blouse. Always have a dozen extra cloth diapers on hand.*

CLOTHING

The more of each necessary item you have, the less frequently you'll have to launder them. On the other hand, too much clothing makes for storage and organizational headaches. When you think about the basics for your twins, balance the monetary cost against the price you pay in creating extra work for yourself. This is also the time to confront the question of whether or not you will dress your twins alike. You may have strong feelings about either option or you may want to talk to other parents of twins to find out what has worked for them.

- six cotton snap undershirts for each baby
- six one-piece, leg-snap pajama sets for each twin
- six receiving blankets for each baby
- two blanket sleepers for each winter baby
- two snowsuits for each winter baby
- two sets of booties (especially for winter babies)
- two hats, suitable to the season, for each twin

While these basics will get you started, few parents or their friends and family can resist the adorable clothing that is out there for little babies. Enjoy this wonderful opportunity to purchase or receive those special gifts like handmade sweaters or baby blankets for your beautiful, new babies.

Twin-Proofing

Your newborn twins will, of course, be unable to get around on their own at first, but "twin-proofing," the process of making your home safe for your babies, can and *should* be started before they arrive. We will go into greater detail about twin-proofing later in this book, but by the time you go to the hospital to deliver your babies, you ought to have completed the first four items on this list.

· Have the telephone numbers of your pediatric office, poison control, the fire department, and, of course, 911 posted at every telephone.

· Be sure that the twins' sleeping spots are not next to any curtain cords or electrical wires that they could grasp or become tangled in.

· Consider any special arrangements that you may want to make regarding your pets.

· Check with the local nursery to be sure that none of your houseplants are potentially dangerous to your babies.

It may seem a little early to be worrying about these next twin-proofing steps, but if you can manage to get them done before the babies are born you'll be glad you did.

• It is not too early to count the number of electrical outlets in your home and purchase safety caps to cover them from exploring baby hands.

• Even if you don't yet have them installed, start thinking about baby-safe latches for cabinets, and safety gates at the tops of stairs and between rooms you won't want your exploring twins to enter.

• Begin to think about storing all poisons, medications, or any dangerous or toxic substances in high, locked, inaccessible places.

There are many topics you will want to discuss *with each other* before the babies come home. Total agreement between parents on all areas of child care is highly improbable, but you are far more likely to have reasonable discussions about all issues, *including* any hot-button topics, before you are confronted with your two very special deliveries.

Things to Think About

• **Can Dad take some significant time off from work when the babies come home?**

You need to consider the longer term implications of Dad being home for the first two weeks or so. Will it mean loss of income and if so, is it manageable? Can you be assured that it will not jeopardize job security? Many employers will be sympathetic to the extraordinary demands of twins, but you need to figure these things out ahead of time.

• **Do either of you have parents or other family members who could help out for the first month?**

If ever there was a time to call out the troops, this is it. However, both parents need to understand the implications of asking family to help out at such a highly emotional moment in your lives. If he has a hard time with your mother or you are uncomfortable with his older sister, talk about it ahead of time.

• **Are you comfortable with family help if it means they will have to move in with you for a while?**

The apartment that seemed so spacious to you as newlyweds may feel very cramped when you bring two babies home. Are you prepared to wait in line for the bathroom or have your in-laws camped out in the living room? If having your extended family in your home makes for too-close quarters and the cost of hotel living for out-of-towners is prohibitive, maybe you have friends who can provide a temporary home away from home for visiting family.

• **Can the family budget be manipulated to allow for hired help in the first two weeks or a month, if that is desirable?**

Some people simply do not have family to help out. While the cost of hiring a baby nurse may be too high for many families, it is

far less costly to hire someone to come in for three or four hours a day to clean, do laundry, and prepare meals that can be frozen and served at your convenience. Even families who can afford a nanny for their newborns may prefer to care for the babies themselves while handing off the household chores.

If any hired help is out of the question, this is another opportunity to interact with your community of friends. There may be a local twins club that would be happy to supply some support, or members of your church, synagogue, or mosque who will willingly step in once they are made aware of a need.

- ## Have you thought about the implications of naming your two babies?

Parents are all over the map on this question. Some seek to emphasize the miracle of a twin birth by choosing rhyming or alliterative names for their twins: Jill and Bill, Marie and Michelle, or Annie and Andrew. Other parents choose to honor a family member on either side of the family in their name choices. Still others seek from the outset to emphasize their twins' individuality by choosing completely unrelated names. Each of these choices has implications in the lives of your unborn babies and it is wise to talk them through ahead of time.

- ## Have you read your health-insurance policy from cover to cover?

Many parents of twins report frustration over dealing with their insurance carriers. It is not uncommon for insurance companies to refuse payment on a claim that appears to their computer to be double billing. First, *read your policy!* Take notes, then speak with a representative of the insurance company and alert them to the fact that you are having twins, so what may appear to be double billing is, in fact, care for two babies. *If both parents have insurance before becoming pregnant, think hard before dropping one policy to save a little money.* You may find that between the two policies your coverage for the babies will be more comprehensive. Some companies cover well-baby visits while some do not. Some companies will not cover two claims for the same diagnosis if they occur within too short a time period. Parents of twins have to be vigilant consumers.

Making It Work for Your Older Children At Home

Women with twins are often on bed rest for extended periods of time. Whether it is in the hospital or at home prior to delivery, a twin pregnancy often presents greater family stress than an impending singleton birth. First of all, in all discussions with your other children, it is important to make your explanations age appropriate, as well as suitable, to your older child's experience. If your four-year-old's grandmother has just had an extended stay in the hospital for an illness, imagine what it might be like for her to hear that Mommy is going to the hospital and *we don't know exactly when she'll be coming home.* Be sure to explain Mom's absence in terms that are both clear and comforting. For mothers on bed rest in the hospital, schedule regular play dates there for mother and child. If Mom is on bed rest but not confined to the hospital, these special play dates can be a time when you are together at home, focusing needed attention on your child before the twins arrive.

After delivery, maybe Dad can take the time he is not at the hospital with Mom to be at home with the older child. Find out ahead of time if your children will be allowed to visit you in the hospital and ask if they can tour the nursery and/or birthing room several weeks before you're due. *If it is your child's preference to stay at home for the days you are in the hospital, try to accommodate that wish.* It is best for very young children to stay in their own homes with a family member or trusted friend whom they know well and who has baby-sat them in the past. Your nine-year-old may be delighted to go to Grandma's for several days until Mommy comes home, but that is not likely to be the case for a younger child.

One Mom's Tale

On Bed Rest in the Hospital for Seven Weeks with Two Small Children At Home

Annie and her husband Paul had two young children when they became pregnant with twins. At twenty-eight-and-a-half weeks, Annie was experiencing several symptoms of premature labor. With two children under four, she had to agree with her obstetrician that any bed rest would be pretty much impossible at home. She was admitted to the hospital and placed on complete bed rest. Fortunately, that did not include her dialing finger, since her telephone would become the command post for seven weeks of marshaling the troops to help care for her three-and-half–year–old son, Ben, and sixteen-month-old daughter, Emily.

At twenty-eight and a half weeks, my obstetrician gave me less than a day to prepare for a hospital stay that would turn out to be seven weeks long. I was pretty much in a panic. I had two little kids at home and had to try to explain that Mommy had to be in the hospital but it was going to be all right.

It was over ten years ago but there are some things you just don't forget. In my seven weeks, I had thirteen roommates and every one of them had something else going on. They never put a woman who had delivered a baby in with me. But I tell you, by the time I got out of there I felt like if someone had given me a stethoscope, I could have walked the halls and seen patients. There were

two other twin moms there during my stay. We were all due about the same time. They were discharged but we all ended up back in the hospital to deliver within forty-eight hours of each other.

One of the hardest things was not being able to see my kids as much as I wanted to. We spoke every night, but they only came to the hospital about once a week. I had a whole wall of their scribbles and pictures right there with my calendar marking off each day. My friends were incredible. I got on the phone and really tapped every resource: There were families we knew from my husband's job, moms from my son's preschool, church friends. A great young girl who baby-sat for us made sure to be at our house every day at five o'clock so the kids could come home. Emily would have spent the day with one of our friends and Ben was at preschool. We set up a week at a time. There was an incredible food-preparation detail. We had a freezer filled with casseroles, even when I came home! Amazingly, the kids ate dinner at home every night I was away and slept at home, too.

It was pretty tough on my husband. In fact, the first night I was in the hospital, Paul had both kids out shopping. Emily was in the cart and Ben was riding underneath. He somehow got a finger stuck in the wheel and they had to race off to the emergency clinic. Not a great first night without Mommy. . . . Paul had so much to deal with and

(continued)

he had bronchitis during that time. I felt absurd—here I was in the hospital, the picture of health—imposing on every person I knew. . . . I was not allowed up or out of that bed at all. I had a million things to do and was not able to do a thing. . . . They were managing the contractions with muscle relaxers and told me that if I could get through seven weeks they would probably let me go home. I have never been more motivated in my life.

When they did let me go home, as eager as I was, it was kind of scary. I was so huge. . . . My mom and dad came and we really worked to keep the kids from jumping on me. I sort of camped out on the couch. We had a friend who continued to come and clean out the fridge each Monday and help with laundry. . . . She was incredible.

One Mom's Tale will resume in Chapter 15 with the birth of the twins.

Chapter 14

PREPARING FOR DELIVERY AND BIRTH

Where to Deliver Your Twins

The delivery of your babies should be discussed and prepared for well ahead of your due date. This means talking about who will be present at the delivery, and *where* it will take place. It is very much in your interest as advocates for your twins to find out what will happen before and after delivery, and to ask about what support services are available for families with twins. If you have not yet done so, be sure to *read your health insurance policy from cover to cover.*

Things You May Want to Know About the Hospital

- Can the father be present in the delivery room if you expect to deliver by C-section? Does that same policy hold for the unanticipated C-section?

- What is the hospital policy regarding the babies being with you in your room?

- Are there staff members specially trained to help you begin to breast-feed your twins?

- Does the hospital offer any financial discounts in the case of multiple births?

· Discuss the conditions associated with visiting the babies in the event that you are released before one or both of them: visiting hours, the number of visitors at a time, etc.

· Can you sleep over in the hospital if you are released before one or both of the babies?

· Is there a hospital tour available for your older children while you are pregnant?

· Can your older children visit you and the babies in the hospital?

· Does the hospital provide any ongoing programs for parents of twins?

· Are they able to recommend any resources in the community for parents of multiples?

It is also important to inquire about the capabilities of the facility itself. On the average, gestation for twins is two to three weeks shorter than it is for singletons: thirty-seven weeks rather than forty. Many hospitals are equipped to handle healthy multiple births after thirty-four weeks gestation. If your doctor anticipates that your twins will be born earlier, it is best to give birth at a medical center that has a level II or level III nursery. These facilities will have a neonatologist on call twenty-four hours a day to handle immediate problems. The neonatologist is a pediatrician who specializes in working with premature infants or full-term newborns who are ill.

Preterm Labor

The presence of any of the following conditions in pregnancy may increase the chances of early labor and delivery of your twins before thirty-four weeks. Be sure to discuss with your doctor the pediatric implications of these conditions:

- polyhydramnios—the presence of excess fluid in the gestational sac

- bleeding episodes or change in vaginal discharge to include blood or mucus

- concerns about the health or growth of one or both babies

- increased frequency of uterine contractions

- a prior obstetric history of preterm delivery

- pregnancy with high-order multiples (triplets or more)

How Far from Home to Hospital?

Having babies, especially twins, is an inexact science and, as mentioned before, your possible early delivery must be kept in mind. Consider a situation in which the physician doubts that a pregnancy will go beyond thirty weeks. The parents live in a suburb, forty miles from the nearest urban medical center. The discussion here should focus on the options available to the family: The expectant mother could stay at home anticipating giving birth at the local facility or she could arrange, possibly with considerable inconvenience, to reside in the city where the hospital has a neonatal intensive care unit (level II or III nursery). Many smaller hospitals use transport systems that will take the babies by ambulance, plane, or helicopter to the more sophisticated facility.

All the factors must be considered. Is the mother on bed rest and can or should she be checked in to the larger facility to await the birth? Are there small children at home who need to be cared for to guarantee the mother's bed rest at any site? Should the parents take their chances and anticipate making the drive when she goes into labor? What is the data on survival rates for infants who must be transported immediately after birth? Common sense tells us that separating the mother from one or both of the babies is not going to be easy on any of them. Once again, the importance of communicating with your doctor about your options can be the difference between calm resolve and anxious uncertainty.

The Right Level of Care for You and Your Babies

LEVEL I

The level I facility is prepared to watch over and care for all patients admitted to the obstetrics service, and has an established protocol for identifying high-risk patients who need to be transferred to a level II or level III facility prior to delivery.

Most level I facilities may also provide continuing care for newborns who have relatively minor problems that do not require advanced laboratory, radiologic, or pediatric consultative services. Level I facilities also provide care for convalescing babies who have returned from level II or level III facilities. They also provide for the stabilization of unexpectedly small infants until they can be transported to the appropriate level II or level III facility.

LEVEL II

The level II facility performs all level I services and most frequently provides the neonatal expertise required to manage otherwise normal newborns from approximately thirty-two to thirty-six weeks gestational age. These facilities manage the care of small, moderately sick neonates who are admitted directly or are transferred in.

Some level II facilities are able to care for the more complicated needs of sick infants but do not have all the necessary care that is available in a level III facility.

LEVEL III

Provides all the care options of level I and level II facilities. The level III can also care for babies born under thirty-two weeks gestational age or under 1,500 grams. These babies will almost always require neonatal medical expertise.

The level III facility provides the most sophisticated care available for babies who are identified as high risk, as well as offering comprehensive perinatal care for mothers.

Information adapted from Guidelines for Perinatal Care, Third Edition (American Academy of Pediatrics, American College of Obstetricians and Gynecologists, 1992)

Who Will Attend the Delivery?

It is important to take the time to speak with your doctor about the personnel who will be involved from the pediatric side. Full-term twins do not always have additional personnel in attendance, but it's different when premature twins are expected. Often, a pediatrician or a neonatologist will be called in to attend to the babies at delivery. There may be a respiratory therapist present or additional nurses who are specially trained to assist with the newborn twins. In a teaching hospital there are likely to be interns and residents called in to assist. On certain occasions the obstetrician will want an anesthesiologist on hand. The position of the babies is a significant factor in determining who is best equipped to deliver your twins. If, for example, one of the babies is transverse and the other is breech, the obstetrician may need to do a breech extraction. You will want to know if your obstetrician is very familiar with this procedure. It is both wise and appropriate to ask your doctor about his experience with the various types of twin presentations. Years ago, there was a general consensus in the medical community that the second twin was more at risk for complications of birth and delivery. Today, advances in fetal monitoring have greatly diminished, if not completely eliminated, those risks. You want your own focus to be on delivering your babies, and this is best accomplished by feeling confident that the medical details are being handled by experts trained to do their specialized jobs. It may sound as though you are gathering enough people to staff your own clinic, but the intimacy of this moment is forged by your connection to your twins and each other; it will not be compromised by having what seems like a small crowd in attendance. Think of it as a rare opportunity to socialize with grown-ups who are as interested in your babies as *you* are.

Vaginal vs. Cesarean Delivery: What Does It Mean to Your Twins?

In a healthy, term infant—whether it is the first or the fourth baby delivered—there is some benefit to vaginal birth. When an infant negotiates the birth canal, its head, which is the largest part of a newborn baby, usually proceeds first, followed by the chest and abdomen. This mechanical compression of the baby's chest allows the fluid that is present in the lungs to be squeezed out, so that when the baby takes

The Right Start

A study published in the *Journal of the American Medical Association* (JAMA) October 2, 1996* states that the likelihood of a successful outcome for a newborn needing intensive care was higher when the pregnant mother was transferred to a level III neonatal intensive care unit (NICU) before giving birth, than if the neonate was transported after delivery.

*"Effect of Patient Volume and Level of Care on Neonatal Mortality"–Phibbs, et al

its first, very-important breath, the fluid is not forced into the little air sacs within the lungs.

We know that the baby delivered by cesarean section may tend to have some mild breathing problems (transient tachypnea of the newborn [TTN], or retained lung fluid) after birth, the result of its not having experienced the compression of the chest that takes place in the course of a vaginal delivery. This breathing difficulty usually corrects itself within twenty-four hours, though some babies do need a little oxygen to help them through the first hours. In even rarer cases, they will need to spend some time on a respirator.

In the case of a premature baby, there can be benefits and risks to vaginal delivery. If a premature twin is in the breech presentation–that is, feet first–delivery through the vagina may not be appropriate. Keeping in mind that the head is usually the largest part of the baby, the breech delivery runs the risk of having the head somewhat delayed in its passage through the birth canal. If either the feet or rear end should deliver first, you don't have the benefit of the baby's head to dilate the cervix and the head may not deliver as fast as it should.

As far as the implications of vaginal or cesarean birth for the second twin, there are many factors to consider. If the first twin has been delivered without incident, the cervix is completely dilated, and the second baby is about the same size, either a breech or vertex (head first) delivery should be pretty uneventful. Most obstetricians are pretty confident of a successful second delivery if the second baby's

head comes down and delivers vertex. All obstetricians would probably agree that the very best case scenario with a twin delivery is two
babies who present vertex for a vaginal birth.

If the second baby is breech and there is concern about head
entrapment, the obstetrician may perform a total breech extraction.
This is a time-honored, extraordinary obstetrical maneuver that has
been in practice since we have had any records of birthing. It requires
the obstetrician reaching up into the uterus and bringing the feet
down in a controlled, gentle fashion. The fetus is guided through the
birth canal, feet first, after the delivery of the first twin. The obstetrician will make this decision regarding the delivery of the second twin
after the delivery of the first baby.

There are also other alternatives. The obstetrician may be able to
guide the breech fetus from the outside of the mother's body:
Through the use of hands on her abdomen, the obstetrician will
maneuver the baby to be vertex for a vaginal delivery. The mother is
then allowed to complete vaginal delivery of the second twin. The use
of ultrasound and other technologies enables your obstetrician to
monitor the undelivered twin so as to make the best decisions regarding delivery.

After the Twins Are Born

It is helpful to anticipate the changing of the guard as your team
shifts from delivery of the twins by your obstetrician to overseeing
their health after birth by their pediatrician. You may want to have one
set of questions for your obstetrician and prepare another list of questions for your pediatrician. Hopefully, most of your questions will be
answered before delivery; however, some questions may persist, so it
will be helpful to write down the few that are left or pop up after the
pediatric interview. After delivery, it's hard for parents of twins to
think about anything but the miracle of their two babies in the here and
now. It is not unusual to hear a new mother comment on the mental,
hormonal, and emotional shift that takes place as she adjusts to the
twins actually existing outside her body. Realizing that your twins now

have a pediatrician, while you as a mother have your own practitioner, is one of the very first steps you take in granting your children their own identities in the family. Once your twins are born, your relationship with your pediatrician shifts instantly from abstract discussion to sharing the responsibility for the health care of two very real lives.

The Premature Twins

While forty weeks is the recognized gestation period for the human infant, any baby, singleton or twin, is considered term after thirty-seven weeks. Those delivered prior to thirty-seven weeks are considered premature. Over one-half of twin pregnancies deliver between thirty-four and thirty-seven weeks. The period from thirty-four to thirty-seven weeks is sort of a gray area as far as discussions of prematurity are concerned, since most of the significant health issues associated with prematurity occur in babies born before thirty-four weeks.

It is important to understand that many of the pediatric health concerns about your twins are not due to their being multiples, but are more likely the result of their being premature. In the following discussion, we will briefly discuss the multitude of problems that are likely to affect twins born before thirty-four weeks, then discuss the few, less significant problems that may effect twins born after thirty-four weeks gestation.

Premature Twins Born At Less Than Thirty-Four Weeks Gestation

Data collected over the past ten years shows a remarkable increase in survival rates for all infants born between twenty-four and thirty-four weeks gestation. While it was once thought that twin infants born prematurely had decreased survival compared to singletons, more recent studies suggest that twin infants, compared to singletons at similar gestational age and birth weight, have similar mortality and complication rates.

Twenty-five years ago, babies born under 1,000 grams and before twenty-eight weeks were often not viable. Now, almost 80 percent of twins born between twenty-four and thirty-one weeks survive. Today, insight into the physiology of premature babies, as well as advances in modern medicine, are keeping pace with the increase in multiple births. It's a wonderful time to be giving birth to twins!

Respiratory Function

The first and most obvious adaptation to life outside the womb is the baby's reliance upon its lungs to supply oxygen. What we look for is the newborn's first gasp to be followed by a deep breath and the first cry. The lungs fill up with air and the baby begins to "pink up." One or both babies may require a little extra oxygen for a jump start. Adequate support of pulmonary function is critical to the premature baby.

Respiratory distress syndrome (RDS) occurs when the baby's lungs have not matured sufficiently to promote adequate breathing. A developmental deficiency in surfactant, a chemical that allows the lungs to expand and stay open, is primarily responsible for RDS. Recent replacement therapy with various commercial surfactant preparations has led to a much improved outcome of this formerly deadly problem. RDS tends to be more of a problem for male babies, probably because their lungs don't mature as quickly in utero as the lungs of a female. The symptoms of RDS can range from mild to severe. In the mildest cases, the baby will receive humidified oxygen. If that is insufficient to provide relief, continuous positive airway pressure (CPAP) is created by inserting a tube into the baby's nose to deliver oxygen. In the most extreme cases, a ventilator that controls the pressure and volume of air is utilized by inserting an endotracheal tube into the baby's windpipe.

In the case of babies born under twenty-eight weeks, there is almost always some respiratory problem, with a 50 percent likelihood that they will develop bronchopulmonary dysplasia (BPD), a form of chronic lung disease. The earlier the gestation, the more likely the twins are to develop this problem. Fortunately, babies can recover completely from this condition, but it does take a long time. The lung takes about two years to develop its full complement of airways and then increases further in size as the body grows, so there is a great deal of potential for improvement in the lung after the babies are born.

Apnea

Apnea, which is not uncommon in premature babies born before thirty-four weeks of age, is defined as a temporary disruption in breathing. It may last for only a few seconds and not present much of a problem or it may be more prolonged (over twenty seconds in duration), be associated with a slowing of the heart rate called bradycardia, and be of much concern. There are many disorders that can cause apnea and your doctor will want to make the appropriate clinical and laboratory evaluations to rule them out. Idiopathic apnea of prematurity is the presence of apnea in an otherwise healthy premature baby. Babies with this type of apnea will grow out of it as they mature. If this diagnosis is made, it can be treated with medication. It's interesting to note that caffeine, which stimulates respiration, is often prescribed to treat apnea. This irony has not escaped the notice of numerous mothers who have commented that they gave up coffee for nine months only to have their newborns become instant "coffee achievers." Typically, once the baby is apnea-free for five to seven days in the hospital, medication is discontinued and the baby is observed carefully. Treatment may be reinstated if significant episodes of the apnea recur. Many parents are able to bring their premature twins home with apnea monitors as well as caffeine, which is given once a day, or aminophylline, a similar drug that stimulates respiration, that is given three or four times a day.

HOME MONITORING FOR APNEA

Financial Considerations:

As soon as you and your twins' doctor anticipate that you'll be needing a home apnea monitor, you should discuss it with the appropriate hospital personnel (discharge planners). The most common delaying factor in the discharge process is funding. The hospital should look into which expenses will be covered by your health-insurance carrier and discuss it with you ahead of time. They may also help to determine if you are eligible for any government assistance. In the case of multiple births, you may find that hospitals, home health-care agencies, and/or medical rental companies will offer you some financial break. You'll never know unless you ask.

What You Need to Know

· Understand the diagnosis. What is the usual course of symptoms and how long should you expect to be monitoring?

· Discuss the purposes, responsibilities, risks and benefits of home monitoring.

· Have you learned how and where to place the monitor, how to attach the monitor to one or both babies, and how to provide the appropriate skin care?

· What do you need to know to carry out a successful home care plan? Do you have an adequate support system? Have you lined up additional caregivers to be trained in the use of the monitor system?

· Do you understand that you must use the monitor when your twins are sleeping, when they are in the car with you, or if they are unattended in a room at home?

· What are the appropriate interpretations of and responses to the monitor alarm? Request that you be given an event recording monitor, as it can be difficult to distinguish true apnea alarms from those that are simply the result of a lead becoming dislodged from your baby's skin. What is your emergency medical plan, including names and phone numbers as needed?

The Cardiovascular System

The cardiovascular system–the heart and the blood vessels that work with the heart–must also adapt to function in the extrauterine environment. In utero, before birth, the blood is obviously not shunted through the lungs for oxygenation. There is a channel called the ductus arteriosus that shunts blood from the right side of the body, where the blood is oxygen-unsaturated, to the left side of the body, which holds the oxygen-rich blood after birth. In a healthy baby, the ductus arteriosus will close within the first twenty-four hours so that the blood is shunted to the lungs. In premature babies this duct may not close naturally, and usually medication is needed. In rare cases surgical closure is necessary.

Other Problems

Other problems that are more likely to effect your twins if they are born before thirty-four weeks include:

· Intraventricular hemorrhage (IVH) is bleeding in the brain. Although it occurs in 20 to 30 percent of babies born before thirty-four weeks, it usually does not result in severe long-term disability.

· Necrotizing enterocolitis (NEC), is inflammation of the intestine that may lead to perforation and sepsis (infection).

· Retinopathy of prematurity (ROP) is retinal damage that usually has little effect on vision.

· Twin-to-twin transfusion syndrome is thought to occur when blood from one twin flows into the other twin through vascular connections in the placenta. One twin then becomes anemic and growth retarded with a decreased blood volume. The other, recipient twin, has an increase in blood volume and is much larger at birth. Complications after delivery are primarily due to growth retardation and premature delivery. This problem occurs almost exclusively in monozygotic twins with monochorionic placentas and therefore is very rare.

For more detailed discussion of these topics we suggest you consult premature infant specific publications.

Twins Born After Thirty-Four Weeks Gestation

Twins born after thirty-four weeks gestation are unlikely to have the significant problems mentioned above but may have some less significant problems that delay their discharge home.

Jaundice

A high bilirubin count and the resultant jaundice is more common in premature than full-term babies and is therefore a frequent pediatric concern for many twins who are born early. Jaundice, which occurs in many newborns, is a yellowish discoloration of the skin. It results from the liver's inability to metabolize bilirubin (which is yellow) as quickly as it is produced. After a baby is born, it begins to break down fetal blood cells and bilirubin is a byproduct of that operation. The bilirubin is then processed by the liver and passed out through the intestines as waste. As the bilirubin level rises, the yellow color appears first in the face and eyes, then moves down to the trunk and to the legs. Premature babies are more likely to become jaundiced than term babies because their systems are immature. Parents should be instructed to be observant of their twins' skin color. In the case of term babies, the pediatrician is likely to monitor the bilirubin count but may not recommend phototherapy (special lights that help the body clear the bilirubin) until the yellow cast to the skin has spread to the legs. In the case of premature twins (born between thirty-four and thirty-seven weeks), phototherapy may be appropriate as soon as the yellow color has spread to the baby's belly. In a full-term baby, bilirubin levels peak between three and five days. Bilirubin levels are measured by the milligram per deciliter (mg/dl) of the baby's blood. If the bilirubin level reaches nineteen or twenty mg/dl, phototherapy is likely to be recommended. In a baby born between thirty-four and thirty-seven weeks, the peak occurs between five to seven days, and it is appropriate to use phototherapy when the level reaches fifteen mg/dl–a sort of preemptive strike against levels that are likely to rise. Some pediatricians may recommend phototherapy at even lower levels of bilirubin.

Either one or both of your twins may need phototherapy. This can be achieved by several effective means: If the babies are otherwise healthy, the use of fiber-optic blankets at home will enable parents to have their twins discharged from the hospital. The hospital or a medical equipment company will supply parents with fiber-optic blankets and instructions for their use. By wrapping the babies in these blankets while they are being cuddled or fed, you are essentially encasing each baby in a layer of light. Fiber-optic blankets tend to work well and have the distinct advantage of enabling you to hold, feed, and bond with each twin during phototherapy. The more traditional option is to place the baby under a bank of fluorescent lights that are available in the hospital nursery or can be rented for home use. If home use of the fiber-optic blanket is not achieving the desired effect, one or both babies may be readmitted to the hospital where intensive phototherapy using lights and a fiber-optic blanket is likely to be successful in lowering the bilirubin levels. A baby with a high bilirubin count will have blood drawn so that bilirubin levels can be monitored. This is standard procedure, as very high levels can have serious implications for your baby's health.

HOME VS. HOSPITAL PHOTOTHERAPY

You should feel comfortable about trying home phototherapy as long as your twins are feeding well, are active, and show no indications of other medical problems. A home health care professional assigned to work with your family should be able to do the following:

- Assess the degree of clinical jaundice
- Draw blood for bilirubin determinations

- Weigh each baby

- Set up and explain all aspects of the phototherapy system that your doctor has recommended for your use.

- There should be follow-up clinical assessments and blood drawing as directed by your doctor.

If bilirubin levels do not decline, your doctor will recommend hospitalization and intensive phototherapy.

It is important to remember that approximately 60 percent of full-term infants become clinically jaundiced over the first week of life. Casual discussion with parents in your doctor's waiting room or even on line at the ATM confirms this; it can be reassuring to hear the veteran parents of year-old twins talk about the successful treatment of jaundice in their babies' first days of life. But those same casual chats can yield an abundance of misinformation. There have been instances where parents were told by well-meaning neighbors that all their baby needed was some "sunshine" to cure jaundice. This led them to allow the baby to sunbathe outdoors, which exposed their newborn's tender skin to overexposure in the sun.

There is also a lot of misinformation about breast-feeding and its implications in the presence of jaundice in newborns. Doctors refer to some cases of jaundice that occur in nursing babies in the first week of life as breast-feeding jaundice. That is distinguished from breast milk jaundice, which may occur later in over a third of all breast-fed babies, and often lasts for up to three months. Mothers who want to nurse twins with either of these forms of jaundice should be encouraged to do so.

In the case of breast-feeding jaundice in full-term babies, it is clear from several studies that there is a close relationship between frequency of nursing and a decreased incidence of elevated bilirubin levels in the first week of life. In other words, the more frequently you breast-feed your twins during the first days of life, the lower their bilirubin levels will be. This is probably because the more frequently a mother nurses during her twins first and second days of life, the earlier her breast milk comes in. New mothers who are nursing their twins should try to feed them as soon as possible after delivery and continue to nurse as often as they wish during those first few days of life. It is a good idea for the new mother to try to nurse the twins at least eight to ten times in a twenty-four hour period to ensure that her breast milk will come in by the third day. Typically, the baby's jaundice will then improve because the breast milk, which is rich in fluid and calories, causes the liver and intestinal function to kick in more effectively.

Regulating Body Temperature

Most healthy babies born after thirty-four weeks don't seem to have much of a problem with maintaining body temperature. Occasionally, one or both twins will be a little cold right after birth and need to be placed in a warming bed or incubator. The incubator is an enclosed, temperature-controlled, infant-size bed. It is usually made of transparent Plexiglas that has porthole openings to allow medical staff and parents to care for the baby. A baby born between thirty-four and thirty-seven weeks may need to be in the incubator from several hours to several days. At this age, infants are often taken out of the incubators for brief periods of time in order to be fed (either by breast or bottle) and held by their parents.

Feeding Your Twins

Whether they are breast- or bottle-fed, it is important to remember that babies born after thirty-four weeks come in all sizes and degrees of maturity. Some twins born at thirty-five weeks are more like premature infants and others are more like full-term babies. Again, there is no exact cutoff; the timing of the last weeks of fetal development is not precise. The healthy premature infant develops the ability to suck, swallow, and breathe in a coordinated fashion between thirty-four and thirty-six weeks gestational age. Most infants born after thirty-four weeks can accomplish this feat with little problem and are ready to nurse or bottle-feed immediately after delivery. Some infants (usually born between thirty-four and thirty-six weeks) may need to be fed by a tube that goes into their mouth or nose and down into the stomach.

Mothers whose newborns cannot nurse right away will need to use a breast pump in order to bring in their milk supply. This should be available in the hospital but a rental machine will probably need to be considered for use at home. Colostrum and breast milk can then be given to their infants by tube. A new mother attempting to provide breast milk for premature twins will need to initially pump her breasts six to eight times a day. Even with two nursing infants, their prematurity may preclude them from sucking vigorously enough to maintain an adequate milk supply even once they start nursing. A breast pump with a double setup allows you to pump both breasts at once so that you might just be able to have a few waking hours when you are not feeding or preparing to feed your newborn twins.

In a few days, these infants will develop the skills to breast- or bottle-feed at least once a day to start. A strategy that often works for the mother who wants to breast-feed her slightly premature twins is to have the twins nurse once a day when they are ready to start. Additional breast-feedings can then gradually replace the tube or nipple-feeding until the infant can be totally breast-fed. There is no easy way to prepare yourselves as parents for the sight of your babies hooked up to feeding tubes, and this is a good time to use the resources that you have to find other parents whose twins have gone through the experience. Take a look at their rollicking one-, three-, or eight-year-olds and remind yourself that you and your beautiful newborn twins will get there, too.

In the case of some extremely premature twins, your physician may recommend commercially prepared human milk fortifiers in powder or liquid form that can be added to

DR. KLEIN COMMENTS ON GOOD HYGIENE AT FEEDING TIME

"Although it is well accepted that breast-feeding results in fewer colds, diarrhea, and illnesses in young babies, the exact mechanism that accounts for this phenomenon is not clear.

Besides all the immunoglobulins found in breast milk, the very fact that breast-feeding moms tend to wash their hands very frequently may also be a contributory factor. Whether your babies nurse at your breast or take a bottle, cleanliness is very important.

If mom has a cold, she needs to take extra precautions as her hands touch her nipples or her baby's mouth. Simply stated, anyone feeding the twins should be sure to wash their hands first."

pumped breast milk to further enhance the babies' nutritional intake. Establishing a breast-milk supply for your premature twins takes some special preparations, but many parents have found it well worth the effort. The babies will get the nourishment they need in those early weeks and the mother will develop the milk supply to nourish them successfully as they become more enthusiastic feeders.

It is helpful for new parents to recognize that the first day after birth is a very dynamic time for a newborn's shifting body fluids. Even infants who are ready to feed (either by breast or bottle) immediately after birth take in only a small amount on the first day. Their weight decreases for several days and then as their fluid intake increases (and the mother's milk comes in if she is nursing) they begin to regain their birth weight. In fact, if a baby doesn't lose a little weight after birth we may be concerned that there is some fluid retention.

Many new parents are under the impression that they should expect six to eight wet diapers a day for each twin right after birth. What usually happens, however, is that the number of wet diapers may actually decrease to two or three per day until their fluid intake increases and they start to have the expected six to eight wet diapers a day.

Bringing Your Babies Home

There are certain criteria that we look for when deciding whether your twins are ready to be discharged. The standards may vary, but this gives you a general impression of what to expect:

- Each baby must be able to maintain his or her body temperature at room temperature.
- Each baby must be taking all feedings—whether by breast or bottle—by mouth.

In the case of premature babies born prior to thirty-four weeks we add the following conditions:

- Their weight gain should be twenty to thirty grams daily for three to five days.

- If they are off respiratory stimulants, they should be apnea-free for four to seven days.

- If they are on respiratory stimulants, they should be apnea-free for three days, and the parents should be prepared and capable of taking care of their babies at home on an apnea monitor.

Most babies born after thirty-seven weeks are able be discharged after a day or two. While many babies born between thirty-four and thirty-seven weeks may also be discharged at that time, some may spend additional days in the hospital before they are ready to go home.

Chapter 15

GOING HOME

Priorities

Chaos is a term with which you'd better be very familiar. Writer Nora Ephron has said that bringing home a baby is like tossing a small hand grenade into a house. Draw your own conclusions about bringing home twins. The more you resist, the more likely you are to be overwhelmed by your newly chaotic environment. If twins are your first children, you cross the threshold of your home as a parent for the first time without the litmus test of previous children to help you gauge the big and little situations in the daily lives of two newborns. If you do have a child or children at home, you have their needs as a constant hum in the back of your mind: Are they feeling left out?

How will you plan William's birthday party? Has Jennifer finished her homework? Has she even *looked* at her homework? Some parents of newborn twins arrive home to a toddler who is suddenly displaced as the baby of the family. There is not a parent of twins who has not thought: How will we survive this?

The best advice to give any family with newborn twins is to prioritize. We've all experienced those moments in our lives when we see a family's devastating loss on TV, and even as we take in the news and share in their sorrow, we think, "Thank heavens my kids are fine; my family is safe; everything is OK." For a brief time we get our priorities straight. All those nagging daily thoughts ("I could use a little more money in the bank" and "Will I ever lose those fifteen pounds?") disappear, and suddenly life is just great–"My kids are fine . . . my family is safe." But inevitably, that instant prioritization of what is truly important fades away and within weeks, days, or even hours, we return to the lesser concerns that make up the complicated litany of day-to-day life. On the far side of all the exhaustion, and all the details of making it through each day with your beautiful new babies, is your deeply rewarding family life. Just try to keep your eyes on the prize!

The First Law of Survival for New Parents of Twins
Designate! Designate! Designate!

- If Mom handles the family accounts, let Dad take them over. It could mean a nap to an exhausted mother.

- Ask your teenager to help you fold his laundry.

- Go over your weekly shopping needs with a friend or extended family member who might handle the family shopping for the first month. Have a friend take over for the next two weeks and pass the task along to volunteers for the first four months of the babies' lives.

- When friends ask if they can help, *say yes first, and figure out what they can do later.* (If you're really on top of this, you may have a list of tasks with you ready to designate. For example, pick up cleaning on Mondays, take the car in for an oil change, weed the garden.)

- Schedule a grocery trip with an older child to choose lunch supplies for her own school lunches. This gives the two of you some special time and teaches her self-sufficiency. (Your designated shopper will take over in the weeks to come.)

- Ask willing friends or family to stock up the freezer with ready-made meals for you to defrost and serve. It is more important that you sit down and eat with your family than cook for them right now.

- Let the babies become familiar with your extended family. If your sister-in-law can take them for a stroll twice a week, use that time to get off your feet.

Remember, people really want to help.

Arriving home with twins carries the matter of prioritizing to a whole, new level. Lists that used to start with "organize family photos" will not surface again for several years. Suddenly your priorities cry out to you quite literally, and with startling clarity. (It may, however, take a little time to distinguish the cry of one priority from the other.) The piles of photos will wait. You have two newborn babies who are utterly dependent upon you for their survival. However it may have been, there must now be a fundamental shift in focus.

Many mothers report success with the "football hold" when feeding their twins.

Particularly with young babies, you may want to hold both babies in your arms, positioning them to cross over each other as they are cradled over your torso.

Growing Comfortable with Feeding Your Twins

The immediacy of your babies' needs will be loud and clear at feeding time. As parents, your approach to feeding your twins should be determined by what works best for your particular family. Many considerations enter into play when parents of twins are deciding whether to breast-feed, bottle-feed (using expressed breast milk or formula), or try a combination of the two. The way you choose to feed your twins is, in part, a family lifestyle decision. Keep in mind that there are possible advantages to the family in both feeding approaches. As is true with all newborns, your twins will respond best to the feeding method or methods that offer *you* the greatest opportunity to be successful as nurturing parents. Your babies will flourish as a result of your ability to relax and bond with them at feeding time.

At Three Weeks of Age You Know Things Are Going Well If. . .

- When seen at two weeks by your health-care provider, both twins (born after thirty-four weeks) have reached or exceeded their birth weight.

- You are able to tell the twins apart. (If this is still a problem, nail polish on the big toe of one baby has done the trick for many parents. Of course, this is only appropriate while they're too young to put their feet into their mouths.)

- The twins (and you) are starting to sleep more during the night than the day.

- You are looking for or have found someone to care for the twins while you both go out to dinner.

- Feeding time has become an enjoyable opportunity for either or both parents to bond with the babies.

Parents should be encouraged to nourish their babies in whatever manner is most comfortable for them. The impression that breast-feeding is the *only* right way to nourish your twins should not be the determining factor in feeding your babies. A mother who, for whatever reason, chooses to bottle-feed her twins should not be made to feel she is failing to do right by her babies. Modern formulas also provide excellent infant nourishment, and bottle-feeding (alone or in addition to nursing) can offer a father the opportunity to more fully participate in nourishing his twins. At a moment in his life when the responsibilities for providing for these two babies is thrust upon him, the father of twins who takes the time out to feed his babies is given a sweet reminder of why he is on that often exhausting treadmill in the first place. Whether using formula or expressed breast milk, when a father shares in the feeding of the twins he is included in a very important aspect of their early life. It is interesting and comforting to both parents when they can compare notes on their twins' individual eating styles. Whatever decision you make, your deep satisfaction at cuddling your hungry babies and watching them thrive will tell you you've made the right choice.

Where there is a strong history of food allergies, your pediatrician may restrict cow's milk and recommend soy formula if the babies are not nursing. Either or both nursing babies might also react to milk protein when the mother is drinking milk. Some breast-feeding mothers with particularly irritable babies may want to eliminate all milk and beef products from their diet for one week in order to see if this results in a calmer baby. Babies can react irritably to the taste or content of breast milk, depending on what a mother eats. The nursing mother who is taking in a lot of caffeine in coffee, tea, or soft drinks is likely to see the effects of that stimulant in her babies. Nursing moms have reported babies who grew suddenly mellow when caffeine was withdrawn from their own diet.

The mother who chooses to breast-feed will begin to nurse her babies shortly after delivery. As we've discussed earlier, approximately 50 percent of twins are delivered at thirty-four to thirty-seven weeks. Babies born at this age may not yet suck vigorously enough to bring in or maintain an adequate supply of their mother's milk. This should not deter a mother from breast-feeding her twins. The babies should nurse first, and then the mother can use a breast pump with a double hookup to begin to express breast milk if necessary. Just as the mother needs to supplement the twins' sucking with the action of the breast pump, the babies may need to have their early nursing supplemented with bottle-feedings of breast milk or formula.

Breast-feeding eight to ten times daily on both breasts for the first couple of days is the very best way to ensure that the breast milk will be in by day three or four. For babies born after thirty-four weeks and feeding by mouth, avoid supplementing the babies' nourishment with water or formula as that is likely to diminish their appetites. It takes *hungry* babies to bring on the mother's milk supply. It is important to understand that there is no finite supply of breast milk. This is strictly a situation of supply and demand. The more the babies demand through sucking, the more milk a mother's breasts will supply. *A breast-feeding mother must be adequately hydrated, drinking at least eight to ten glasses of fluid each day.* Cultivating the technique to breast-feed twins requires commitment from a mother, but rest assured that a woman's body is designed to accommodate the nursing needs of both her babies. Finding the time to breast-feed your babies will take support from family, friends, and maybe even colleagues at work. But in the long run, what may seem like an indulgence will prove to have been a highly pragmatic approach.

While the feeding of two babies may appear an overwhelming task at first, it has hidden benefits: hopefully, the needs of hungry twins will preclude any possibility of a mother jumping back into a full schedule before she should. Do not underestimate the benefits of enforced rest. Most of us are conditioned to work at an unnaturally overzealous pace, and a new mother is not immune to the seductive lure of a clean house or a stack of completed reports in the "out" basket of her home office. But no mother should settle for an unrested body that staggers through an overbooked day. Remember, no matter how frequently people tell you to rest up before your babies are born, the profound exhaustion experienced in the early weeks or months of your twins' lives can only be remedied by a daily commitment to getting off your feet.

Feeding Strategies

Generally, the strategy for feeding twins is to find out what works for you and go with it. If you're breast-feeding,

DR. KLEIN COMMENTS ON FEEDING ONE TWIN AT THE BREAST AND ONE ON THE BOTTLE

"There are mothers who report to their pediatricians that one baby seems to prefer the breast, while the other is more enthusiastic about the bottle. If she is content with this situation and both babies are gaining weight and appear to be thriving, then I don't see a problem. If a mom feels uncomfortable about this—if she fears it indicates some disparity in the care or support she is providing her twins—a pediatrician or breast-feeding consultant can look further into the circumstances surrounding feeding time, ranging from the mother's diet to the nursing environment to the order which the twins are fed. Perhaps the bottle baby will feed vigorously on breast milk from a bottle. A baby who has switched from breast to bottle can still get Mom's cuddling at feeding time. You should feel comfortable about bringing this or any feeding dilemma to your pediatrician."

one possibility is to nurse one baby on one breast then follow with the second baby on the other breast, feeding each for ten to fifteen minutes. At the next feeding, be sure to switch sides to maintain an equal milk supply. One baby may be a more vigorous feeder than the other.

In a second scenario, one baby nurses at both breasts to ensure that one breast does not become engorged due to imbalanced demand. The second baby is then fed expressed breast milk or formula from a bottle. At the next feeding, the babies switch, with the bottle baby taking the breast this time. After breast-feeding is well established, many mothers find it convenient to nurse both babies at the same time, holding them on a pillow, or holding them in a "football hold" under each arm.

The Second Law of Survival
There's a Reason They Call Them Pacifiers

When you settle in to feed your babies, you may choose to feed one while the second sleeps beside you. The problem is that there is no guarantee that the other twin won't wake up hungry before you're ready for her. Sucking appears to relax and comfort babies, so this is the moment you don't want to be caught without a pacifier or two.

When you are trying to establish a feeding schedule for the twins of every two to four hours and one or both start clamoring for food after an hour and a half, this is the ideal time to try the pacifier.

Many pacifiers (and bottle nipples) are designed to be orthodontically correct, and their calming properties will simplify things at feeding time.

Half the battle is won by finding a quiet place where you and the babies are least likely to be distracted. Creating a comfy spot in the babies' room is a good idea: You may decide to have your rocker or easy chair in the nursery. In fact, you may want to provide adequate seating in the babies' room for Mom and Dad to comfortably feed the twins at the same time. Establish a routine that includes having your personal supplies at arm's reach: bottles (if you're using them), your book and reading glasses, the portable phone (with the ringer off), a glass of water, and two pacifiers, for example. Have several spare pillows to support your arms as you cradle one or both of the babies and be sure to support your back. It is important to see to your own comfort when feeding your twins. Remember, you're in this together and relaxed parents are a real bonus to hungry babies.

The Third Law of Survival
Back to Basics

The insistent cries of two hungry babies can compromise your better judgment when it comes to saving your back from undue stress. Particularly when you are just getting your feeding rhythms established, your comfort is as important as the babies'. Get in the habit of sitting smart.

• Even though your babies are not yet heavyweights, lift them as though they were. Bend at the knees and use your arms—not your middle back—to support them.

• Make sure your back is supported when you settle in to feed the babies. Do not sit with an unsupported back and lean in to your hungry babies.

• Remain conscious of relaxing your neck and shoulders as you hold the babies. This is your time to release, not accumulate tension.

For breast-feeding mothers, once your breast milk is in, the babies are likely to need to nurse every two to four hours during daylight. If you are bottle-feeding, feed each twin two to four ounces every two to four hours during the day. In either case, at nighttime let them sleep until either or both of them awakens, and then feed them. The feeding of twins, whether by breast or bottle, presents the family with a unique set of circumstances. You cannot feed them both on demand or you will be doing little else but feeding babies for the first few months. (Of course, it may feel like that anyway.) In the beginning, you can let the demands of the first hungry baby dictate the feeding schedule; in other words, feed the first hungry baby then feed the second baby right away. Even if one baby is sleeping, it should be awakened and fed. When the parents of twins discuss sleeping arrangements for the babies, they often express concern about one baby waking the other. In fact, this may be the good news! You actually want both babies awake so that they can both be fed. While this is in direct opposition to the "if it ain't broke, don't fix it" school of twin care, it is the best way to get your babies on the same schedule.

Different feeding styles are among the first things you'll notice regarding the individuality of your two newborns. You may find that one twin (the squeaky wheel) does indeed regulate herself, and awakens at three-hour intervals demanding to be fed. This baby may be a more vigorous eater than her brother, who is less demanding. The twin who feeds enthusiastically is the natural recipient of your delighted attention. Then, when you go to feed the second, less-lively eater, you may not be as persistent in your feeding attempts. There is a tendency to allow the less enthusiastic eater to stop sooner, especially when that baby is the second to be fed. Once you recognize that this behavior exists, you may want to purposely feed the less vigorous eater first. This goes a long way toward assuring both babies an ample opportunity to feed and bond with either parent. Feeding time is a perfect example of an opportunity for a parent's insightful intervention to ensure both babies the bonding time and encouragement they need.

Making It Work: A Look At the Needs of Your Other Children

If there are other children at home, you will want to include them in the lives of the twins in age-appropriate fashion. There are many task-centered moments that are opportunities for older siblings to become acquainted with the new babies. A little one can bring you diapers or sit in his own rocking chair with a baby doll as you feed the twins. An older child can help with many of the household chores.

Interestingly, fathers report a renewed pleasure in relationships with children already in the home when newborn twins enter the picture. While siblings are likely to be primed for the arrival of the twins, it is very important to take steps to ensure that they are more invested in, than threatened by, the newcomers. Just as you have made provisions for the twins, so must you provide for the needs of your other children at this unique moment in your family's life. Siblings, whether they are toddlers or teenagers, will need to have assurances that their parents are still there for them. This is readily accomplished by providing them with your undivided attention at designated times in *their* schedules. The certainty of this special time is an invaluable aid, providing parents with a concrete goal to offer their children (and themselves). It is no longer a question of asking a child to wait indefinitely for your attention–the "maybe later" that parents offer guiltily and children hear with dread. Instead, you and your children will come to anticipate the satisfying payoff of a schedule that includes a designated period of time that they (not the twins, or your job, or the house, or *anything or anyone else*) have your undivided attention. It is equally important for *both* parents to establish special time with their other children.

The designated time will need to be daily for a young child. For your five-year-old, no matter how hectic it has been at the dinner hour, he needs to know there is a time in each day that he will have each parent's undivided attention–perhaps it will be Daddy giving him his bath each night. Maybe after bath time your daughter knows she can count on Mom to read her a story (more likely several stories!) before tucking her in. For your teenager, a weekly event might be more meaningful. It could be going out to lunch with Mom every Saturday, or staying up late one night a week to hang out with Dad and watch a video.

This is not about supplying elaborate treats for your children. It is about providing your children with the bedrock knowledge that you are there for them. There are three key elements here: first, that the time be consistent (if you say you'll be putting her to bed each night, then make every effort to make it happen); second, that it be about

One Mom's Tale
The Twins Come Home

continued from page 176, Chapter 13

I delivered my twins by cesarean section at thirty-seven weeks. I had a son and a daughter, Jeff and Molly. Both the babies were able to come home with me and then the circus really got going! There was no time to ponder what effect my being away for those weeks had on Ben and Emily, my older children at home. I can't say that I felt any guilt at the time . . . but the deficit is more apparent to me now. Every time I see an eighteen-month-old toddler, I realize I came home with two babies when I already had a preschooler and a tiny thing toddling around holding onto my pant leg. Suddenly there were two more. We were really winging it. No nanny, no housekeeper—I was on my own. I nursed at first because I really felt I had to, but it got a whole lot easier when I made a decision to switch to formula. We had a production line and would make twenty-five little feeding bottles at a time. It was great to have Paul able to help feed the babies.

The advice at my twins club was to take it a minute at a time. And as the weeks turn to months, it becomes ten minutes at a time and then half an hour. . . . You just creep along making a little progress each day. If you insist upon looking at the whole picture, you get overwhelmed. As far as my two older children were concerned, I think we kind of were all together in feeling a little miffed that we were suddenly this big family that required so much work. As soon as the doctor gave me the go ahead to be out and about with the babies, we were in those car seats and we were gone. I had been isolated for long enough. We got the double stroller, Emily held on, and we were off to the park. In retrospect, with a toddler at home, I'd recommend that parents get a triplet stroller. Emily did kind of get bounced too quickly out of her baby spot. But she adapted by becoming very much the little mommy. She truly helped to care for those babies. She's good at it, and she is also good at letting us know how good she is at it. We are very lucky. I suppose it could have gone the other way, but she loves little children and is wonderful with them. I know there was an impact on Ben, too, but he had already begun to have his own little social life emerging. He had pals and loved to have play dates.

Paul and I worked very hard to make sure everyone was getting attention and that they all got some individual time. But I will tell you they are all very capable and very self-sufficient children. They all seem to make good decisions and I'm very proud of them. But in the first year . . . You know how they always tell you God doesn't give you more than you can handle. . . . My response was that I was sure he had gotten me confused with someone else!

that child; and third, this is not the time to enlist your child's aid in warming formula for the twins or putting together their cribs. The dramatic entry of twins into the family is a time to rally the troops—and your troops are much more likely to feel generously about meeting the needs of the twins if their own need for love, attention, and guidance is not wanting.

When You Don't All Come Home Together: One Or Both Twins Remains in the Hospital

Pregnancy is a time of heightened emotions for parents. A multiple pregnancy further increases the stakes. You're playing the waiting game. The twins' due date looms large on the calendar—the day the waiting will stop and your family's new life will begin. There is excitement, anticipation, even apprehension. Above all, there is the implicit sense that the birth of the babies will propel you into the next stage of your lives. But if one or both of your twins is unable to leave the hospital, you may find yourselves playing a whole new kind of waiting game.

Medical problems may dictate the need for one or both twins to remain in your hospital's nursery for days, weeks, or even months. This presents logistical and emotional uncertainty for the whole family: How will you bond with both twins? Will you be able to nurse them both? What about the other children at home? Perhaps the most difficult scenario is when only one baby is able to come home with you. There is just no way a mother is going to be able to give those babies "equal" attention, nor should she expect it of herself. There may be days that a mother is unable to get to the hospital. *That is OK.* Maybe Father or Grandma can go to the nursery and hold the baby or touch him in his isolette. The staff in the hospital nursery is highly skilled: They are there to see to your baby's health and to support your needs to love and bond with your baby. If your child's medical condition warrants it, you may be able to hold and feed her. The families who are most successful at negotiating this trying time recognize early on that they must have realistic expectations of themselves and each other. The mother who thinks she is going to make it to the hospital, other twin in tow, for every daylight feeding of her baby needs to be counseled about having more realistic expectations. Consult your pediatrician about questions and concerns, not only for the hospitalized twin, but your whole family. Your hospital is likely to have a family support system that may include a family advocate, social worker, parent support groups, and parent-to-parent programs. Any or all of these resources are there to help your family through a crisis or to provide general information.

There are many things you can do to participate in the life of your baby who remains in the hospital. If it is your intention to breast-feed your hospitalized son, express milk for him. Take your child's picture and keep it with you. Show it to your other children. Call your baby by name. Speak to her when you visit the nursery and let her become familiar with your voice. If hospital regulations permit, bring your other children to see their sister. Answer your children's questions about the twins honestly—reality is preferable to the scary fantasies they'll create if you try to shelter them. Try to stay calm as an individual and united as a couple. Take care of your health and work steadily toward the time you'll all be together.

The Fourth Law of Survival
Compromise

Remember chaos? While chaos may be the prevailing force in your life, compromise is the key to your mental survival. An unmowed lawn or dishes in the sink or even toys all over the living-room floor are a small price to pay for the opportunity to feed your babies in a quiet room away from the chaos.

Chapter 16

SETTLING IN AT HOME

Two Weeks and Counting

While most adults reach a certain degree of detachment from the anniversary of their own birth (the big "0s"–forty, fifty, and the like–being notable exceptions), having newborn twins at home wrenches you unerringly back to near obsession with noting the anniversary of each of their achievements. You have undoubtedly recognized the miracle of their first twenty-four hours upon the earth, just as you've made careful note of the first smile, the first time they looked into your eyes, the first time they grasped your finger, their first attempts to reach out for each other, even the first dirty diaper.

Making it through each day is a noteworthy accomplishment. By the time you have been home for several weeks, you no longer refer to your babies exclusively as "the twins." Each is likely to have had his own significant moments, her own individual responses to you and to their environment. You know that whereas James likes to be loosely swaddled and startles at the sound of the doorbell, Rebecca can sleep through the "1812 Overture" *and* the dog barking along. Almost without realizing it, you are transitioning from the dizzying newness of adding two new members to your family to the more reflective examination of what it all means.

What are the ramifications as far as your marriage is concerned? How will you manage financially? Will the demands of family require

DR. KLEIN COMMENTS ON TWINS' SLEEPING ARRANGEMENTS

"I know people don't follow it to the letter, but . . . I usually encourage new parents not to have their babies sleeping with them. There is the potential for rolling over on one of the babies, or of having everyone's sleep compromised, and that includes the twins!

A baby is highly sensitive to the scent of its Mom, particularly if she is breast-feeding. The proximity of Mom's scent as your twins drift in and out of sleep acts as a lure to complete alertness.

Whether they are going to co-bed or have separate sleeping arrangements, I recommend that very young twins sleep either next to the parents' bed or in their own room. The purchase of a nursery monitor will keep you alert to the twins' needs, and everyone will have a better chance at a little uninterrupted sleep."

you to reassess your career or educational goals? The implications of adding twins to the family are further reaching than the casual observer would imagine. After the joggers in the park admire your two-seater stroller and speculate about your diaper bills, they wish you good luck, and you are the ones who go home to the twenty-four/seven of life with two new babies. Once you have had your babies home with you for several weeks, it is not unusual to find that the stream of well-wishers has dwindled to a trickle of the few steadfast friends and family members who are prepared to hang in there for the duration. We've discussed the importance of accepting the generosity of that support team, but inevitably it is the parents who bear the greatest responsibility in developing successful strategies for the day-to-day life with their children and each other. It is important to return to that primary relationship because it can and will have such a strong impact on the lives of your twins.

Your Couple Relationship

The dynamics within the family make a significant impression upon the physical and emotional health of your twins. Each time your physician sees his two, small patients, they are his conduit to viewing the family unit as a whole. Each family has its own threshold of tolerance for such scrutiny. Some parents are extremely receptive to this psychosocial approach to the overall health of the family, while some may view it as an infringement on their privacy. As we have discussed earlier, part of your responsibility in choosing the right pediatrician is to have a grasp of his child-care philosophy. You don't need to agree with everything he says, but it is helpful to understand that he brings to his practice a point of view honed by experience as a physician and perhaps as a parent. If you find yourself distinctly at odds with his outlook over an extended period of time, you may want to look for another pediatrician. But inquiries about your lifestyle are frequently the most effective way to problem-solve when your twins are concerned.

Put It on the List!

The world can be divided into those who make lists and those who don't. New parents of twins would be wise to grab their pencils (or dry-erase markers) and come on board with the most zealous list makers. The purchase of a dry-erase board for the kitchen is a modest investment to make in your twins' care—and your sanity!

The changing of the guard can be a frenetic experience. As Mom, Dad or a caregiver comes on shift, babies may be cranky, hungry, wet, soiled, in need of medication, or any combination of the above. A quick look at a list on the dry-erase board can save precious moments and lots of confusion.

Your lists (one for each twin) might include:

- time of last feeding
- amount consumed
- what was eaten (for your older babies)
- time and duration of last nap
- time medication was taken (if applicable)

If you are not naturally inclined toward list making, it may take some effort to get used to this idea, but give it your best shot and you are likely to be pleased with the results.

Certainly, the early months of parenting twins are enormously challenging; but does a new mother necessarily need to be bone weary every single day? This is where the team approach can be very helpful. Parents and their pediatrician should take the time to talk about what you laughingly refer to as the twins' sleeping schedule. Or think about what factors are leading to excessive fatigue on the part of the mother. What factors, you may ask. Well, how about I just gave birth to two babies after carrying them around for nine months! Doesn't that pretty much account for all the exhaustion I could ever hope to have? Well, yes and no. The early months of parenting twins is unquestionably one of the most physically draining experiences you are likely to endure. But it does get easier in time and you can make it a little easier on yourself in the present. In fact, just as people tended to overschedule themselves before they even thought about having babies, new parents often have unrealistic expectations of themselves, each other, and even the babies once they are born. That is further exacerbated by the assumption that as new parents of twins, you can kiss the idea of any real relaxation good-bye.

But the truth is that the undeniable joy of having your twins does not mean you have to give up having *some* balance in your life. We've talked about the importance of setting priorities when you come home from the hospital, but the best-laid plans have a tendency to slip away as days turn to weeks and weeks slip into months. What starts as a few hectic days with couples barely seeing each other can turn into a pattern of failed communication. Sometimes your pediatrician is also a detective as you search together to find the clues to an improved daily routine for the whole family.

For example: A mother brings her twins in for a checkup and in the course of the examination she reveals to the doctor that she is exhausted and at her wit's end. The babies are sleeping most of the day and are up all night. She can't remember the last time she had a discussion with her husband that was not about schedules, and they are both getting eerily familiar with the pizza delivery guy. The first thing the doctor might do is take a detailed description of what goes on in the household in the course of a day:

- When do the babies wake up?
- What do they do when they wake up?
- Are they hungry?
- Who feeds them when they first wake up?
- When do the babies go down for the night?

The outcome is that the doctor realizes these babies are up until 11:00 P.M. each night because Dad doesn't get home until late in the evening and that is his only time to be with the babies. Meanwhile, a pattern is emerging that has Mom frustrated and tired, Dad feeling that his time with the babies is very limited, both parents failing to get any real couple time, and one too many half-eaten pizzas in the refrigerator.

The longer this process goes on, the more difficult it is to change and the greater the frustration all around. Mom is at home going through the difficult process of establishing a feeding schedule for the babies while Dad is at work imagining all the wonderful time he is missing with the babies. When they are finally together with both babies they never get around to discussing the reality of both their days. It is not easy to be sitting there with your milk letting down at the sound of your baby's cry and forcing yourself to wait for an hour until it is time for a feeding. So the blissful time Dad imagines he is missing is not *quite* the real picture. And the daily interaction Dad is having in the business world may have frustrations that he no longer feels free to express at home. The essence of the *coupledom* that brought you together as helpmates and lovers—and gave you the courage and passion to start a family—is under siege. The bottom line is that without effective communication, long-term estrangement between couples sometimes takes root in the tiny shadows of two precious, new lives.

The pediatrician might advise these parents to feed the twins every two to four hours during the daytime. That means that if one of the twins seems hungry or cranky an hour after feeding, she may need to be held off. Particularly with twins, you sometimes have to draw that line in the sand and make a commitment to get them on a feeding schedule. At first glance, this may seem too difficult, maybe even unkind, to a hungry baby. But the baby who is always snacking is never really hungry, nor is she ever completely satisfied. Is there someone other than Mom to take the "squeaky wheel" for a stroller ride, cuddle, or play? Being away from the cries of a hungry baby will keep Mom's milk from letting down and perhaps give her some solo time with her other twin, an older child, or even a relaxing bath. If Mom is on call by herself, she might be able to distract the baby with play or a pacifier.

While one parent may be most likely to take the twins for checkups, it is very important to communicate with the absent parent about the guidelines or suggestions your pediatrician may offer regarding feeding or sleeping. In the case of the Dad who looks forward to his late-evening time with his children, he may need to adjust his expectations—giving up his Saturday morning basketball game so that he gets that weekend time with the babies and uses weeknights to hear about the twins' day in the course of couple time with his wife.

When one twin is still hospitalized several weeks or even months after birth, the strains upon the couple relationship are even greater. This is the time to seek any and all outside support you can. The Family Leave Act, signed into law by President Bill Clinton, is designed for just such a situation. We've talked about the need for flexibility on the part of families with twins, but this same flexibility may need to extend into the workplace. Depending on the medical condition affecting one or both twins, hospitalization could go on for an extended period of time. Parents in that situation are understandably torn as to where they are most needed. That constant anxiety leads to a feeling of distraction that makes you less effective no matter where you are. It's like the old song says: "How can you be in two places at once when you're not anywhere at all?" The neonatal intensive care unit (NICU) is working twenty-four hours a day to assure the best possible outcome for your baby who is still in the hospital. Truly, the greatest gift you give your baby is to take care of yourself and each other.

Keeping the Family Healthy

The first thing to remember is that when healthy young babies get sick, it is usually because they have been exposed to somebody who is ill. Plain and simple, it is best to keep anybody with the sniffles away from the babies. If either or both parents have a cold, they should be very careful about hygiene. Anyone in the family should wash their hands and wear a mask if they have respiratory symptoms. These masks are available at any drugstore and are very effective. The simple act of hand washing is often what stands between you and whatever virus happens to be floating around. The child with a cold wipes her nose and touches the baby. Grandma covers her mouth when she coughs and two minutes later she touches the baby. It might sound almost too fastidious, but when both twins get colds at the same time, you won't think so. A convenient pump bottle of antibacterial soap at the kitchen sink, along with paper towels for hand drying, is a great idea. Young siblings can be encouraged to be attentive to their hygiene with a chart on the fridge that awards them a star when they remember to wash their hands before cuddling their young twin siblings. Let family members get into the habit of using their own hand towels. Children can choose their own color or maybe have a special monogrammed towel just for them.

Parents also should get used to washing their hands between taking care of one and then the other when one of the twins is sick. Realistically, the period of infectivity frequently takes place before you have a hint of illness in either, so colds in babies are not uncommon. There is really no data that tells us this kind of communal sharing of a virus is more common between twins than any other brothers or sisters with shared toys and close contact.

Some Tips for Your Sibling Teen Sitters

CONSIDER HAVING YOUR TEEN TAKE A BABY-SITTING COURSE

These classes stress safety, common sense, and, in the case of a medical emergency, how to best respond until trained medical personnel arrive on the scene. Many classes offer certificates of completion that will make your child an attractive baby-sitting candidate to neighbors and friends.

BE CLEAR ABOUT THE TERMS OF YOUR AGREEMENT AND STICK TO THEM.

Caring for eight-month-old twins might not mean having them in the room while you watch your favorite sitcom. And pay up right away!

ALWAYS HAVE EMERGENCY NUMBERS NEXT TO THE PHONE, OR PROGRAM THEM IN WHERE APPROPRIATE

Poison control, 911, your pediatrician, and a number where you can be reached should be immediately available.

DON'T HAVE YOUR TEENS SITTING FOR INFANTS LATE INTO THE EVENING

They may like to push the limits on their own bed times, but young teens get tired and cannot be relied upon to be awake and focused enough to care for two infants at midnight.

Bringing Your Children at Home into the Loop

To your children at home, new twins are like a picnic in the rain: the good news and the bad news all in two sweet, but occasionally soggy, packages. Hopefully, your young children have been exposed to what to expect through pictures, books, hospital tours, and talk with parents. But all the attention and time that goes into getting your four-year-old ready for her new baby brother and sister cannot fully prepare her for the enormous change that is about to take place in the family dynamic. The firstborn child displaced by the arrival of twins is naturally conflicted by the upheaval. Well-meaning friends and family have tried to make amends for all the attention going to the twins but, again, after the first rush of little gifts, attention, and words of praise "for such a wonderful big sister," the harsh reality sets in: There is not always a lap for me because *guess who is in it!* Older children have been heard to comment "It's the twins, it's the twins. It's *always* the twins!"

It is very important to recognize that feelings of jealousy are normal and appropriate. Imagine the reaction of the wife whose husband comes home and says "Sweetheart, soon I'll be bringing home two new, little wives to be a part of our family, But don't worry, there's plenty of love for everybody and I'll still love you just as much as I ever did and you'll get to love them too!" Well, it plays just about as well to your four-year-old. The lifelong thread of love and attachment between siblings is part of a complex and ever-changing pattern. Your babies are too young to manifest the alliance within the family that is sometimes perceived by other siblings, but they do still have each other in a most basic sense. Mommy and Daddy are together and the twins are together, so the older sibling may very reasonably ask, "Who is *my* partner?" It is not uncommon for the firstborn to feel lonely in the midst of all the excitement.

Most young children—say, from three to seven—can be effectively coaxed into showing their "love" for the babies because they are so deeply invested in wanting to please their parents. But the young child constantly asked to kiss the babies, or pat the babies, or tell Grandma how much she loves the babies is essentially playing a role with the expectation that it will make her parents proud of her. There is very little in the way of real affection in that role playing. The young firstborn child always experiences some displacement, but when twins are on the way, a five-year-old may have already endured several weeks of his Mom's need for bed rest. Gone are the outings to the park, and Mom leaning over the side of the tub to make funny shapes with his shampoo-covered hair. By the time the twins have been home for several weeks it is very important for parents to reestablish a routine with their other children.

Always be sure to keep your child's daycare or preschool teacher appraised of developments at home. And ask them to update you on any changes in the child's behavior at school. The potty-trained three-year-old may suddenly start having accidents at preschool and his teacher will be much better equipped to handle it if she knows there are new twins at home. It is very common for young children to ask for a bottle again or to ask to nurse. Parents should be prepared for the full complement of behaviors, from hostility toward friends and family to a hypercritical fixation on "being good" or doing everything right: "Look, Mom and Dad—I never spill or draw outside the lines, and I can tie my own shoes." Just as adults do not fall instantly in love in the deepest sense of the word, siblings need time to develop affection for one another. Don't underestimate your twins' ability to work their magic upon their older siblings. The early smiles and gurgles from your twins that melt your heart may have a similar defrosting effect on their five-year-old sister.

The rule of thumb is to allow your children to express their feelings about the twins, and expect that they will range from resentment to amusement to the blossoming of real affection. The hard-and-fast rule is that all feelings are fair game, but physical aggression that could hurt the babies is never acceptable. Your young children may need to channel their feelings in some physical outlet, but overt or covert thumping or pinching is not an option. Be ready to answer questions about why the singleton is not a twin; if you love the twins twice as much; how come when their school friends come over they just want to play with the twins.

Socializing with friends or organized activities outside the orbit of the twins can be helpful, but try not to change their current child care any more than necessary. If you were considering a new preschool that coincides with the birth of the twins, you might want to rethink making such a substantial change. The first six months may be the most difficult on your young child. Conversation that elevates their status without diminishing the twins can be very successful in foster-ing good sibling relationships. Offer ample opportunity for commiser-ation and support: "It's fun feeding the babies but it sure can take a long time." Some parents report the beginnings of real kinship once the babies begin to be more fun to play with. Let your children take pride in the skills they are sharing with their little siblings. Just as your focus shifts from seeing "the twins" to seeing two individuals, your children are likely to have similar feelings. They may experience greater rapport with one twin. That's O.K. Try, where possible, to engineer opportunities for older siblings to have outings with one twin at a time, even if it is half-an-hour of play in the living room. And most important, give your children the gift of patience with their questions, feelings, and behavior.

Many scouting, community, and first-aid organizations are offering baby-sitting safety programs for preteens and young teens. Certainly you want your older children to pitch in and pull their fair share in the family without financial compensation, but hiring your older chil-dren (sometimes in tandem with a responsible friend) to care for your twins can be a real win/win situation. Older siblings love having an opportunity to earn money while providing you with an opportunity for some couple time–and their baby brothers and sisters with a lov-ing caregiver. Teens report typical earnings of $2.50 to $5.00 per hour, and they appreciate the chance to be recognized in their roles as help-mates to hardworking parents.

Preteens, ages ten to twelve, can be hired as "mother's helpers"–on hand to entertain the twins for an hour or two during the day when a parent is at home but would like some uninterrupted time to work or rest. *Preteen sitters, even the most competent, are not recommended for twins under school age. Older siblings may be very capable of helping out with infants when necessary.*

One Family's Story
One Twin in the Hospital and One At Home

Carol & Vince's twin boys, Alex and Nicky, were born at thirty-one weeks. They are now twelve-and-a-half, and Carol says she is trying to adjust to becoming the mother of teenagers. She spoke about her experience with having one son in the hospital for two weeks and the other transferred by ambulance to a NICU [neonatal intensive care unit] nursery at another hospital where he remained for five months.

My first recollection is that it was so odd coming home from the hospital empty-handed....

I didn't really get to see either of them at first. They were both delivered by C-section and I remember a nurse sort of showed me these two little, green bundles and said, "Here they are!" and then whisked them away. I had all these expectations of cuddling them and it just wasn't like that. The next time I got to see them was about four-and-a-half hours later. They wheeled Alex into my room in his Isolette.... I remember hearing his little monitor beeping as it rolled down the hall. I saw him before they transported him to another hospital with an NICU, but I never got to hold him. I didn't see Nicky until after that. He was in an Isolette too. He was a little jaundiced and ended up staying in the hospital for the first two weeks. Vince went to see Alex right away at the hospital he had been transported to and I remember they told him at the NICU to get a Polaroid camera and take pictures of Alex to

bring to me. I had them with me the whole time Alex was hospitalized.

I was released from the hospital after four days and I remember telling Vince I wanted to go home at night because I just didn't want to see anyone. I was not ready to talk to anybody right away. But soon, a very natural pattern emerged.... My mother would take me to the hospital to nurse Nicky and then we'd drive over the hill to the hospital that Alex had been transferred to. After a few days I got a double breast pump and started pumping and freezing breast milk for Alex in sterile bottles. It actually reached a point where there was no more room in the freezer. But if anyone touched my milk supply in the freezer I would flip.... It was like our hoard of gold.

As it happens, Alex never did nurse, but in a way that gave Vince an excellent opportunity to really connect with him. After two weeks Nicky came home, and that was wonderful. Once Alex was ready to take nourishment by mouth, Vince would feed him my breast milk from a bottle. That time with Alex was very, very important to my husband. It was difficult but eventually I came to look at our situation in a more positive light. Alex had the benefit of my breast milk and the benefit of wonderful time with his father. They developed a closeness that has never changed. In fact, once Alex came home, we tended to kind of pair up that way. If we were going out, Vince would tend to have Alex and I would take Nicky. I remember becoming aware of that and trying to

(continued)

sort of impose a conscious change but for the most part we did kind of follow the path that had been established early on.

Alex's care felt very collaborative . . . and from the beginning, the communication from the hospital was fantastic. There was the neonatologist, our pediatrician, the thoracic surgeon, the head NICU nurse assigned to Alex's case, all the other nurses, and several specialists who were brought in to consult.

I found that I only wanted to communicate positive things with friends and business associates. After the first month the hospital really encouraged us to bring friends and family to scrub in and get as close to Alex as they and we felt comfortable with. We developed a real camaraderie in the NICU with other parents whose babies were having a difficult start. There was a Korean family that spoke no English but we became friends and exchanged gifts as our children's condition improved enough for each to be moved from the most serious level NICU to an interim care unit where Alex actually spent the most time.

Eventually time kind of lost all meaning. At first you really sort of lived for it. In the first few hours of Alex's life they told us he'd have to be in intensive care for ten to twelve days and it sounded like an eternity. At twelve days he was still in there and looked like he was almost worse off and they told us it would be ten to twelve weeks. By the time we hit twelve weeks we had stopped asking. We knew there was no way his medical team could really assess that. . . . He was very slow coming along. It was a roller coaster every day.

There wasn't a time I wasn't thinking of Alex and wanting the boys together but we just worked at projecting a positive outlook . . . just knowing that he would be home with us eventually. And there were times I felt very torn that I could not be in two places at once. But I just could not see exposing Nicky to everything at the hospital. . . . They certainly worked at providing the most sterile environment possible, but we both picked up colds there. Other people did, too. It was not the place I wanted to bring a healthy child. We had one at risk and we felt that was all the risk we were willing to take. But except for a time that Vince and I were both sick, I don't think he missed a day of visiting Alex.

Vince and I were somehow balancing each other's emotional needs. When I was losing it he would really come through with a very positive outlook and when it reversed I could do the same for him. Though I didn't think of it at the time, I have to say that it was the hand of God, or whatever you want to call it, that lifted us up and kept us caring for each other. As the weeks turned into months there was just something that carried us forward and kept us from becoming completely unglued, because both of us were wrung dry. . . .

Connecting with Alex was a little hard when he came home. But I'll never forget those first twenty-four hours. My parents were with us and I remember turning to Vince and saying, "I don't think he's ready to come home. I think we have to bring him back." I remember feeling he had caregivers who were better equipped than I was to help him. [Alex] could not relax that first night. . . . We were so thrilled to have him with us but you could just feel the tension in his little body. His back would arch and he'd scream. I really felt like I was not the best person to care for him. And we'd been through colic with Nicky so we were used to crying. . . . But of course, it was really just a matter of time.

And as far as their relationship within the family, I've never really second-guessed how things might have been different if Alex had not had so many problems when he was born. But I do remember thinking around the time they turned three that they seemed to kind of discover each other. Sort of this realization that "I've got a buddy here." Suddenly they got very engaged with each other for long periods of time. And their communication with each other was remarkable. We'd really sit back and marvel. And it's interesting that Alex has always been comfortable with our leaving to go out as long as he had Nicky there. But Nicky seemed more attached . . . less willing to let go.

As far as Alex's development, we came to trust our pediatrician's judgment that he was doing fine. I'm sure it can be different for every child, but our doctor reassured us that in Alex's case there was no timetable that we had to follow . . . that as long as he was developing one skill after the next in an appropriate sort of developmental order that he was doing really well. But by the time he started reading really early, ahead of everybody else, we felt a sort of amazing confirmation that his mind was certainly O.K. and his body, his physical aptitude, just needed its own pace to catch up, which it has.

If I was to offer advice to any parents going through the experience of having one baby at home while one was hospitalized, I'd say this is going to teach you the meaning of patience, and it is the most important thing you can learn. Your baby will come along at its own pace. You have to care for the one at home and take comfort that he is at home. You really have to let go of your expectations and the sooner you do that, the better off you'll all be. Think of it as a roller-coaster ride and just make sure you and your husband strap yourselves in with one seatbelt.

Chapter 17

YOUR TWINS FROM BIRTH TO TWO MONTHS

Your Growing Twins

Correcting for Early Delivery

After your twins are born, your pediatrician will begin to plot their growth on a growth chart. The growth chart is a graph of the range of normal height, weight, and head circumference and may be broken down into two charts: one from birth to three years, and the second from two years to eighteen years. In appendix B you will find sample growth charts for three sets of twins. We have limited the age range in those charts to eighteen months for purposes of this book.

Let's take the hypothetical example of twins who are born six weeks before their due date. We describe those babies as being born at a gestational age of thirty-four weeks. We plot them on their growth curve at their actual age. But six weeks later, when their due date arrives, we also begin to plot their growth curves from what we call their corrected age (calculated from the expected date of delivery). Parents of premature babies, particularly those who must remain hospitalized, sometimes get very tuned in to the plotting of these curves, particularly if their twins' weight appears to be below average for an infant of its age.

This tendency to focus on your babies' weight is understandable, particularly in the anxious early weeks of a premature infant's life, because there is so little that a parent can feel is concrete evidence of the baby's increasing well-being. But it is easy for a parent to grow obsessed with weight gain and we know that particularly in the case of a premature baby in the hospital, we will see weight fluctuate from day to day. There are two important factors to remember:

- You still need to correct for your twins' age. They may have been born two weeks ago, but if they were born six weeks early, there is still a need to correct for their gestational age.

- While the babies are being weighed daily, a single measurement of weight loss does not have much significance. Only a trend of weight loss or gain over time is helpful in assessing each of your twins' health.

Parents of significantly premature babies are well-advised to relax their concern with weight gain from day to day, especially once the babies get home. It is usually not a good idea to have an infant scale at home. There are stories of concerned parents walking into a butcher shop and weighing their babies on those scales. The pediatrician is likely to be closely monitoring the babies' progress with checkups every week or every other week at first. The twins will be weighed and measured and have their head circumference marked down on their charts. In the case of one baby who has been discharged several months after his twin, there is likely to be a real disparity in size as well as development. This is a part of the continuing challenge of supporting each twin's right to his own distinctive size, temperament, and range of skills.

Your Very Young Baby

If the hospital has discharged your twins at thirty-four weeks or older, they should have a normal startle reflex, be

DR. KLEIN COMMENTS ON INFANT STIMULATION PROGRAMS

"I am most likely to recommend an infant stimulation program for babies who are significantly premature, usually under thirty weeks. If this is the case with your twins, you might ask your pediatrician for his recommendation. These programs are offered by occupational or physical therapists, or other health-care professionals who specialize in the developmental needs of premature babies. It can be very rewarding for parents to work with a specialist who is trained to teach you gentle exercises, positioning, and other ways to interact with your babies that will help to advance their development."

able to suck and swallow, and have normal breathing capabilities. They may look at your face but not really be tracking yet; they may smile in their sleep, but not responsively; and they will probably start making sounds other than crying, though those sounds may not be too distinct yet.

There will be some ability to lift and turn their heads, though that really varies. As far as muscle tone is concerned, babies born at less than thirty-four weeks may not yet be quite on par with the term baby. Premature infants born at less than thirty-four weeks are often hypotonic: as they lie on their backs, their arms and legs are in extension. As babies develop in utero from the second trimester to term, they begin to assume the fetal position with arms flexed and legs drawn into the abdomen, like little balls. Your premature twins may not have completely developed this ability in utero so you need to become their personal trainer. Your goal is to work gently but steadily to help your babies into that flexed position, particularly when they are on their tummies. The current pediatric recommendations are for your babies to sleep on flat surfaces (no pillow) on their back. They need to practice being placed on their tummies at least two to three times a day for a ten-minute session with their knees and arms tucked gently under their bodies. Remain with them while they are in this position. Talk to them from a position slightly above their heads. This will encourage each baby to push up and to work at lifting her head.

The Social Smile

There are few things in your life that compare to the first time you get a smile of recognition and pleasure from your babies: This is different from the reflexive smile that you have watched play across their faces in sleep. This is the smile that tells you they are happy to see you, or that something has truly tickled their fancy. This is the looking-around smile that is a response to all the smiling and singing and cooing you have used to reach out to your twins. This milestone usually occurs by six to eight weeks of age (corrected age for premature babies).

Sleeping More At Night

Contrary to what many say, there is no correlation between your twins eating solid food and sleeping through the night. Your eight-week-old babies are likely to be taking in ample nourishment by bottle or breast and as a result are ready to go a little longer between feedings. One of the first challenges faced by you and your babies is the development of a rhythm that will eventually lead to all of you sleeping through the night. Your babies had many months of daily movement (yours) before their birth to lull them into a restful state. By the time they are six or eight weeks old they are beginning to learn how to quiet themselves.

Sleep as far away from the twins as is comfortable for you. A baby monitor will let you hear your babies without being in superclose proximity. Babies are acutely sensitive to the smell of their mother's breast milk and the scent of the breast-feeding mother may be enough to urge your twins to wakefulness. Make their sleeping environment as dark and calm as possible: no lights except for a night-light. If you hear them whimper or gurgle a bit, don't rush in to them. Babies, like adults, wake and fall asleep again several times throughout the night. One of their biggest jobs is to learn to comfort themselves back to sleep. So don't entertain them, and only change them if they are really wet or soiled.

Looking from Side to Side

Your babies will begin tracking your close movements and they will look into your eyes. In the early weeks they will have the ability to focus that is approximately the distance from their head to Mom's face while nursing or being held for a bottle. At around eight weeks, your twins will start to follow a moving object within a visual radius of 180 degrees.

DR. KLEIN COMMENTS ON PARENTAL CONCERNS ABOUT THE DPT IMMUNIZATION

"Many parents voice concern to their pediatrician about the whole cell pertussis component of the diphtheria, tetanus, pertussis (DTP) vaccine and associated side effects. In some babies, the vaccine can cause a reaction that includes fever. In rare cases, high fever can lead to a brief seizure but will not have long-term consequences. Pertussis, or whooping cough, can be fatal to an infant and does still occur, even in the United States. A new acellular pertussis vaccine has recently been approved for young infants and has fewer associated side effects. Whether the pertussis vaccine causes brain damage in infants is highly controversial. There are children who have developed brain damage around the time they were administered the pertussis vaccine, but we do not have the evidence that definitively links the two events."

Parental Questions and Concerns

Fevers

If one or both of the twins feels warm to the touch and you suspect a fever, take a temperature under the arm with either a mercury or digital thermometer. Other means of temperature-taking are not as reliable. Place the thermometer in the baby's armpit for five minutes. With an uncomfortable or crying baby, simply hold the thermometer in place as you cuddle or rock the baby to comfort him. If the temperature is above 99°F, then you will need to take a rectal temperature. This is easily done with your baby on her back, her legs held gently up and together. Put a little petroleum jelly on the tip of a rectal thermometer and insert it about one inch into her rectum for three minutes. Hold the thermometer gently in place by letting it rest between your index and middle fingers as your hand lies outstretched across the baby's bottom. If the rectal temperature is equal to or greater than 100.4°F and your baby is less than two months of age, seek medical attention immediately.

Breathing Sounds

By the time babies are four weeks of age, they will have begun to secrete mucus in the lining of the nose. The airway is so small that even if there is just a little mucus in there, they can start to make a lot of noise when they breathe. Parents may mistake this for a cold or think there is some other problem. If there are other symptoms, such as a runny nose, cough, or fever, then one or both of your babies may indeed have a cold. Observe them while they are feeding: If they have to stop sucking to take a breath, that is the strongest indication that the nasal passage is clogged. Saltwater nose drops can be purchased over the counter and they usually relieve the clogging.

Feeding

Once you've made it to the two-week mark at home with your babies, you have probably grown more confident about their overall care and feeding. If your twins go in for a checkup after two weeks at home and they are both gaining weight adequately, it is a pretty safe assumption that they are both eating well. Your doctor may ask how much the babies are eating. Term infants—as well as babies born at thirty-four to thirty-six weeks, and eating well enough to be discharged from the hospital—should nurse ten to fifteen minutes on each side at every feeding.

Even after a few weeks, your twins born at thirty-four weeks may not nurse vigorously enough to maintain an adequate milk supply. In that case, nurse first and pump immediately after. As the twins gets closer to term, this problem usually corrects itself, but not always. Start with the side that you stopped with the time before. Nurse or feed every two to four hours during the day, timing from the start of one feeding to the next. If the babies are asleep four hours after the start of their last feeding, wake them even if they've just been asleep for ten to fifteen minutes and feed them. Nursing both twins should take thirty to forty minutes each. At night, feed the babies when they wake up. If one awakens for a feeding, rouse the other one to feed as well. If the mother does not have enough breast milk, she can try switching breasts every five minutes for a full thirty minutes of nursing both babies. And she might also try to nurse every two hours for just a few days until the milk supply has improved. *The rule of thumb is to switch breasts frequently to increase milk supply, but don't increase the length of time you nurse at each feeding.*

If Mom feels that all she is doing is breast-feeding, that will eventually have an effect on Dad. Soon nobody is happy and Mom may stop breast-feeding sooner than she had hoped. In fact, if a father supports the mother's desire to breast-feed the twins, nursing is likely to go on longer than it otherwise might. Your pediatrician can root like mad from the sidelines, but the pediatrician's encouragement is far less significant than the father's support in the long run. There is an increased time factor in feeding your twins no matter what method you use. There is no data that describes an average length of time that mothers nurse their twins. The goal here is to have two thriving babies who are gaining weight, *and* a successfully functioning family. Either breast- or bottle-feeding can make for happy, healthy babies.

"When I see a family with twins, one of the things we always discuss is the importance of looking at their babies as individuals. Each twin has come into the world with a partner but is still unique. During the course of the well-baby visit I try to ask my questions as they pertain separately to each baby. Then we speak in a more general way about "the twins." Early on, it is not unusual for parents to come in and begin talking about their experience, saying "the twins are *this*. . . " or "when should we expect the twins to do *that*." I always try to steer the conversation to their observations about first one baby and then the other.

Usually the measurements for height, weight, and head circumference of each baby will have been completed and recorded on their individual growth chart by the time I come into the examining room. I prefer to initially observe each baby in its parents' arms. So I ask Mom or Dad to sit in a chair holding one baby at a time. If the mother needs to stand with her baby so she can rock her, that's fine; we do what is

Your Noisy Babies

Babies at this age are beginning to make a whole barnyard of sounds: They are gasping, snorting, grunting, cooing, and sucking loudly. By now you have probably come to recognize a whole litany of cries from each of your babies. If your noisy baby becomes unusually quiet, you should mention it to your pediatrician. But for the most part, you can sit back and enjoy the show.

Immunization

Immunization is one of the most important elements of pediatric care. There are numerous illustrations of how the introduction of immunization practices are linked to the decline of a given disease. In recent years, the introduction of the *Haemophilus* B conjugate vaccine (Hib) has almost wiped out a bacteria that is one of the causes of meningitis. Rubella, once a major cause of birth defects, has been almost completely obliterated.

Visiting the Doctor

The Well-Baby Visit: Birth to Two Months

The checkup, or well-baby visit, is an important opportunity for your pediatrician to assess your twins' health on an ongoing basis. Each doctor has an individual approach, but you can count on several components being present in any pediatrician's routine: Your twins' height, weight, and head circumference will be plotted on a growth curve that is a permanent feature of each babies' medical chart. They will be plotted for their actual age, and for their corrected age if need be. There are likely to be inquiries about eating and sleeping and an opportunity for you to ask any questions you have about your babies' progress.

Immunizations: Birth to Two Months

You will find a detailed immunization chart from birth to age six in the back of this book. Look there for specifics regarding each immunization.

The first hepatitis B (Hep B) vaccine is given any time between birth and two months, with a second dose given between one and four months.

The first diphtheria, tetanus, pertussis (DTP) vaccine is given at two months of age.

The first *Haemophilus influenzae* type B (Hib) vaccine is given at two months of age.

The first poliovirus (OPV or IPV) vaccine is given at two months of age.

The Growth Curve

Each of your babies will be weighed and measured for height and head circumference. These three measurements will be plotted on a graph that is called the growth chart. Your pediatrician can share that information with you so that you can have a visual impression of each baby's growth relative to himself over time as well as relative to other babies. It is important for parents of twins, especially if they are nonidentical, to anticipate different rates of growth in their twins. The curves differ for boys and girls so if your son and daughter are of equal weight, that does not mean they are at the same point on the growth curve. As your pediatrician assesses your twins' growth patterns over time, any number of patterns may emerge. The plotting of the growth curve is a sort of jumping-off point for discussions regarding all aspects of your babies' lives,

comfortable. Since I like to begin the visit with the baby on his parent's lap, I tell this to my families at their first visit. If I observe that at each subsequent visit a mother with twins walks into the examination room with one baby held by her caregiver, and she puts the other baby down in its carrier and sits down alone, I may begin to think that this mother is feeling a little overwhelmed, even depressed and detached from her babies. I'll try to steer our conversation to a discussion of what is happening at home. Maybe she is in need of more support than she is getting, and we can brainstorm a little bit about finding her some help.

If both parents are not available, it is helpful if there is another adult at the visit to help out. I have a form that I use as a guideline for the visit, but I don't let it rule our conversation. As we talk, I put the appropriate notes in the baby's chart. I ask about questions or concerns that they want to address and we may go into detail right then, unless their question involves the physical exam. If it doesn't happen to come up in the course of the conversation, I'll always ask about how the baby is feeding

(continued)

and sleeping and the life of the family in general.

Then we go on to discuss development. We talk about what the baby has done so far and what to expect in the future. I may make suggestions about feeding or sleeping, and it is not unusual to inquire about what kind of support is available to the family. If I feel there are unexplored options as far as help for tired parents, we may talk about them. We discuss what immunizations, if any, are going to be given at the visit, and what the complications might be. I have parents sign forms giving permission for their baby's immunization.

If the baby is on medication, we review that and talk about any past medical history, where appropriate. If there was some problem or issue discussed at a prior visit, I will bring it up to see what resolution, if any, there was. Of course, each progressive visit encompasses additional elements of the baby's development.

I talk about safety issues at almost every visit.

Sometimes I think I may repeat things too frequently, but I feel it is important to stress everything from car safety to pool safety to baby-proofing the house. I begin to talk about baby-proofing at the four-month visit because

including feeding, sleeping habits, and their individual temperaments. This book's appendix includes growth charts for three sets of twins born at twenty-seven weeks, thirty-four weeks, and at term.

Safety

Safety issues for your twins will grow more complex as increasing mobility makes their world larger. To start, you must look at the world of the very young baby and make immediate adjustments to that environment. Keep these same issues in mind when visiting a friend's home or traveling with your young twins.

Twin-Proofing Your Home

As we said in the first chapter, by the time your babies come home, you need at least the following safety precautions:

- Emergency phone numbers next to every phone

- Cribs and changing tables placed safely away from electrical wires, cords, and curtains

- Pet and plant safety

- All toxic substances stored in a high, locked cabinet.

It may seem early to be concerned about your babies swallowing poison but you should have two bottles of syrup of ipecac in your home (one for each twin). Never administer ipecac without the advice of a doctor or poison control center.

- Never leave the twins unsupervised at bath time or near any water.

· Keep all small objects such as coins, buttons, nuts, popcorn, grapes, and small toys (like Legos) away from your twins' grasp. Older sibs should be instructed never to leave their own toys in the twins' increasing reach.

· Be very careful about choking safety. Never place jewelry chains around the neck of an infant. Do not tie pacifiers on a ribbon or string to pajamas or other clothing.

· Do not leave your twins unattended on any surface. *They may surprise you by rolling over for the first time, and you don't want it to be onto the floor from their changing table!*

· Never leave your infant in a playpen that has one side down.

In the Car

There are numerous consumer publications that can help you decide on the right car seats for your twins. While convenience and aesthetics play a part in this purchase, safety is your primary concern. When you have twins, you will need to strap one car seat into the center position of the rear seat and the other in the right, rear passenger area. This will enable you to have at least some access and visual contact with both babies. The car seats face back for babies that are this young, and are securely strapped in place. You can purchase special mirrors that clip to the visor in the front and attach by suction to the rear window, allowing a great view of front- or rear-facing car seats.

Babies should never be held on a lap in a moving car, even for a few seconds. And of course, you must not leave them alone in the car even to run into the gas station while you are at the pump. Police stations in towns all across the

that is when babies will usually start to reach for things that they invariably put in their mouth. I like to give parents stickers with the number of the local poison control center to place on their telephones. By the nine-month visit, when babies are likely to be crawling around, I am really hoping that all the twin-proofing of the house is complete.

Then I move on to the complete physical examination of the baby: top to bottom, stem to stern. . . . At four or five months, and sometimes before that, I begin the exam with the baby on its mother's lap. I like to take a little time to play as we start the physical. When the baby is old enough, I may hand him one or two tongue depressors to hold and then we'll play with them. Play is instructional for me and tends to be calming for the baby. I begin the exam by listening to the chest because I want to make sure I get to that, even if the baby becomes restless or upset during the exam. I listen to their lungs to make sure there is no wheezing—no questionable sounds. I listen to the heart to make certain there are no abnormalities there. I then listen to the abdomen and examine it with my hands.

(continued)

While the baby is on the parent's lap, I remove the diaper and examine the baby's genitalia, and also the hips to make sure they are moving correctly. I stretch out their legs to make sure they are of equal length, and put the diaper back on. I ask the parent to hug the baby by placing their arms over the baby's arms. While the baby is comfortably restrained, I look at the ears, nose, and throat. I look in the mouth to see if teeth are coming in.

Depending on the age, I may hold the baby upright in order to make sure that he can support his weight on his legs. In an older baby, I may ask to see how she is walking. At this point, the typical examination of one baby is pretty much completed and I go on to the second twin.

At the end of the visit, we will discuss any problems that are the result of prematurity if that is the case; we'll talk about any referrals to specialists when needed; and discuss any medicine that needs to be prescribed or refilled. At that point, I usually leave the exam room and my nurse will follow up with the appropriate immunizations, hemoglobin measurement or tuberculosis testing as needed.

United States have received calls from panic-stricken parents who have locked their keys inside the car with an infant. Also, consider buying a sun shade that will protect your young babies from overheating while riding in the car.

Tender Skin

If either of your twins has a diaper rash, it will usually respond to a zinc oxide cream. If diaper rash does not respond to zinc oxide, ask your physician for further suggestions. There is no need to apply any other lotion, oils, creams, ointments, talc, or corn starch on your babies' sensitive skin. Both talc and corn starch can clog your babies' pores and can be breathed in through the nose. It is also a good idea to turn down the hot water temperature in the house to 120°F or below. Just in case there is an accident, you will be very thankful that the water was no hotter. Also, keep your young twins out of direct sunlight. If you are out on a sunny day, be sure they have on hats or are in a shaded area. Do not use sunscreen on babies younger than six months.

Smoke

Babies should not be exposed to cigarette smoke. Smokers should do so outside your house, and they should wash their hands and face and remove their outer clothing before holding the baby. Ideally, babies should never be in a room, car, or enclosed area where anyone has smoked.

Foods to Avoid

Babies under one year of age should not be given honey, as it has been known to cause botulism in the immature digestive system. Whole milk, fish, citrus fruits, and egg whites should also be avoided, as there seems to be a higher likelihood of developing allergic reactions to these foods if they are introduced too early. We'll discuss food allergies in greater detail later on.

SIDS

Sudden infant death syndrome (SIDS) is defined as the unexplained death of a previously healthy infant. It usually occurs when they are asleep. Death from SIDS is unusual before one month of age and the peak incidence occurs between two and four months of age. Almost all cases of SIDS (95 percent) occur by six months of age.

While we have not yet been able to definitively state the cause of SIDS, we do know several facts of which parents should be aware:

- SIDS is not caused by suffocation or choking.

- SIDS is not contagious.

- SIDS is not caused by the diphtheria, tetanus, pertussis (DTP) vaccine, or other immunizations

SIDS is associated with sleeping in the prone position. Parents should put their babies down to sleep on their backs, on a firm mattress, with no blankets under the baby. No pillows or stuffed toys should be in the crib of a young, sleeping infant. Your baby should not be overbundled, and the room temperature should feel comfortable to you.

ROUNDTABLE TALK

PRESENT AT THE DISCUSSION ARE:

Dr. Connie Agnew
Jill Ganon

DR. KLEIN COMMENTS ON THE GROWTH CURVE

"The growth curve is a tool that your pediatrician uses as a measure of your twins' health. A child who is growing well is invariably healthy. If one or both of your twins is not growing well, your doctor may not immediately know *why,* **but examination of the growth curve will very definitely suggest the need for further evaluation of the patient."**

DR. KLEIN COMMENTS ON THE DANGERS OF CIGARETTE SMOKE

"We know that smoking during pregnancy is hazardous to mother and baby. But the parent who smokes around young babies continues to jeopardize the children's health as well as their own. There are numerous risks to infants: increased colds, ear infections, sudden infant death syndrome (SIDS), and other breathing problems are all associated with exposure to cigarette smoke. *I cannot overstate the importance of raising your twins in a smoke-free environment."*

Tom & Sarah
Laura & Nick
Joan & David
Robert & Grace
Kate & Matt

TOPICS FOR DISCUSSION ARE:

Managing Day to Day

JILL: O.K. So tell me a little about the day to day.... How do you manage?

KATE: All I can say is that if we ever had another one it would be a piece of cake. Thank goodness my mom has come down from Canada. I'm a twin and my mother has a lot of experience. My sister who lives near her has had two kids in the last five years so my mother has plenty of recent experience, too.

MATT: But this is her first out-of-town assignment...

JOAN: I think it might be different if our friends were having babies now. I've felt kind of isolated.... I was on bed rest for a long time as well as being home recovering with the twins after their birth. I didn't know a whole lot about baby care, and I'm in the medical field [Joan is a psychiatric nurse]. Now I'm on leave from my job and I've found it very hard to find someone who is "twin capable" to give me a break. We end up mostly having friends and family come in to sort of help out while we're there. The days can get pretty long.

LAURA: The day-to-day.... Let's just say I've been doing my marketing on Fridays at midnight. Sometimes it feels like people just don't understand. A friend will say, "Come on over with the babies." If I plan to be there at noon, I have to be up at 5:00 A.M. to be there on time. Christmas Day was a perfect example. We didn't make it to brunch until 1:30, and that was with both of us getting ready. You really do need to get some help once in awhile.

NICK: The first few weeks were great. Laura's mom took off a week and my folks came in from Ohio. But since then . . . Laura's mom takes a day off here and there. I take off in the morning and get home at 7:30 or 8:00 P.M. It would be nice to afford a nanny but we can't. And we kind of thought people in the old days pulled it off. We don't have to buy in to this more pampered–no pun intended–society. But I should say that Laura's parents will come any evening we need them. But we still never get any place on time.

LAURA: And my parents know the routine. They can walk in and take over in an instant. This is just normal to us. I've never been the mother of just one child. And I also really get a lot of support from the twins club. Meetings alternate between having speakers and support groups. You can break into a smaller group of moms with twins the same age as yours and you just talk about what the babies are doing: Mine aren't sleeping throughout the night, etc. You get some questions together and go back into the larger group and ask those moms how they've handled things, what stroller works for you. And it is a great resource for buying used clothes and things that you need in twos! I knew there was a national club so I just called information and eventually found two local L.A. clubs.

TOM: Our relatives are all in New York. When it comes to getting help we advertise, but it is rough. We've hired people from agencies at $10 to $15 an hour and they are incompetent. You'd think that someone who is supposed to be able to care for twins would be able to change a diaper without getting poop all over the blanket. . . . We really try to get at least a few hours a week for each other. I'm a musician and it was always my intention to stay at home during the day but, honestly, this situation with our babies being so premature has pretty much done in my business. Fortunately, Sarah makes a lot more money than I do. So we're squeaking by and I figure we'll recover sometime later on.

ROBERT: We felt so fortunate that we were able to take the boys home from the hospital with us. Grace's mom came to help. Grace was breast-feeding so I was just a shuttle service . . . from mom to the crib and from the crib to mom. But we also made a conscious decision that we wanted to be the ones to raise our children. Sometimes it's nuts. But every Saturday, no matter what, we go out. Except last Saturday we decided we'd rather sleep than go out. . . . But you know how you always hear about how the stress of twins can just make your marriage fall apart? We've become more focused around our kids and our marriage is just better.

Chapter 18

YOUR TWINS FROM THREE TO FOUR MONTHS

Your Growing Twins

Exploring Their Environment

The amount of stimuli coming in to your twins' world is far greater than their ability to send signals back out. By the time they are three months old, they are already trying to mimic your voices and speak back to you. They are learning to use their limbs in a more coordinated fashion, and are likely to stare at their own hand. Both babies are probably indicating interest in more of their environment. They are working hard and can become cranky or even appear bored in reaction to overstimulation at this age.

Babbling and Laughing

Babies learn speech by imitating—that is why it is so important to talk with your twins. Their responsive smiles are now accompanied by cooing, babbling, and the use of sounds to get your attention. Your twins may laugh as a sign of pleasure or amusement. There is a tremendous range of expression in these beginnings of speech. The impression that your twins are mimicking you sometimes is probably pretty accurate.

Hearing

Infants with normal hearing almost always produce well-formed, single-syllable sounds (though they sometimes repeat), such as "da," "na," "bee," and "ya-ya," before eleven months of age. If either of your twins does not begin to make these or similar sounds before eleven months of age, this should be considered a sign of possible impaired hearing and an audiologic assessment should be made. Your twins may begin to pay attention to and show pleasure at music.

Purposeful Grasp and Voluntary Release

At three months, your twins are likely to grab a tiny fistful of your hair and give a mighty tug, but it is still strictly hit or miss from a developmental standpoint. By four to five months they will be able to voluntarily release their grasp of held objects. They will purposefully reach for, swing at, or grasp for objects but are not yet efficient enough to reliably grab an object that interests them.

Bring Hands Together into the Midline

By three to four months you may notice your twins bringing their hands together over their tummies and then to their mouths. Previously, they may have inadvertently found their hands, but this marks a more purposeful ability to control motor skills. If your babies have not yet begun to put their hands in their mouths for comfort or exploration, they are likely to do so now. At four months they may also start to transfer objects from hand to hand.

Parental Questions and Concerns

Diaper Rash

Diaper rash is a common problem for babies of any age. It usually responds well to over-the-counter zinc-oxide ointment. If there is a lot of discomfort, place the baby in lukewarm water for five or ten minutes at a time, several times a day. Most infants find that very soothing.

There are studies showing that babies who use cloth diapers are less inclined to develop rashes. However, parents—especially parents of twins—need to consider the additional work and possible added expense of diaper service for two infants, keeping in mind that diaper rash is usually very easily treated.

Babies are also inclined to get yeast infections or monilial dermatitis in the diaper area. It classically shows up as a very bright, red area of skin that is surrounded by little, red spots. This can be treated by an over-the-counter antifungal medication or a prescription medication ordered by your doctor.

Different Temperaments and Different Development

In just one day, a pediatrician seeing several sets of twins is going to hear one parent's concern that the babies are not sleeping enough. The next parent will be concerned that the babies appear to be sleeping to much. What's a doctor to say? The answer is that there is no such thing as the perfect set of twins: We have no perfect baby model. There is a broad range of normal when it comes to babies. As long as your twins are eating, healthy, and growing well, whatever they're doing is O.K. Of course, what is perfectly swell for each of them may not make life particularly easy on the rest of the family!

There are certain temperaments that babies may exhibit at particular moments in their development: the crying or the sunny baby; the anxious or the placid baby. While we like to look back and draw a straight line from the sunny baby to the relentlessly optimistic ten-year-old, we may be imposing our subjective viewpoint more than we realize. The baby who could bring down the nursery walls with her cry can become a remarkably composed five-year-old. For the parents of twins, this may be of particular interest. The implications for twins are obvious. There is an understandable, even an inevitable, tendency to compare and label: the leader and the follower; the big one the little

DR. KLEIN COMMENTS ON SLEEPING THROUGH THE NIGHT

"Like adults, babies will awaken several times in the course of the night. If they have not yet learned to fall asleep inside the crib and are used to falling asleep in their parent's arms, they will not be able to go back to sleep when they wake up inside their crib. I usually recommend the use of a transitional blanket for helping babies to comfort themselves and learn to fall back to sleep. I can't say it is completely successful every time, but many parents have had great results.

At some point—when the babies are about four months of age and starting to reach for and grasp things—each baby can be given a small, flannel blanket (about 18" by 18"), maybe with a border of soft satin which will feel wonderful to the touch. For the first week, Mom sleeps with the blanket to give it her comforting scent. The following week,

one; the bright one and the physical one. The reality is far more fluid, or at least it should be. The twin who is labeled "the good eater" is going to have certain expectations thrust upon her so that even when Grandma comes to visit, she will expect to settle in for a whole bottle at a feeding. If she is feeding the twin who has been labeled "the fussy one," she has the reasonable expectation that this twin won't feed as enthusiastically. And so a cycle of self-fulfilling prophecy begins. The twin with the greater large-motor skills chases the ball while the other twin has quiet time. The quieter baby waits for the new diaper every time because he just doesn't make such a fuss. The temptation to label any child can come from the most loving impulse: the desire to know deeply what your child is about. But the consequences of doing this with your twin infants can also have an impact on how they will relate to each other in years to come. You are into the first year of a lifetime of inevitable comparisons: It is kind of built into the system when you have twins. You do your twins and yourselves a great service by trying to remain flexible in the way you perceive and relate to each of them. This is not easy to do, but it is a gift that you can give to your twins on a daily basis.

Sleeping Arrangements

As your twins grow larger, they may start to interfere with each other if they are in the same crib. It is not unreasonable to expect them to wake for a changing and feeding once during the night. If one or both is still waking two or three times a night, you may want to think about how you can help your babies to learn to comfort themselves back to sleep. This is the point where parents need to consider that they are going to the babies too soon, denying them the opportunity to learn how to wake up and feel secure enough to go back to sleep without any time from Mom or Dad. Your pediatrician may ask you about your babies' daily feeding schedule. By the time they are three months old, they should be eating less frequently as they can consume more at each feeding. If they eat too frequently during the day, every time they wake up they assume it is time to eat. Speak with your pediatrician about guidelines to help your twins to develop the rhythm of daytime wakefulness and nighttime sleeping.

Should the Babies Be Separated If One Is Sick?

The period of incubation for most viral infections is quite variable, ranging from a few days to several weeks. Trying to separate your twins when one shows symptoms of a cold is usually a case of too little too late. Very young babies, even in the same crib, are not likely to interact with each other that much, and you can certainly put them at either end of the crib to ensure that they won't be touching each other's faces or grasping for each other's toys. Be sure to wash your hands after caring for each twin, especially when one is ill.

Cradle Cap

The dry, scaly crust that can often occur in a baby's hair with an associated rash on the face is thought to be caused by a yeast infection in the scalp. Cradle cap is the body's reaction to that infection. You can lightly rub mineral oil into your baby's scalp, comb out the flakes, and then wash the hair immediately with baby shampoo. *Do not use baby oil, which is absorbed by the skin.* Cradle cap also responds very well to over-the-counter medicated shampoo, or your pediatrician can prescribe a special shampoo as well as a medicated cream to put on the rash if needed.

when Mom or Dad holds the twins while nursing or giving a bottle, the babies get their blankets to hold onto while they fall asleep. *As soon as the baby is asleep,* she is placed [on her back] in the crib, with the blanket either still held in her grasp or right next to her. Remember, this blanket goes in to the crib *next to your baby, not under her.* The third week, Mom or Dad should watch each twin intently and place them in their cribs *just as they are about to fall asleep.* The fourth week, let your babies be a little more awake, and place them in their cribs with their blankets after their feeding. For several subsequent weeks allow your baby to be more awake before you put her in the crib with her blanket. The object, of course, is to have your twins associate falling asleep with this soft, wonderful-smelling, transitional blanket. So, in the middle of the night the baby wakes up, grabs the blanket, and is self-comforted back to sleep."

Visiting the Doctor

Immunization: Three to Four Months

The second hepatitis B (Hep B) vaccine is given between one and four months.

The second diphtheria, tetanus, pertussis (DTP) vaccine is given at four months of age.

The second *Haemophilus influenzae* type B (Hib) vaccine is given at four months of age.

The second poliovirus (OPV or IPV) vaccine is given at four months of age.

Safety

Basic Twin-Proofing

- **Security Gates**

   Be sure to use security gates at the top and bottom of the stairs, as well as to cordon off any area in the house to which your twins should not have access. This is particularly important with twins, because you cannot guarantee that they will both be doing their exploring in the same area of the house at the same time. In fact, you can almost guarantee that they won't!

- **Corner Covers**

   This is a simple way to make all those sharp corners a lot less lethal. Mount on cabinets, tables, corners, etc.

DR. KLEIN COMMENTS ON KEEPING LITTLE BABIES CLEAN IN THE BIG, DIRTY CITY

"It may be different in other areas of the country but here in a large, urban center with so much dust and smog, I recommend that parents bathe their babies every day. It is important to remember that, even in parts of the country where the winters get very cold, you can bathe your babies daily without worrying about their catching a draught or a cold. You catch colds from germs, not from being cold!"

- **Electrical Outlet Covers**

  Be sure to cover all outlets to which your twins have access, and that includes surge protector strips that many people use with their computers. You can purchase outlet caps or swivel covers that automatically cover the outlet when you pull the plug.

- **Doorknob Covers**

  These flexible covers slip onto doorknobs and prevent children from turning them, while remaining easy for adults to squeeze and turn.

- **Drape and Blind Cord Windups**

  We've already discussed the importance of not placing the crib next to exposed cords, but these devices can prevent a real tragedy in the world of your increasingly curious twins. Use them throughout your home.

- **VCR and TV Locks or Covers**

  Save your entertainment center from prying fingers.

- **Scatter Rugs**

  Tack down scatter rugs to prevent slipping on hard floors.

Twin-Proofing Your Bathroom

- **Toilet Lock**

  The toilet is often of great curiosity to exploring babies and must be locked closed from your twins, who might easily topple into trouble. The lock installs and

---

DR. KLEIN COMMENTS ON THE IMPORTANCE OF TWIN-PROOFING AND GENERAL SAFETY

"At the four-month well-baby visit, as babies are beginning to grab items and put them into their mouth, I discuss the implications of that developmental milestone as far as the babies' environment is concerned. I like to go into greater detail about baby-proofing the home and other aspects of safety.

As a physician, I have had to treat infants who were injured, some severely, in accidents that could have been prevented through baby-proofing in the home. It can be a terrible tragedy that I'd love to see all families spared. And I must stress to parents of twins that by the time those babies are mobile, scooting off in opposite directions, you will find great comfort in having prepared a safe environment for them.

Every home is different. Some families choose to call a professional baby-proofing company to go through the entire house and develop a list of recommendations that you can implement, or in some cases hire the same

(continued)

company to do the whole job. You can also adopt a twin's eye view of the world by crawling about your home and seeing what looks inviting: an edge of a tablecloth to tug, the fishbowl on a low bookshelf, the books themselves, a coffee table that showcases your treasured ceramics.

If you have not yet done so, this is the time to choose a closet with a lock to provide a twin-proof (as well as teen-proof, and holiday and birthday gift-proof) spot for toxic substances, dangerous objects, and certainly any firearms that are in your home."

detaches easily for adults or older children in the house. *The basic rules for water safety apply here: Do not allow your babies access to this or any standing pool of water.*

- **Nonslip Mats for the Tub or Shower**

Safety mats provide traction in slippery tubs or showers and are important for the whole family.

- **Bath Spout Cover**

Soft covers can adapt to most tub spouts. It cushions and insulates against bumped heads. This is especially effective for the twin tub time that can get a little hectic.

Twin-Proofing Your Kitchen

- **Stove Guard**

Protect your twins from reaching out and touching a hot burner, even though it has been turned off. Stove guards mount easily and remove for cleaning or when not in use.

- **Oven Lock**

Made from material that can withstand the heat of the oven, this lock will prevent your twins from opening the oven at any time, but still allow for easy access by an adult.

- **Drawer and Cabinet Latches**

A must for keeping two sets of hands away from sharp knives, glassware, and cleaning supplies. *Remember that dishwasher soap and even regular dish soap could be dangerous to your babies. Keep them locked away.*

Twin-Proofing the Twins' Bedroom

We've already discussed basic crib and changing table safety. The following items may be helpful as you work with your twins to establish longer sleeping patterns:

- **The Nursery Monitor**

  Many parents find the nursery monitor reassuring. There are monitors on the market today that have wrist receivers so you can hear the babies while you're in any room in the house.

- **Night-Light**

  Be sure to have a low light source in the twins' bedroom—enough light to change a diaper but not so much as to entice your babies into activity. Some night-lights feature a silent switch, and will shut off automatically after giving your babies time to drift off to sleep. Place the light near the door to the bedroom.

ROUNDTABLE TALK

PRESENT AT THE DISCUSSION ARE:

Dr. Alan Klein
Tom
David
Robert
Matt

TOPICS FOR DISCUSSION ARE:

Do Husbands Feel Acknowledged for Their Role?
Do You Have a Favorite?

TOM: I have to say that sometimes I feel like their butler. . . . But I just put those feelings away because I'm always their advocate and I'll always do what needs to be done. Friends and family would send cards and call, and in my situation it was kind of crazy. We had three babies [premature triplets born at twenty-six weeks] and they were so small and in the NICU [neonatal intensive care unit]. I couldn't hold them except for putting my hand in through the porthole of the Isolette. We'd been trying for so long to have a baby. . . . Well, I had a friend whose wife had also just given birth and I finally asked him, could I come over and hold your baby? I needed grounding. . . . I needed a goal of what to feel when you hold a child. It was wonderful.

ROBERT: It can feel like a thankless job. . . . But we wanted so badly to have a baby. As fathers we are really out there doing all the legwork. Our wives are there with the babies really needing to be served by us. We'd been trying for so long to get pregnant. We'd had a miscarriage and we really both wanted these babies. We were very excited and wanted to take every precaution. I was there for all of it. I went to every doctor appointment . . . everything.

ALAN: I think I'm hearing that even though you were involved, I'm not sure you were acknowledged.

ROBERT: I was acknowledged by my wife but nobody else. She has told me she could never have gone through it without me. Unless you've been through it you cannot understand. Especially with infertility and then multiple babies. I set up every appointment and asked every question. I didn't want my wife to go through anything but labor. Bed rest was crazy. . . . I'd get her out to an appointment then home and in bed, then I'd get back and make her dinner and then it would start all over again. I kept track of all the billing and it was complicated. People don't realize. It was extremely nerve-racking.

TOM: Since you'd had a miscarriage you sort of had that fear. It never occurred to me. I just had faith. But when the kids were finally born, and they were so premature and we were told we'd probably lose all of them. [They had triplets, one of whom died at eleven days.] I had so many feelings and one of them was terror at starting all over.

MATT: My wife was on bed rest for two weeks. She is pretty mentally tough and I don't think she was looking for me to do that much. I think she found it pretty frustrating because she couldn't get around. I suppose I did try to wait on her because I didn't want her to do anything. She didn't seem to need a lot of support . . . or maybe she did and I didn't realize it. I felt very involved but I never felt like she was going to break down. I tend to worry more than she does anyway so I was kind of prepared for anything she might have needed anyway. And we called the doctor with the slightest problem. I think I felt appreciated to the degree that it was relevant to me. Actually, some of my friends thought it was odd that I went with her to the doctor appointments. But I was sensitive to the fact that there was risk associated with her pregnancy and I have a very low tolerance for uncertainty. I felt better being there.

ALAN: I think there is a sense among the general public that pregnancy is very much an experience that is owned by women. But with all of you having wives on bed rest, you were very much involved. You played a much bigger role and I'm wondering if other people–your friends and family–knew the extent of your involvement.

DAVID: If I was acknowledged by anyone at all it was my wife Joan. I worked with a guy who told me that the day his child was born he and his wife got out of bed and she fixed his breakfast and then they went off to the hospital and he waited in the waiting room. But that was awhile ago.

ALAN: Do you guys have a favorite?

MATT: We don't. But I think it might be because my wife was a twin and she always had the sense that her sister kind of got more attention . . . always a little wilder . . . the squeaky wheel kind of thing. So we really work to make sure that doesn't happen. I mean, one has a couple of irritating points and the other has different irritating points and we just deal with it.

DAVID: I had a thought that while I see them as individuals I also see them as parts of a whole, and if one wasn't there I'd really feel that something was missing. Even when we look at them and try to see who seems to have the physical characteristics of my side of the family, it doesn't feel like an issue of favoritism. . . . Not like I'd prefer that one.

ROBERT: I'll just say I don't have a favorite. . . . I cannot imagine one without the other. But one of them just grabbed me. It's funny. One of them looks like her and one of them looks like me. I seem to favor the one that looks like her and she seems to spend more time with the one that looks like me. I have a few theories. Maybe subconsciously I feel I'm afraid to get too close to the one that looks like me. Or maybe the same way I'm attracted to my wife, I'm drawn to the boy that looks like her.

DAVID: We named the boys after their grandfathers and my family appears to favor the child named after their side of the family.

TOM: Well there's one I definitely have more fun with. You don't love your kids the same . . . but you love them the same amount. They just do different things to me. I couldn't say which I love better. My son is into everything and I love that about him . . . although I try to discipline him and he just laughs at me. Yet my daughter melts my heart. She is more needy but she snuggles into me. . . . I love them differently.

ALAN: With families with two children one frequently is identified as the mother's child and one as the father's, and in my practice it isn't static: It really tends to move back and forth. It will be interesting to see how it develops with your twins.

TOM: Well, I think if you put it in those terms, Samantha is more mine because my wife, at least in my mind, seems to favor Michael. He looks like her father and Sarah lost her father when she was very young. There is just some bond she has. She has such warm and loving memories of her father.

MATT: Maybe it is a question of who you bond more with. My son John didn't have serious problems but he had a problem with eating enough. He was smaller and needed more attention. And I think that my wife thinks *I* can get John to eat more than she can, so it ends up that I spend more time with him.

TOM: There are times I feel more affection for one than the other, but it does go back and forth.

ROBERT: It seems like we all have in common the fact that we were ready and we all really wanted our kids. And with twins, if you aren't ready for it, I can't imagine how you would cope.

Chapter 19

YOUR TWINS FROM FIVE TO SIX MONTHS

Your Growing Twins

Teething

The appearance of your babies' first teeth can happen anywhere from three to eighteen months. If your twins are identical, you can expect to see similar dental characteristics between them. Your pediatrician will be looking to see that the teeth are appearing in an appropriate order. Resist the temptation to let your babies go to sleep with a bottle of milk or juice as either will promote tooth decay, even in young babies, after the teeth have erupted.

Changes in Growth Patterns and Growth Rates

At five or six months, you are likely to see that the rate of growth as indicated in your twins' growth charts is going to decrease. In other words, they are not going to grow quite as fast. As a rule of thumb, your pediatrician will expect the weight gain in the first six months to round out to approximately an ounce a day. After six months, that drops to an ounce every other day for the rest of the first year.

In the case of premature twins, we may still be correcting for the expected date of delivery: your five-month-old babies who were born four weeks early will be at a four-month range in growth and development. Hopefully, over time their growth and developmental capabilities will go into the range that no longer needs correcting. The degree of prematurity is a factor: Once your twins move into the normal growth range, and are growing at a normal rate for their actual age, your pediatrician may decide it is no longer necessary to correct. If your twins are two months premature, that two months is very significant when we are looking at a baby who is five months old. However, as your twins grow up, those two months grow less meaningful. By the time your twins are five years old, those two months will have become inconsequential.

Increased Social Behavior

By the fifth month, laughter may be a regular feature as your twins show great pleasure in playing with you. Your babies are increasingly interested in sustained social contact, and may show their displeasure loud and clear if contact is broken before they are ready. Babies at this age are beginning to show excitement at the sight of food.

Sitting Unassisted

The six-month-old baby won't get to a sitting position unassisted but, placed in position, may sit unaided for awhile. Of course, placed side by side, your twins may grab at each other and tend to support or topple each other over. They begin to sit on their own with their backs rounded, supporting their weight on their hands, which are placed palm down in front of them.

Transferring Objects from Hand to Hand

At about five-and-a-half months, babies begin to transfer objects from hand to hand. Your baby is likely to observe and compare held objects.

Parental Questions and Concerns

Starting Solid Food

Your babies will be ready for the introduction of solid foods sometime between their fourth and sixth months. If solids are introduced too early there is a greater likelihood that an infant will become allergic to them. Don't succumb to pressure to start solids too soon because you think the babies will sleep through the night. The introduction of solids depends on the readiness of each baby's digestive tract. Term babies are usually ready by five months, but this is certainly something that every parent will want to discuss with their own pediatrician. For the premature baby, a corrected age of between four and six months is usually appropriate.

You are likely to perceive your twins' increased interest in watching you eat. Once again, the wonderful power of babies to mimic is at work as they watch you chew and begin to imitate the chewing motion. Introduce one food at a time so you will know what food isn't working if either twin has a reaction to it. It is also a good idea to feed both babies the same foods just to try to simplify your already complicated world. If one of your twins doesn't like squash, but both like carrots, feed them carrots for now.

Help with Feeding

If there is any time that help is important, it is at feeding time. The more organized you are, the better off you'll all be. If you have to prepare the cereal after nursing one or both babies, so much time goes by that it is as though you were into another feeding. Have the solid foods ready before you sit down to nurse or offer a bottle. Each baby should have his own spoon and bowl in order to minimize the spread of illness. If you're nursing, of course you'll be holding one or both babies, but if they are taking a bottle, now is a good time for them to be in a baby chair.

Even with little babies, it is important to begin to establish meal and snack times, so that food does not become a tool of behavior modification. Mealtimes for your twins can be an organizational challenge, but they can also be an opportunity for wonderful time with each baby.

Allergies

It is helpful to understand that there can be a genetic predisposition toward developing allergies. If Mom is allergic to walnuts, that does not mean that either twin will be allergic to walnuts, but they may be inclined to develop allergic reactions. If you have a history of respiratory allergies in the family, it is wise to try to create a dust-free environment for your children. Eighty percent of children who do have allergies are allergic to dust or dust mites, and it is possible to delay the onset of allergy to dust by limiting early exposure.

MOST COMMON FOOD ALLERGENS

(limit exposure before one year of age)

berries	chocolate
citrus fruits	egg white
milk	shellfish
tomatoes	wheat
nuts (nuts should not be given before four years of age due to choking hazard)	

LEAST COMMON FOOD ALLERGENS

(customary beginning foods for young babies)

apples	apricots
barley	cooked carrots
oats	peaches
pears	plums
rice	squash

formula or breast milk, so solids should supplement, not supplant, that important nourishment. If your pediatrician feels that the babies are putting on weight a little too fast, he may recommend that you reverse the order and give the solid food first. In the third week of solid foods try another cereal, like barley or oatmeal. In the fourth week try sweet potatoes and, if all is going well, slowly introduce other appropriate foods, one new food per week. Stay with single ingredient items as you introduce the other food groups: green vegetables, fruits, and meats. Hold off with fruits until your twins are enthusiastic about several other foods. Fruits are sweet and one or both of your twins may have a sweet tooth and resist other foods once he realizes sweet tastes are an option."

The Child-Rearing Taboo: Favoritism

"It is the elephant in the middle of the room that nobody wants to acknowledge . . ." The bottom line is that parents frequently *do* have favorites. This is the case where any siblings are concerned and it can certainly be the case with twins. (There, we've said it.) As your children grow and develop and their temperaments change, the child who was a favorite of one parent may lose that status as the parent finds reason to favor another. A parent's choice of a child as a favorite may take place on a conscious level but it is just as likely to be subconscious. Often, a parent singles out a child for reasons that are not clear. Sometimes the reasons are painfully apparent though a parent may be uncomfortable with what such favoritism says about themselves. Parents can easily find themselves charmed by a strikingly beautiful or wonderfully kind child. Sometimes a parent's fierce protection of the child they perceive as less gifted or less obviously endowed can lead to favoritism. Sometimes the reasons are far more subtle and fluid and never rise to consciousness. The parents of twins are likely to choose different favorites and they may shift their positions. Talking with your mate about your feelings may provide you with revelations that ultimately enhance your parenting of both babies. But remember that however infrequently such feelings are acknowledged, they are very common. The parents who anticipate them are best equipped to handle them when they arise.

Negotiating the World with Your Twins

Remember to leave plenty of time. Parents of one young child are often troubled by how long it takes to get out of the house. As far as trying to rush anywhere, twins are double trouble. Your best bet is to leave yourself plenty of time to accomplish even modest goals. Just know that there is no such thing as running to the market for a minute if you're doing it with your twins. Give yourself an extra hour just to account for getting in and out of the car at either end of your travels. You are going to have many happy moments out and about with your beautiful babies, so be sure to give yourself lots of time to enjoy them.

Vomiting and Diarrhea

Diarrhea is often difficult to distinguish from regular bowel movements in breast-fed babies since their movements are typically quite loose. An increase in the volume and/or frequency of bowel movements may indicate that your baby has picked up some kind of stomach flu. In most cases, both vomiting and diarrhea are self-limiting and require no specific medication.

Blood in the bowel movement is reason for extra concern and you should call your pediatrician. It may indicate the presence of a bacterial infection that needs to be treated with an antibiotic.

Loose stool can be treated by manipulating the diet and using what many pediatricians refer to as the BRAT diet: Bananas, Rice, Applesauce, and Toast. (Of course, with younger babies, eliminate the toast.)

The primary concern with vomiting and diarrhea is dehydration. The signs of dehydration are a lack of tears, dryness of the mouth, decreased urination, and, in extreme cases, dehydration can result in skin that can become "tented" or remain as though still held between your thumb and forefinger after you are no longer gently compressing your baby's skin. *Call your physician for specific instructions at the first sign of dehydration.* Usually, dehydration can be treated or prevented with electrolyte replacement solutions that are readily available in your supermarket or pharmacy.

Visiting the Doctor

Immunization: Five to Six Months

The third hepatitis B (Hep B) vaccine is given between six and eighteen months.

The third diphtheria, tetanus, pertussis (DTP) vaccine is given at six months of age.

The third *Haemophilus influenzae* type B (Hib) vaccine is given at six months of age.

The third poliovirus (OPV or IPV) vaccine is given between six and eighteen months of age.

Safety

Burn Safety

As stated previously, parents of young babies should turn their hot-water heaters down to below 120°F so that if your baby is burned, it will be less serious than it would otherwise be. When running a bath for the twins, run the cold water first, then the hot. When turning the water off, do the opposite, never allowing only hot water to run into the tub. Before putting your babies in the water, be sure to swish the water around to avoid any hot spots. Never add hot water with the babies in the tub.

Be very conscientious about keeping babies away from hot beverages at home and certainly in a restaurant, where a server could inadvertently spill hot coffee or tea on one of your twins.

When using the stove, use the back burners first, and turn all pan handles away from the front of the stove if you use the front burners. If your baby does get burned, place the burned area under running cold water for at least five minutes.

Choking

Although it may seem early to discuss these things, be very careful about the dangers of choking on raw carrots, raw celery, bacon, peanuts, nuts, and popcorn. Grapes and hot dogs are not recommended for children under four years of age unless they are skinned and cut up into tiny pieces.

Sunburn

As far as sunburn is concerned, your babies should not be in direct sun if they are under six months of age. At six months, choose a sunscreen made especially for your babies' sensitive skin, and don't allow them to be exposed to the hottest sun of the day. It is a good idea to dab a bit of sunscreen on an arm or leg of each baby and wait several hours to make sure there is no adverse reaction.

ROUNDTABLE TALK

PRESENT AT THE DISCUSSION ARE:

Dr. Connie Agnew
Dr. Alan Klein
Jill Ganon
Tom & Sarah
Nick & Laura
Joan & David
Robert & Grace
Kate & Matt

TOPICS FOR DISCUSSION ARE:

The Financial Impact of Parenting Twins

JILL: Can we talk a little about financial implications of having twins?

JOAN: Our finances . . . we go back and forth from being in denial . . . sort of we'll be O.K. once I get back to work . . . to "Oh my God! What are we going to do?" . . . And just when you think you're getting out from under, something comes up. This week it was an emergency with our dog . . . $200 a day for intensive care.

NICK: We love our doctor but medical costs are a concern, particularly with Laura not working. Now that we only have my insurance, for some bizarre reason it doesn't seem to be covering well-baby care, immunizations, and things like that. Is anybody else experiencing that?

JOAN: Our insurance stopped paying on one of the babies because they kept asking, "Why are you sending one baby to the doctor twice in one day?"

LAURA: Our insurance company kept complaining that we were submitting duplicate charges.

NICK: It is mass confusion since the boys were born five months ago. It is amazing that the insurance companies just don't comprehend twins.

ROBERT: I find it helpful to keep very strict records and to really scrutinize all bills. I have definitely found billing errors. It's really crazy. You make too much money to qualify for low-income help, but suddenly you're down to one income and your expenses skyrocket.

TOM: You learn really quickly that the computer doesn't think.

SARAH: You really have to read your policies. I knew our situation would be complicated so I got a second policy. We find that we get a lot of denied claims at first because the babies go to the doctor so frequently.

TOM: It is still rough because our second policy has turned out to be our primary [one] because I am older, and that seems to be the way they work it. The only way we could manage a second policy was with a huge deductible. But we also have California Children's Services (CCS) and Medi-Cal. In California, any baby born under 1,200 grams may qualify for both. You do have to qualify through diagnosis and financial screening. Our babies also qualify for SSI [Social Security Income] due to their low birth weights. But there is an income factor there, too.

ALAN: I was under the impression that even someone with a substantial income would qualify at least for CCS because the health-care bills, especially hospital bills, are so staggering.

TOM: That is true but there is a level beyond which they do not cover.

ALAN: In general, I counsel couples to put significantly premature twins, born at less than thirty-three weeks or so, on both their policies if possible. I know it is difficult. The cost of their care is usually so high that even your 10 or 20 percent responsibility can amount to a lot of money.

TOM: I don't know if people understand that there are caps to what insurance companies will pay. You really need to research that ahead of time if you can, especially with the potential for enormous costs with a multiple birth.

ALAN: Another option no one has mentioned yet is the possibility of asking for a discount.... I can't remember anyone here ever approaching me.

JOAN: But you can bet we will now!

ALAN: Well, you should ask. I have families who do, and a lot depends on their insurance. It used to be that I could give everyone who had twins a discount. Now, a lot of insurance already grants a discount over my usual charge so it is not as easy to discount it further. But depending on your personal financial situation, it can be reasonable to ask.

ROBERT: I asked for discounts. The worst they can do is say no. In many cases, when you have twins they will either write off the balance or discount it. We'd start with the business office and they would put us through to the supervisor or sometimes directly to the doctor. We were not turned down and the least we received was a discount. It depends on what the insurance pays and what the original discount was. If insurance has paid 90 percent of a $1,200 [bill], chances are they'll write off the balance or most of it. Sometimes it really feels like a matter of survival.

ALAN: In my practice, I offer discounts to anyone who has real financial hardship. Sometimes we work out long-term payment plans. But it is important to understand that there is a clause in the insurance contract that doctors agree to that says if there is no charge to the patient, there can be no charge to the insurance company. So a complete discount is virtually impossible.

JOAN: As a nurse, I always ask doctors if they give professional discounts. It is less likely now than it used to be. In retrospect, I wonder if it was wise to have dropped my insurance to go on my husband's policy. I thought I was paying this unnecessary fee for my own coverage, but we might be better off if I'd kept it. It just was not something I thought through prior to becoming pregnant.

Chapter 20

YOUR TWINS FROM SEVEN MONTHS TO ONE YEAR

Your Twins' Development

Thumb Finger Grasp and Voluntary Release

At about eight months your babies will begin to grasp objects between thumb and forefinger, as well as discover the thrill of uncovering a hidden toy. By one year of age, babies will have the ability to turn the pages of a book. They have the ability to release an object when it is requested by another person.

Responding to Requests

At seven months, your babies are likely to respond to your verbal request ("Can you give me the block?") if it is accompanied by the gesture of your outstretched hand. By twelve months, your verbal request ("May I have the block?") will be responded to without any need for accompanying gestures.

Your Social Babies

At seven months of age, your twins may show a preference for one parent over the other, but both parents should be assured that is only temporary. Babies will show real individuality now, and have their own personal responses to each social contact with family, friends, and other babies. Around this time, your babies may get a lot of enjoyment from play with a mirror. By about ten months your twins will be responding to their names, waving bye-bye, and playing responsive games like peekaboo and patty-cake. Your year-old twins may be engaging in make-believe play, like pretending to drink from a cup or read a book.

First Words

At seven months you will hear the beginnings of polysyllabic vowel sounds, and between ten and twelve months you may hear words with repetitive consonant sounds like "mama" and "dada." Your year-old twins may have some additional words in their vocabularies.

Motor Skills

By seven months your babies may support most of their own weight, and you can observe them bouncing actively. Not every baby learns to crawl. Some lift themselves to a standing position and eventually begin to just walk. But if your twins are going to crawl or creep, they are likely to be pretty mobile by ten months. Walking readiness continues to advance as one or both babies may begin to pull themselves to a standing position and then walk or "cruise," holding onto furniture for support. Next, they will begin to walk with you holding one of their hands, until taking one or two unassisted steps.

Parental Questions and Concerns

Putting Twins in Day Care

Children in a day-care setting outside the home are definitely exposed to more colds, but each baby's world must grow larger at some point and *whenever* that happens, the baby is vulnerable to whatever bug happens to be out there. Decisions about day care should be made keeping several factors in mind: parents' work situations, the family's finances, and the availability of help to come to your home.

The social aspect of day care for your twins is not significant this early in their lives, and their opportunity to socialize with each other is a definite plus as they move out of their first twelve months and into their toddler years.

Motor Development

By six-and-a-half to seven months of age your twins are probably rolling from their tummies to their backs and from their backs to their tummies. By seven to eight months your twins are sitting without support. They are working at pulling together the elements of control over their bodies in order to attain the next developmental milestone. You'll see them beginning to rock back and forth on all fours in preparation to crawl. Again, some babies will take their first steps at ten months after only several weeks of crawling, while some will pull to a stand and just start walking at twelve months without ever having crawled. It is the appropriate connecting of each of these activities that tells you your babies' development is as it should be.

Questions from Strangers

We are all captivated by twins. As parents, you have now entered a segment of the population that is more knowledgeable about, and sensitive to, twin issues than your average shopper in the checkout line. Along with admiring looks and pleasant comments, parents report remarks from "Wouldn't you just know that the boy would be the more beautiful baby?" to "Gee, they look tiny. Are they OK?" It is important to develop your own protocol for dealing with remarks from strangers, or even casual friends. If your twins were premature and you get tired of hearing about how small they are for their age, don't hesitate to tell the inquiring stranger that your seven-month-old twins are five months old.

Weaning

Sometimes, one or both twins will wean themselves spontaneously. In that case, the mother may need to express milk to avoid engorgement. But if the mother is making the decision to begin weaning, it should be done in a manner that spares her the discomfort of engorgement.

Weaning can be most effectively accomplished if done over a period of several weeks. The first week, stop the noontime feeding; the second week, stop the early evening feeding; the third week, stop the bedtime feeding; and, finally, stop the morning feeding. The morning feeding is saved for last as that is the time that the mother is likely to have the greatest milk supply and risks engorgement.

It is often easier to have the father or another caregiver give the bottle when Mom is attempting to wean. While mothers often worry that their babies will go hungry, they almost never do. With Mom not there, they simply become hungry enough to accept a bottle and will soon be quite content with the new arrangement. If the mother is the only one available at feeding time, putting the baby in a high chair rather than cuddling in the recognized nursing position may make the baby more receptive to accepting a bottle.

Visiting the Doctor

Immunization: Seven Months to One Year

The third hepatitis B (Hep B) vaccine is given between six and eighteen months.

The fourth diphtheria, tetanus, pertussis (DTP) vaccine is given between twelve and eighteen months of age.

The fourth *Haemophilus influenzae* type B (Hib) vaccine is given between twelve and fifteen months of age.

The third poliovirus (OPV or IPV) vaccine is given between six and eighteen months of age.

The first measles, mumps, rubella (MMR) vaccine is given between twelve and fifteen months.

The first varicella zoster virus (Var) vaccine is given between twelve and eighteen months.

Safety

Finalize Twin-Proofing for Your Active Babies

Now that your babies are getting around and beginning to explore, you can see why it is important to be a few steps ahead of them when it comes to safety. With their increased mobility, you can no longer tell yourself you have an eye on them: There is no guarantee they will stay where you put them!

THE PERILS OF EXERCISE EQUIPMENT

The treadmill that is designed for your health can be very dangerous to your twins. This is another case where two, tiny explorers can get into real trouble. Babies should have absolutely no access to treadmills, stationary bikes, workout stations, hand weights, or barbells. These fitness tools are very enticing to babies, perhaps because they are attracted to your physical activity when *you* use them.

POOL AND JACUZZI

If you are fortunate enough to own a pool or Jacuzzi, it should be in a gated, enclosed area. Even then, there should always be a protective pool cover securely anchored in place whenever the pool is not in use. Inflatable wading pools are no exception: Never allow your twins to play in the yard with a filled wading pool unless they are supervised by an adult. A baby can drown in several inches of water.

DR. KLEIN COMMENTS ON BABY WALKERS

"Baby walkers present a particular danger because they move so fast and can allow babies to scoot their way into trouble really quickly. *This is especially true with twins, when they are more than likely to take off in two directions at once!* The best-intentioned and most diligent parent is no match for twins in baby walkers. There are wonderful, new stationary centers you can buy for your twins with plenty of stimulation but no wheels."

WINDOWS, BALCONIES, AND PORCHES

Windows are very dangerous to babies who like to hoist themselves up for a better view. *Remember, a screen is not an adequate barrier for an enthusiastic infant, and your twins can create better access than the singleton baby whether by happy accident or collaboration.* Keep windows closed unless they are blocked by baby-safe window guards.

ROUNDTABLE TALK

PRESENT AT THE DISCUSSION ARE:

> *Dr. Connie Agnew*
> *Dr. Alan Klein*
> *Jill Ganon*
> *Tom & Sarah*
> *Nick & Laura*
> *Joan & David*
> *Robert & Grace*
> *Kate & Matt*

TOPICS FOR DISCUSSION ARE:

> *Out in the World with Your Twins*
> *Reflections on a Year with Your Twins*

NICK: Our boys are identical and you just don't ever really forget that they are twins. They are fourteen months now and they tackle each other and go back and forth doing the same things. And I have to say they get an enormous amount of attention when we just go out to the mall.

LAURA: In talking to lots of other parents with twins, it seems that identical twins seem to reach developmental milestones very close to the same time . . . more so than fraternal twins. These guys were walking within a week of each other . . . they stood unassisted on the same day.

NICK: You can sort of identify with celebrities, though I think its maybe more difficult with twins. People stare at celebrities but they stay away. But put identical twins in a stroller and nobody has any qualms about coming right up to you and asking a million questions. It's kind of flattering, but sometimes you're really in a hurry. Of course, if you just have one or if we take separate strollers and split up when we get to the mall, no reaction whatsoever. But the double stroller is a sideshow.

TOM: We'll have Sammi in pink and Michael in jeans and people will still come up to us and say, "Wow, twins . . . boy and girl. Are they identical?" [laughter]

JILL: Do you give a lot of thought to how they are dressed?

LAURA: Our boys usually wear similar things. Overalls, but each one has a different color shirt. It's kind of fun at a family party or something. But knowing my family and not wanting to deal with "who is who?" all day, I'll make sure one is in white socks and one in red, or something like that. And also, if we're at home and I want to know which one is running off, I can't see their faces, but I can look at the socks and know—there goes Kevin!

JILL: Do they communicate in a special way with each other?

TOM: I don't know if they use their own language, but we have their cribs end to end and they sort of grab at each other. You can hear them laughing. They only do it when they are by themselves. If they catch me poking my head in, it's over. Whatever it is they are communicating, they both find it really funny sometimes.

MATT: I think our guys are communicating. They are not yet a year old. They look at each other and make all sorts of noises, they fight over toys, roll over each other. They will literally shake each other sometimes . . . they are very funny.

LAURA: We have their cribs end to end. If by some miracle they are napping at the same time. I'll hear giggling when they wake up and I'll peak in their room, and they are in their cribs looking like jailed inmates. And in the high chair . . . God forbid one starts laughing. They'll look at each other and start to howl. Forget trying to feed them.

JILL: So how would you sum up the year?

MATT: For us, I'd say that other than the fact that we now have two kids, everything was the same for us. I travel a lot so when I get home I like to stay home. It's like Joan said, sometimes you look at them and say, "How did we do that?" Especially now that they are ten months old—out of the slug stage. . . . Now they really know you and each other and are doing things. It's incredibly exciting. If anything, our relationship is better.

KATE: Like Matt says, things haven't changed that much. I'm just more tired than before.

TOM: I'm incredibly aware of how much they've developed and how different they are from each other. My son is very independent, but my daughter will really pull and cry if she wants my attention.

JOAN: I've gone back to work part-time so now we have sitters who come in. That is a big step. Sometimes they scream when I leave, sometimes they don't. They are going through some separation issues. Sometimes David will walk into the bathroom and they're just outside the bathroom door, crying and crying. Of course, now Paul can reach the knob so he'll just open the door and see if his dad's in there.

MATT: Now I say we never get to go to any of the parties that we never went to anyway. . . . This is the greatest thing we've ever done. If anything, our relationship is better. We have someone living in to help with the kids, and it's been strange getting used to having somebody living with us. But she goes her own way on the weekends. Once the kids are in bed, our life is the same as it always was, except we're much more tired. I think it's great.

JOAN: The boys are such an important part of our family, and my marriage is more important to me now. It's sort of like everything is more important in a balanced way. I'm not sure if it's because we had twins but I think it is. Having twins stopped us from being these two little people with big jobs. If we'd just had one, I think I would have pretty much taken care of the baby, and David would have done his thing at work and of course loved the baby. But we wouldn't have become the kind of team we are now.

LAURA: At first, I didn't have the self-confidence as a mother to do it alone and was always asking for help. But now, fourteen months have passed and there is the sense that if we can do two [babies], we can do anything. It's so much fun, there's so much love, and now they are at the point where they're really responding. They'll hug me . . . sometimes I have to laugh at what it must look like as I walk across the living room with one on each leg . . . or else they are following me around like ducklings.

DONALD: So much has happened since we first knew we were pregnant. We're so involved with Samantha and Michael, and they are making such incredible progress. You don't necessarily realize how much Brian [their third son, who died eleven days after birth] is a part of our lives until we think about maybe leaving L.A. and we realize it would feel like we were abandoning him. . . . He's a sort of a guardian angel. We had to make the decision to take him off life support and it was excruciating. We still wonder if we did the right thing because we went through the process with our daughter, too. We were ready to take her off life support. You have to understand, they were so tiny. . . . Sarah was holding her one last time, and Samantha just wouldn't stop staring at Sarah. We finally decided to do a CAT scan, and that gave us hope that at least her condition wasn't deteriorating. And now she is a little behind her brother but she is growing and doing really well. And she was almost taken off life support. That's as heavy as it gets. It's hard not to feel that maybe there could have been a miracle for Brian, but his problems were so much more severe. . . . He's a big part of our prayers. . . . He'll always be a part of our family.

NICK: On some level, I kind of look at it like a job. There are times all of us in the work world don't like our job, but you learn to have some perspective. Laura is a full-time mom and I know how incredibly hard she works. She is the one on call for these boys Monday through Friday, and it might mean sometimes she's up through the night, but I'm there with her and the boys on weekends. I know it is tough on Laura.

LAURA: It's absolutely worth the bloodshot eyes, and I wouldn't trade it for anything. As a couple, we've learned so much.

IMMUNIZATION SCHEDULES

RECOMMENDED CHILDHOOD IMMUNIZATION SCHEDULE[1]
United States, January-December 1997

Vaccine ▼ Age ▶	Birth	1 mo	2 mos	4 mos	6 mos	12 mos	15 mos	18 mos	4-6 yrs
Hepatitis B [2,3]		Hep B-1							
			Hep B-2			Hep B-3			
Diphtheria, Tetanus, Pertussis [4]		DTaP or DTP	DTaP or DTP	DTaP or DTP			DTaP or DTP [4]		DTaP or DTP
H. influenzae type b [5]			Hib	Hib	Hib [5]	Hib [5]			
Polio [6]			Polio [6]	Polio		Polio [6]			Polio
Measles, Mumps, Rubella [7]						MMR			MMR [7]
Varicella [8] (Chicken Pox)						Var			

Shaded bars indicate range of acceptable ages for vaccination.

Approved by the Advisory Committee on Immunization Practices (ACIP), American Academy of Pediatrics (AAP), and American Academy of Family Physicians (AAFP).

Necessary footnotes are provided below.

[1] This schedule indicates the recommended age for routine administration of currently licensed childhood vaccines. Some combination vaccines are available and may be used whenever administration of all components of the vaccine is indicated. Providers should consult the manufacturers' package inserts for detailed recommendations.

[2] **Infants born to HBsAg-negative mothers** should receive 2.5 µg of Merck vaccine (Recombivax HB) or 10 µg of SmithKline Beecham (SB) vaccine (Engerix-B). The second dose should be administered +/− 1 month after the first dose.

Infants born to HBsAg-positive mothers should receive 0.5 mL hepatitis B immune globulin (HBIG) within 12 hours of birth, and either 5 μg of Merck vaccine (Recombivax HB) or 10 μg of SB vaccine (Engerix-B) at a separate site. The second dose is recommended at 1-2 months of age and the third dose at 6 months of age.

Infants born to mothers whose HBsAg status is unknown should receive either 5 μg of Merck vaccine (Recombivax HB) or 10 μg of SB vaccine (Engerix-B) within 12 hours of birth. The second dose of vaccine is recommended at 1 month of age and the third dose at 6 months of age. Blood should be drawn at the time of delivery to determine the mother's HBsAG status; if it is positive, the infant should receive HBIG as soon as possible (no later than 1 week of age). The dosage and timing of subsequent vaccine doses should be based upon the mother's HBsAG status.

3 Children and adolescents who have not been vaccinated against hepatitis B in infancy may begin the series during any childhood visit. Those who have not previously received doses of hepatitis B vaccine should initiate or complete the series during the 11-12 year old visit. The second dose should be administered at least 4 months after the first dose and at least 2 months after the second dose.

4 DTaP (diphtheria and tetanus toxoids and acellular pertussis vaccine) is the preferred vaccine for all doses in the vaccination series, including completion of the series in children who have received +/− 1 dose of whole-cell DTP vaccine. Whole-cell DTP is an acceptable alternative to DTaP. The 4th dose (DTP or DTaP) may be administered as early as 12 months of age, provided 6 months have elapsed since the third dose, and if the child is considered unlikely to return at 15-18 months of age. Td (tetanus and diphtheria toxoids, absorbed, for adult use) is recommended at 11-12 years of age if at least 5 years have elapsed since the last dose of DTP, DTaP, or DT. Subsequent routine Td boosters are recommended every 10 years.

5 Three H. influenzae type b (Hib) conjugate vaccines are licensed for infant use. If PRP-OMP (PedvaxHIB [Merck]) is administered at 2 and 4 months of age, a dose at 6 months is not required. After completing the primary series, any Hib conjugate vaccine may be used as a booster.

6 Two poliovirus vaccines are currently licensed in the U.S.: inactivated poliovirus vaccine (IPV) and oral poliovirus vaccine (OPV). The following schedules are all acceptable by the ACIP, the AAP, and the AAFT, and parents and providers may choose among them:

1. IPV at 2 and 4 months; OPV at 12-18 months and 4-6 years

2. IPV at 2, 4, 12-18 months, and 4-6 years

3. OPV at 2, 4, 6-18 months, and 4-6 years

The ACIP routinely recommends schedule 1. IPV is the only poliovirus vaccine recommended for immunocompromised persons and their household contacts.

7 The second dose of MMR is routinely recommended at 4-6 years of age or at 11-12 years of age, but may be administered during any visit, provided at least 1 month has elapsed since receipt of the first dose and that both doses are administered at or after 12 months of age.

8 Susceptible children may receive Varicella vaccine (Var) at any visit after the first birthday, and those who lack a reliable history of chickenpox should be immunized during the 11-12 year old visit. Children +/− 13 years of age should receive 2 doses, at least 1 month apart.

Adapted from the American Academy of Pediatrics. Active and Passive Immunization. In: Peter G. Ed. *1997 Red Book; Report of the Committee of Infectious Diseases.* 24th ed. Elk Grove Village, IL: American Academy of Pediatrics; 1997; 18-19

GROWTH CHARTS

Boys: Birth to 18 Months Physical Growth Percentiles

O Baby's Actual Age
★ Baby's Corrected Age

TWIN BOY "A" BORN AT 27 WEEKS GESTATION

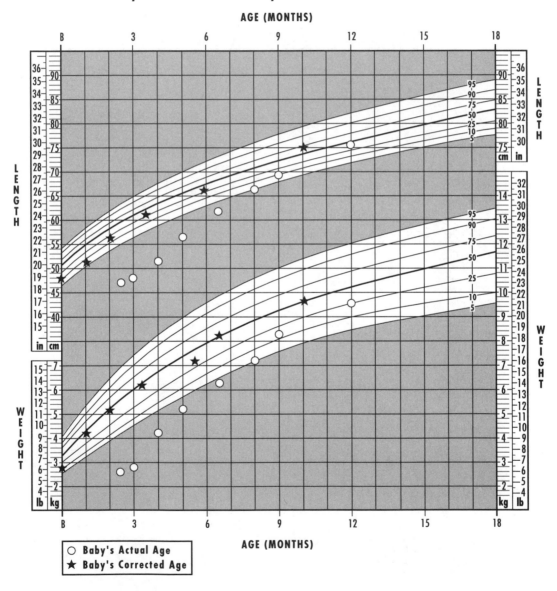

Boys: Birth to 18 Months Physical Growth Percentiles

○ Baby's Actual Age
★ Baby's Corrected Age

TWIN BOY "B" BORN AT 27 WEEKS GESTATION

Boys: Birth to 18 Months Physical Growth Percentiles

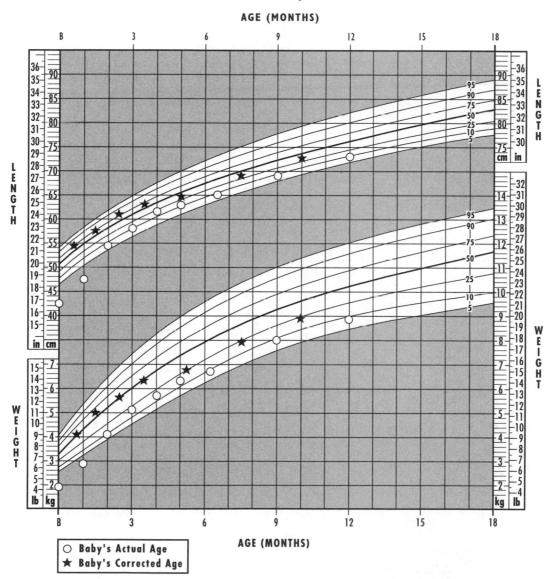

AGE (MONTHS)

○ Baby's Actual Age
★ Baby's Corrected Age

TWIN BOY "A" BORN AT 34 WEEKS GESTATION

Boys: Birth to 18 Months Physical Growth Percentiles

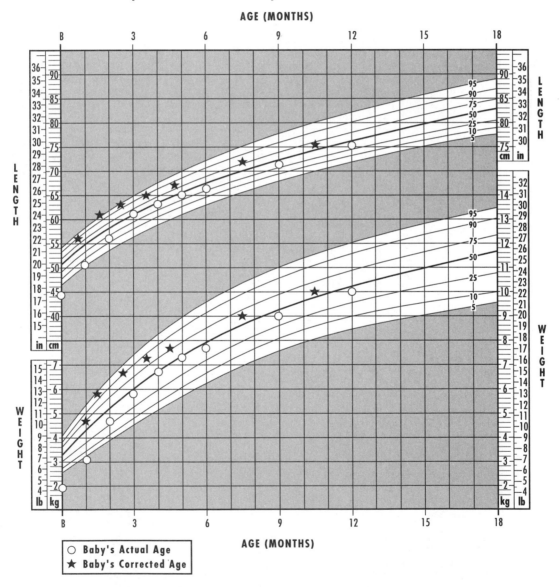

○ Baby's Actual Age
★ Baby's Corrected Age

TWIN BOY "B" BORN AT 34 WEEKS GESTATION

Boys: Birth to 18 Months Physical Growth Percentiles

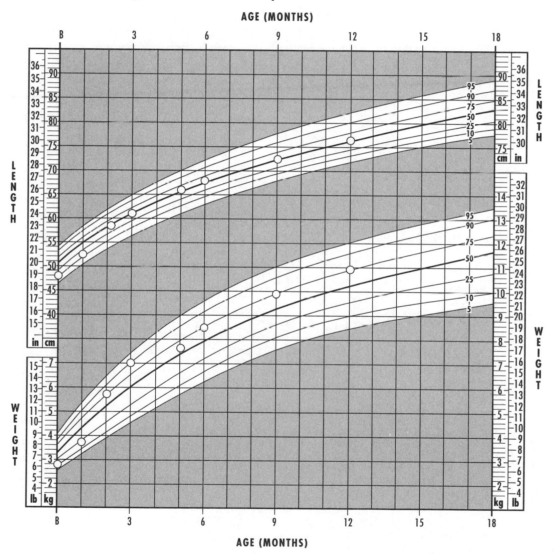

AGE (MONTHS)

FULL TERM TWIN BOY

Girls: Birth to 18 Months Physical Growth Percentiles

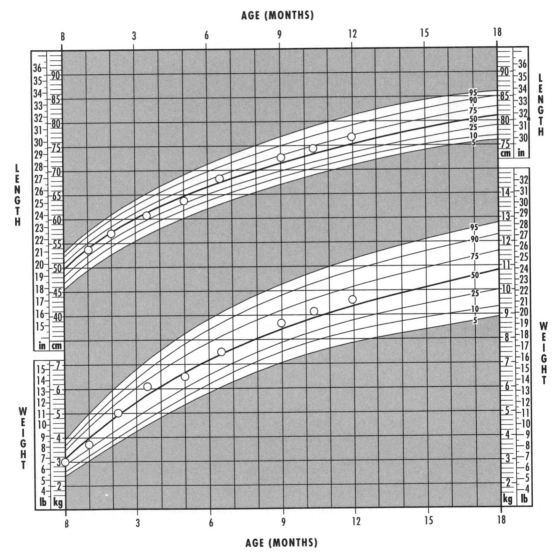

FULL TERM TWIN GIRL

MIDTRIMESTER RISK FOR CHROMOSOME ABNORMALITIES

Maternal Age	Risk For Trisomy 21[1,2]	Risk For Trisomy 18[3]
15	1:1215	1:4734
16	1:1210	1:4716
17	1:1205	1:4695
18	1:1198	1:4668
19	1:1189	1:4632
20	1:1177	1:4584
21	1:1160	1:4521
22	1:1140	1:4443
23	1:1114	1:4341
24	1:1081	1:4212
25	1:1040	1:4053
26	1:990	1:3858
27	1:930	1:3624
28	1:862	1:3357
29	1:784	1:3054
30	1:700	1:2727
31	1:613	1:2388
32	1:526	1:2049

Maternal Age	Risk For Trisomy 21[1,2]	Risk For Trisomy 18[3]
33	1:442	1:1722
34	1:365	1:1422
35	1:296	1:1152
36	1:236	1:921
37	1:186	1:726
38	1:146	1:567
39	1:112	1:438
40	1:86	1:336
41	1:65	1:255
42	1:50	1:195
43	1:38	1:147
44	1:28	1:111
45	1:22	1:84
46	1:16	1:63
47	1:12	1:45
48	1:8	1:33
49	1:6	1:24
50	1:5	1:18

The numbers provided in this table are approximate risks based on data currently available. These numbers are population-based risk estimates and should not be presented as a woman's individual risk.

These numbers represent the estimated risk for a fetus with Down's syndrome or Trisomy 18 at midtrimester.

Approximatelly 23 percent of Down's syndrome fetuses[2] and 70 percent of Trisomy 18 fetuses[4] will be lost between midtrimester and term.

[1] Cuckle, H.A., Wald, N.J., Thompson, S.C.: Estimating a woman's risk of having a pregnancy associated with Down's Syndrome using her own age and serum alpha-fetoprotein level. Br J Obstet Gynaecol 1987 94:387.

[2] Data from [1] adjusted for 23% loss rate: Hook, E.B.: Chromosome abnormalities and spontaneous fetal deaths following amniocentesis: futher data and associations with maternal age. Am J Hum Genet 1983 35:110-116.

[3] Estimate from Foundation for Blood Research.

[4] Hook, E.G., Cross, P.K., Schreinemechars, D.M.: Chromosomal abnormality rates at amniocentesis and in live-born infants. J Am Med Assoc 1983 249:2034-2038.

RESOURCE GUIDE

Organizations

Center for Study of Multiple Birth (CSMB)
Suite 464
333 E. Superior St.
Chicago, IL 60611
(312) 266–9093
http://pubweb.acns.nwu.edu/~lgk395/csmb.html
E-mail: lgk395@nwu.edu (Dr. Louis Keith, director)

A public charity organized in 1977 in support of medical and social research in the area of multiple births.

International Twins Association (ITA)
c/o Lynn Long or Lori Stewart
6898 Channel Road, NE
Minneapolis, MN 55432
(612) 571–8910 or (612) 571–3022

A nonprofit agency promoting the spiritual, intellectual, and social welfare of twins throughout the world.

The International Society For Twin Studies
Adam P. Matheny, Jr., Ph.D.
c/o The Louisville Twin Study
2301 S. Third Street
Louisville, KY 40208
http://kate.pc.helsinki.fi/twin/ists.html
E-mail: apmath01@ulkyvm.louisville.edu

An international, multidisciplinary organization, established to further research and social action in all fields related to twin studies.

Minnesota Center for Twin and Adoption Research
University of Minnesota
Department of Psychology
75 East River Road
Minneapolis, MN 55455

Mothers of Supertwins (MOST)
P.O. Box 951
Brentwood, NY 11717
(516) 434-MOST
http://www.familyresource.org/most/
E-mail: MOSTMOM@nyc.pipeline.com

A nonprofit organization serving the needs of families expecting multiples or already parents of triplets, quadruplets, or quintuplets.

The National Organization of Mothers of Twins Clubs, Inc. (NOMOTC)
P.O. Box 23185
Albuquerque, NM 87192-1188
(505) 275-0955
http://www.nomotc.org/
E-mail: nomotc@aol.com (Executive Office)

A nonprofit nationwide network of parents of multiples clubs sharing information, concerns, and advice.

Parents of Multiple Births Association of Canada (POMBA)
240 Graff Avenue
Box 22005
Stratford, ON N5A 7V6
Canada
(519) 272–2203
Fax: (519) 272–1926
http://www.pomba.org/
E-mail: pomba@cyg.net or office@pomba.org

A nonprofit organization whose purpose is to act as a general information source and liason between parents and agencies, health caregivers,
and educators.

Sidelines
(714) 497–2265
http://home.earthlink.net/~sidelines/
E-mail: sidelines@earthlink.net

A nonprofit organization providing education, referral information, support, and advocacy services for women experiencing complicated pregnancies.

Twin Days Festival
Twin Days Festival Committee
P.O. Box 29
Twinsburg, OH 44807
(216) 425–3652
http://www.visi.com/~johnr/twins.html

An annual festival for twins of all ages in Twinsburg, OH.

Twin Services
P.O. Box 10066
Berkeley, CA 94709

(510) 524–0863
Fax: (510) 524–0894
Se habla español
http://www.parentsplace.com/readroom/twins/index.html

Offers free counseling and referral services.

The Twin to Twin Transfusion Syndrome (TTTS) Foundation, Inc.
411 Longbeach Parkway
Bay Village, OH 44140
(216) 899–8887
http://eagle.nest.boise.id.us/projects/ttts/ttts.htm
E-mail: TTTSFound@aol.com

A nonprofit organization providing educational, emotional, and financial support to families before, during, and after pregnancies diagnosed with TTTS.

twinsight
Eileen M. Pearlman, Ph.D./Director
1137 2nd Street, Suite 109
Santa Monica, CA 90403
(310) 458–1373
Fax: (310) 451–8761

Dr. Pearlman, who is an identical twin, works with multiples of all ages and their families. *twinsight* offers counseling, psychotherapy, workshops, and consultations via phone or in person.

Twinless Twins International Support Group
c/o Raymond W. Brandt, Ph.D, Ed.D.
11220 St. Joe Road
Fort Wayne, IN 46835
(219) 627–5414
http://www.fwi.com/twinless/
E-mail: ebero@interaccess.com

A support group serving twins (all multiple births) who suffer from the loss of companionship of their twin.

The Twins Foundation
P.O. Box 6043
Providence, RI 02940
(401) 729-1000
http://www.twinsfoundation.com
E-mail: twins@twinsfoundation.com

A nonprofit membership organization and research information center on twins that includes a national twin registry and a quarterly newsletter.

Magazines, Newsletters, and Books

Twin Pleasures Publishing
E-mail: TwinGma@brownetwins.com
(800) 894-6257

The Browne Twins Series
by Patricia Frechtman, illustrated by Ric Harbin
Board books written about a real set of twins by their grandmother. These books are designed for twins and their sibs, as well as peers, teachers, and the extended family.

Additional materials such as a baby book designed for parents of twins, party supplies, video, and free quarterly newsletter, "From Our House to Yours," are also available.

Our Newsletter (published quarterly)
Center For Loss In Multiple Birth, Inc.
(907) 746–6123

CLIMB
c/o Jean Kollantai
P.O. Box 1064
Palmer, AK 99645

TWINS magazine (published 6 times each year)
5350 South Roslyn Street
Suite 400
Englewood, CO 80111
(800) 328–3211
http://www.twinsmagazine.com/

Twins World Magazine
(219) 627–5414

The Twins Foundation Newletter (published quarterly)
The Twins Foundation
P.O. Box 6043
Providence, RI 02940
(401) 729-1000

Twin Services' Publications
(510) 524–0863
*Your Twins' First Year: A Survival Kit for New and Expectant Parents;
Surviving with Toddler Twins: A Handout Collection for Parents; Twins in
School, Apart or Together; Twin Care: A Handout Collection*

Maternity Needs

Girdles and Support Hose

Gottfried Medical
P.O. Box 8966
Toledo, OH 43623
(800) 537–1968

Custom vascular support hose; prescription required

IEM Orthopedics
P.O. Box 592
Ravenna, OH 44266
(330) 297–7652

Custom maternity lumbo-pelvic support

Jobst Support Hose
P.O. Box 653
Toledo, OH 43697
(800) 537–1063

Vascular support hose available at retail outlets; custom maternity girdles and support hose with prescription

Medi Support Hose
76 Seegers Road
Arlington Heights, IL 60005
(800) 633–6334

Vascular support hose available at retail outlets; custom support hose with prescription

Breast Feeding

Cozy Cuddles Nursing Pillow
(416) 299–5507

Nursing comfort pillows with convenient washable covers

La Leche League International
(847) 519–9585
http://www.twinsmagazine.com/

Many useful items for nursing such as: several styles of nursing pillows, baby cups for tiny infants who have trouble sucking, breast shells for women with inverted nipples, nursing pads, posture correct nursing stool, heat pads, lanolin cream for sore nipples, milk freezer bags

Lact-aid International Incorporated
(423) 744–9090

Supplemental feeding system provides oral sucking therapy for infants, as well as nutritional supplementation

Maternity and Nursing Additions
(800) 571–5837

Medela
(800) 435–8316

Breast pumps and nursing aids; directs customers to most convenient
rental station and/or breast feeding consultant

Two by Two
(800) 526–2594

"Nursemate" pillow designed to comfortably support two nursing babies

White River Breast Pump
(800) 824–6351

Breast pump with kit to allow for simultaneous pumping of both breasts;
directs customers to most convenient local pharmacy for rental; shipping
to rural areas can be arranged

Products That Will Help You to Care for Your Twins

Baby Carriers

The Better Baby Sling
The Better Baby Sling Company
P.O. Box 11709
London SE14 5ZR
UK
44–171–635–7900 (from the US)

Baby carrier allows for carrying twins in three different positions

Tot Tenders Inc.
(800) 634–6870

Front baby carrier, "Gemini," can be used for carrying babies together or
may be separated to carry babies individually

Child Proofing and Safety

Office of Information and Public Affairs
Publication #202 ("The Safe Nursery—A Buyer's Guide")
U.S. Consumer Product Safety Commission
Washington, DC 20207

KidCo
(800) 553–5529

One Step Ahead
(800) 950–5120

Perfectly Safe
(800) 837–KIDS

Rev-a-Shelf
(800) 762–9030

Right Start catalog
(800) 548–8531

The Safety Zone
(800) 999–3030

Clothing, Bedding and General Baby Care

Jan's Custom Knits
(408) 637–3269

Baby blankets for multiples

The Natural Baby Company
(609) 771–9233

Bedding carriers, strollers, diapers, covers, knapsacks, footwear, lamb-skin, wool items, books for parents, nursing clothes

Pretty Small: Tiny Clothes for Tiny Babies
Mrs. Gwen Lloyd
93 Chadderton Drive
Chapel House, Newcastle Upon Tyne
NE5 1HP
UK

Lovely baby clothes specially designed for premature or small infants

Strollers

The Baby Jogger
(800) 241–1848

Side by side stroller, "Twinner," available with quick release wheels and several wheel sizes

Perego strollers from Janet Bleyl
(209) 474–3073

Wholesale dealer of Perego twin and triplet strollers at reduced cost

Two by Two
(800) 526–2594

"Connect Two" connects two umbrella style strollers

UNI-USA
(800) 832–2376

Twin in-line stroller, large wheels suitable for jogging

Free Products

Beechnut Food Corporation
(800) 523–6633

New parent pack available to mothers of multiples, includes information on newborns and product coupons

Evenflo
(800) 356–2229

Gift package of feeding products to parents of multiples, coupons for bottles, informational brochures on breast and bottle feeding

Playtex
(800) 222–0453

Ask to speak with consumer affairs multiple birth program; free gift package of disposable nursing kit.

Index

Note: Page numbers with an *f* indicate figures; those with a *t* indicate tables.

Abdomen
    backache and, 87, 101, 112, 123, 203
    evaluation of, 33
    exercises for, 55, 56f, 59, 59f
    expansion of, 78
    itching of, 30
    pain in, 51, 112
    size of, 30
Abortion, 23
Abruptio placentae, 103
Accutane, 16
Acetaminophen, 17
Aerobics, 55
AFP (alpha-fetoprotein) test, 80–81
Africans
    sickle cell anemia in, 23
    twins among, 2, 9
Age, maternal, 10, 82–83
    diabetes risk and, 116
    Down's syndrome and, 89, 279t, 280
Airbags, 168. *See also* Car seats.
Airplane flights, 92–93
    dehydration on, 92
    radiation exposure during, 20
    tips for, 83–84
Alcohol use
    during pregnancy, 14
    preterm labor and, 104

Allergies
    food, 200, 233, 253–254
    immunization, 225
Alpha-fetoprotein (AFP) test, 80–81
American Indians, twins among, 2
Aminophylline, 185
Amniocentesis, 67, 89f
    fetal gender and, 94
    indications for, 89
    miscarriage risk with, 89, 90
    scheduling of, 87
    triple marker test vs., 80–81
Amniotic fluid, 76, 85–86
    imbalances of, 103
    leakage of, 138
    volume of, 126
Ampicillin, 45
Anemia, 63, 79
    banked blood and, 126
    family planning and, 22
    iron supplements for, 28
    test for, 35, 80
Anencephaly, 80. *See also* Neural tube defects.
Anesthesia
    epidural, 142–144, 146
    general, 146–147
    regional, 142
    spinal, 146

Anorexia nervosa, 19
Anticonvulsants, birth defects with, 16–17
Antidepressants, breast-feeding and, 156
Apgar test, 149
Apnea, 185–186
    drugs for, 185, 194
Appetite, changes in, 43, 63, 76, 132
Arthritis
    evaluation of, 33
    family planning and, 22
Asians
    thalassemia in, 23
    twins among, 2, 9
Aspirin, during pregnancy, 17, 77
Asthma, 22

Baby blues, 152
Baby carriers, 169, 288
Baby-sitters, 215
Baby walkers, 265
Backaches
    from abdominal weight, 87, 101, 112, 124
    feeding and, 203
Banked blood, 126
Bathroom safety, 169, 243–244
Bedding, 168
Bedrest, 105, 107, 126, 127, 133, 174
    hospitalization for, 175–176
Betamethasone, 105–106
Biceps exercise, 60, 60f
Birth coach, 91
Birth control, 20–21
Birth defects, 90. *See also specific types, e.g.,* Spina
        bifida.
    diabetes and, 116, 117
    drug-related, 15–17
    ethnicity and, 23
    rubella and, 23
    umbilical cord and, 148
Birthing classes, 91–92, 129–130, 141
Blacks
    sickle cell anemia in, 23
    twins among, 2, 9
Bleeding
    after delivery, 149–150

during early pregnancy, 51–53
    gums, 64, 79, 87, 100, 113
    intraventricular, 187
    labor and, 138
        preterm, 104, 179
Blood clots, 52–53
Blood tests, 35, 90
Blood transfusions, 126, 187
Body temperature regulation, 192
Bottle-feeding, 192–194, 198, 204. *See also*
        Feeding.
    posture and, 203
    strategies for, 198–203, 226–228, 252–253
BPD (bronchopulmonary dysplasia), 184
Bradley childbirth classes, 91–92. *See also*
        Birthing classes.
Bras, 49, 78
BRAT diet, 255
Braxton-Hicks contractions, 112–113, 125, 132
    labor and, 137–138
Breasts
    engorgement of, 151
    exam of, 33, 80, 88
    mastitis of, 151
    support for, 49, 78
    tenderness of, 48–49, 64
Breast-feeding, 150–152, 192–193, 198–202,
        204
    antidepressants and, 156
    caffeine and, 200
    football hold for, 198f, 202
    hydration for, 201
    jaundice and, 190–191
    positions for, 198f
    posture and, 203
    resources for, 287–288
    strategies for, 198–204, 226–228, 252–253
Breast pump, 151, 192–193
Breathing problem(s)
    infant, 181, 184–186, 226
        apnea as, 185–186
        smoking and, 234
    maternal, 47–48, 64, 79, 124
Breech birth, 144–145, 145f, 181–182
Bronchopulmonary dysplasia (BPD), 184

Bulimia, 19
Burn safety, 256

Caffeine
    apnea and, 185
    breast-feeding and, 200
Calcium
    leg cramps and, 100
    during pregnancy, 27–28, 28t
Carbohydrates, 26
    sources of, 26
Carpel tunnel syndrome, 99–100, 113, 125
Carriers, baby, 169, 288
Car seats, 167–168, 231–232
Cephalosporin, pregnancy risk with, 45
Certified nurse-midwife (CNM)
    choice of, 41
    during labor, 141–142
Cervix
    dilation of, 106, 139, 140f
    effacement of, 139, 139f
    incompetent, 10
Cesarean delivery, 144–148
    bikini cut for, 147
    personnel for, 147
    vaginal vs., 180–182
Checkups, pregnancy
    at 8 weeks, 49–50
    at 12 weeks, 65–67
    at 16 weeks, 79–81
    at 20 weeks, 87–89
    at 24 weeks, 101–102
    at 28 weeks, 114–115
    at 32 weeks, 125–126
Chest pain, 47
Childbirth classes, 91–92, 129–130, 141
China, birth control in, 2
Chlamydial infections
    diaper rash with, 239
    tests for, 34
Chocolate, 19
Choking, 256
Chorionic villus sampling (CVS), 67, 68f
Chromosomal defects. *See* Genetic disorders.
Cigarettes. *See* Tobacco use.

Ciprofloxacin, 45
Clomiphene citrate (Clomid), 9, 11
Clothing, 170
CNM (certified nurse-midwife), 41, 141–142
Colostrum, 192
Condoms, 20
Constipation, 25, 46–47, 64. *See also*
    Gastrointestinal problems.
Contractions
    Braxton-Hicks, 112–113, 125, 132
        labor and, 137–138
    during labor, 139–140
    oxytocin and, 143, 148
    in preterm labor, 104
Couple relationships
    intimacy and, 134–136
    twins' impact on, 93–95, 210–214
Cradle cap, 241
Cramping, 51
Cribs, 168
C-section. *See* Cesarean delivery.
CVS (chorionic villus sampling), 67, 68f
Cystic fibrosis, 23, 65

Danazol, birth defects with, 16
Day care, 262–263
Dehydration. *See* Fluid balance.
Delivery, 137–149. *See also* Preterm labor.
    Braxton-Hicks contractions and, 137–138
    cesarean. *See* Cesarean delivery.
    depression after, 152–156
    early, 102–106, 222–223
    gestational diabetes and, 117–118
    preparation for, 177–182
    recovery after, 149–150
    stages of, 139–148, 140f, 144f–145f
    stories about, 127–130
    ultrasonography for, 145–146
    vaginal, 180–182
Demerol (meperidine), 142
Dental exam, 20
Depression
    postpartum, 152–156
    symptoms of, 153
    treatment of, 155–156

DES (diethylstilbestrol), 22
Diabetes, 103
  family planning and, 22
  gestational, 115–119
    diagnosis of, 116
    diet for, 115, 117
    effects of, 117–118
    risks for, 116
    sweets and, 25, 118–119
    symptoms of, 116
    test for, 80
    treatment of, 118–119
Diagnosis, pregnancy, 8, 31–35
  ultrasonography for, 35–37, 36f
Diaper(s), 169, 194
  rash, 232, 238–239
Diarrhea, 255
Diet. *See also* Nutrition.
  BRAT, 255
Diethylstilbestrol (DES), 22
Dilantin, birth defects with, 17
Diphtheria, tetanus, pertussis (DTP) vaccine, 225,
    229, 233, 242, 256, 264
  schedule for, 271f, 271–272
Discharge, from hospital, 194–197, 206
Dizygotic twins, 7f, 7–8
Doctors. *See* Health care providers.
Down's syndrome
  alpha-fetoprotein test for, 80–81
  chorionic villus sampling for, 67
  maternal age and, 89, 279t, 280
  risks for, 89, 279t, 280
Dreams
  REM sleep and, 111
  vivid, 77, 132
Drugs
  FCA categories for, 15–16
  pregnancy risk with, 15–17
  for preterm labor, 105–106
Drug use, during pregnancy, 13–14
DTP (diphtheria, tetanus, pertussis) vaccine, 225,
    229, 233, 242, 256, 264
  schedule for, 271f, 271–272
Ductus arteriosus, prematurity and, 187
Dyspnea, during pregnancy, 47–48

Eating disorders, pregnancy and, 18–19
Ectopic pregnancy, 23
Edema, 99–100, 125, 132
Effacement, cervical, 139, 139f
Einstein, Albert, 14
Emergency instructions, 50. *See also* Safety.
Environmental toxins, 19–20
  home safety with, 171, 230–231
Ephron, Nora, 196
Epidural anesthesia, 142–144, 146
Epilepsy, drugs for, birth defects with, 16–17
Episiotomy, 143, 148
Estriol test, 80
Estrogen
  skin changes with, 32
  vaginal discharge and, 76
Ethnicity
  birth defects and, 23
  twins and, 2, 9
Exercise(s)
  diabetes and, 115, 117
  equipment for, 265
  Kegel, 125
  during pregnancy, 53–61, 56f–61f, 79

Family
  dynamics, 210–214
  help from, 172
  illness in, 214–215, 226, 241
  planning for, 20–21, 122, 135–136
  twins' impact on, 93–95, 134–136, 257–260
Family Leave Act, 214
Fathers
  bonding by, 207–208, 248–249
  childbirth classes for, 91, 141
  during delivery, 141, 147–148
  on fathering, 120–122, 245–248
  reactions of, 73–74
Fatigue, 31, 43–44, 79, 124
Favoritism, 247–248, 254
FDA drug categories, 15–16
Feeding, 150–152, 192–194, 204. *See also* Breast-
    feeding.
  help with, 252–253
  hygiene for, 193

posture and, 203
strategies for, 198–204, 226–228, 252–253
Feet swelling, 78, 87, 101, 132
Fertility treatments, 10–12, 21
counseling for, 95
fraternal twins from, 12
miscarriage with, 81
selective reduction after, 96
Fertilizers, as toxin, 19
Fetal heartbeats
assessment of, 80, 88, 101
monitor for, 104, 141
twin diagnosis by, 31–32
Fetal hiccups, 123
Fetal movements, 31, 86, 99, 111–112
Fever, 226
body temperature vs., 100
during early pregnancy, 51–52
Fluid balance
airplane flights and, 92
for breast-feeding, 201
after delivery, 149
edema and, 99–100
feet swelling and, 78, 87
during pregnancy, 25, 26, 44
preterm labor and, 104–105
vomiting and, 46, 255
water retention and, 31
Folic acid
dietary, 28t
neural tube defects and, 27
Food allergies, 200, 233, 253–254
Food and Drug Administration (FDA), 15–16
Food cravings, 63, 79
Football hold, for breast-feeding, 198f, 202

Gamete intra-fallopian transfer (GIFT), 11–12
Gardnerella vaginalis, 113
Gastrointestinal problems. *See also specific types,*
e.g., Morning sickness.
of infants, 255
during pregnancy, 25, 46, 79, 87, 100, 113
Gaucher's disease, 65
Genetic disorders
alpha-fetoprotein test for, 80–81

chorionic villus sampling for, 67, 68f
family planning and, 21–22
risks for, 279t, 280
screening for, 23, 65–66, 88–89
German measles
birth defects with, 23
test for, 35
vaccine for, 228, 265, 271f, 271–272
Gestational diabetes, 115–119
diagnosis of, 116
diet for, 115, 117
effects of, 117–118
risks for, 116
sweets and, 25, 118–119
symptoms of, 116
test for, 80
treatment of, 118–119
Gestational sac, 8f, 9f, 89
GIFT (gamete intra-fallopian transfer), 11–12
Glow of pregnancy, 63–64, 79, 87, 100, 113
Glucose tolerance test, 117
Gonadotropins, 11. *See also specific types, e.g.,*
Human chorionic gonadotropin.
Gonorrhea test, 34
Group practices, 39–40. *See also* Health care
providers.
Growth rates, 229–230, 233, 250–251
charts for, 273f–278f
Gums, bleeding of, 64, 79, 87, 100, 113

Haemophilus influenzae B vaccine, 228, 229, 242,
256, 264
schedule for, 271f, 271–272
Headaches, 77–78, 87, 101
Health care providers
for cesarean, 147
choice of, 37–40, 90–91, 127, 162–165
roundtable on, 71–73
for delivery, 180
hospital choice and, 177–179
insurance issues with, 173–174, 177, 258–259
interview with, 164–165, 182
levels of care and, 191
team approach to, 165–167
while traveling, 93

Hearing assessment, 238
Heartbeats
    assessment of, 80, 88, 101
    monitor for, 104, 141
    twin diagnosis by, 31–32
Heartburn, 46, 79, 87. *See also* Gastrointestinal
    problems.
Hemophilia, 65
Hemorrhage. *See* Bleeding.
Hemorrhoids, 124, 133
Hepatitis B vaccine, 229, 242, 255, 264
    schedule for, 271f, 271–272
Hiatal hernia, 47
Hib vaccine, 228, 229, 256, 264
    schedule for, 271f, 271–272
Hiccups, fetal, 123
Home safety. *See* Safety.
Honey, danger of, 233
Honeymoon of pregnancy, 86–87, 100, 112
Honikman, Jane, 155
Hospital(s)
    care levels of, 191
    choice of, 177–179
    discharge from, 194–197, 206
    intensive care unit at, 219–221
Hot flashes, 100, 113
Human chorionic gonadotropin (HCG). *See also*
    Gonadotropins.
    pregnancy tests for, 34, 80
Huntington's chorea, 66
Hydration. *See* Fluid balance.
Hyperemesis gravidarum, 46. *See also* Morning
    sickness.
Hypertension, 22, 48, 125, 103
Hyperthyroidism. *See* Thyroid disorders.

Ibuprofen, 17, 77
Immunization(s), 228
    at 2 months, 229
    at 4 months, 242
    at 6 months, 255–256
    at 1 year old, 264–265
    reaction to, 225
    schedule for, 271f, 271–272
    varicella zoster, 265

Incline press exercise, 58, 58f
Indigestion, 46. *See also* Gastrointestinal
    problems.
Individuality, 228, 247–248, 261–262
Infant stimulation programs, 223
Infertility. *See* Fertility treatments.
Insurance issues, 173–174, 177, 258–259
Intensive care unit, 219–221. *See also* Hospital(s).
International Childbirth Education Method,
    91–92. *See also* Birthing classes.
Intimacy. *See also* Relationships.
    after childbirth, 134–136
Intrauterine devices (IUDs), 20–21
Intraventricular hemorrhage, 187
In vitro fertilization (IVF), 11
    miscarriage with, 81
Iodine, dietary, 28t
Iron, dietary, 28, 28t
IUDs (intrauterine devices), 20–21

Jacuzzis, 265
Jaundice, 188–191
    breast-feeding and, 190–191
    phototherapy for, 189–190

Kegel exercises, 125

Labor. *See also* Delivery *and* Preterm labor.
    gestational diabetes and, 117–118
Lactation. *See* Breast-feeding.
La Leche League, 287
Lamaze classes, 91–92. *See also* Birthing classes.
Lanugo, 98–99, 123, 137
Leave of absence, 172
Leg cramps, 100, 113
Ligament(s)
    pelvic, 132
    progesterone and, 54–55
    round, 87, 101
Lochia, 149
Low birth weight babies, 258. *See also*
    Prematurity.
    dietary protein and, 25
    smoking and, 14
Lupus, 22, 103

Macrodantin, 45
Magnesium, dietary, 28t
Magnesium sulfate, for preterm labor, 105
Mask of pregnancy, 32
Mastitis, 151
Maternity blues, 152,
Measles, mumps, rubella (MMR) vaccine, 265,
    271f, 271–272
  schedule for, 271f, 271–272
Membranes, ruptured
  delivery after, 106
  during labor, 141
  preterm labor and, 104
Meningitis, 228
Meperidine, 142
Midwives, 141–142
  choice of, 41
Migraines, 77–78. *See also* Headaches.
Milk products, 26
Miscarriage, 81
  amniocentesis and, 89, 90
  risks for, 51, 102
  smoking and, 13
  vanishing twin syndrome and, 8, 36–37,
    53
MMR (measles, mumps, rubella) vaccine, 265,
    271f, 271–272
  schedule for, 271f, 271–272
Monitor
  for fetal heartbeats, 104, 141
  for nursery, 245
Monozygotic twins, 7f, 7–8
Mood swings, 25, 79
Morning sickness, 45–46, 65, 76. *See also*
    Gastrointestinal problems.
  food cravings after, 63
  vitamin B_6 for, 46
Mothers
  age of, 10, 82–83
    diabetes risk and, 116
    Down's syndrome and, 89, 279t, 280
  bonding by, 207–208, 248–249
  nutrition for, 23–28, 28t
  previous pregnancies of, 23
Mucus plug, 141

Mumps immunization, 265, 271f, 271–272
Muscular dystrophy, 65

Nasal congestion, during pregnancy, 47, 65, 79,
    87, 100, 113
Native Americans, twins among, 2
Necrotizing enterocolitis (NEC), 187
Neural tube defects
  alpha-fetoprotein test for, 80
  folic acid and, 27
Niacin, dietary, 28t
Nigeria, 2, 9
Nipple discharge, during pregnancy, 49, 65,
    79
Nonsteroidal anti-inflammatory drugs
    (NSAIDs), 17, 77
Nosebleeds, 47
Nursing. *See* Breast-feeding.
Nutrition
  diabetes and, 115, 117
  diet for, 26–27
  food cravings and, 63, 79
  placental, 89
  during pregnancy, 23–28, 28t
  preterm labor and, 103
  problems with, 18–19
  stretch marks and, 64

Obstetrician. *See also* Health care providers.
  choice of, 37–40, 90–91, 127
    roundtable on, 71–73
  while traveling, 93
Oligohydramnios, 103
Over-the-counter (OTC) drugs. *See also* Drugs.
  pregnancy risk with, 15–17
Ovum transfer fertilization technique, 12
Oxytocin, 143, 148

Pacifiers, 202
Paint, as toxin, 19, 171
Pap smear, 34
Pediatrician. *See also* Health care providers.
  choice of, 162–164
  interview with, 164–165, 182
Pelvic exam, 33–34, 115

Pelvic tilt exercise, 57, 57f
Pergonal, for infertility, 11
Pertussis vaccine, 225, 229, 233, 242, 256, 264
    schedule for, 271f, 271–272
Pesticides, as toxin, 19, 171
Phenobarbital, birth defects with, 17
Phosphorus, dietary, 28t
Phototherapy, for jaundice, 189–190
Physical exam, 20, 32–35
    at 8 weeks, 50
    at 12 weeks, 66–67
    at 16 weeks, 80–81
    at 20 weeks, 88–89
    at 24 weeks, 101–102
    at 28 weeks, 114–115
    at 32 weeks, 125–126
Physician. See Health care providers.
Placenta(s)
    abnormalities of, 103, 103f, 104f
        smoking and, 14
    amniotic fluid and, 86
    delivery of, 148
    development of, 37
    functions of, 37f
    gestational sacs and, 8f, 9f, 89
    previa, 103, 103f
    for twins, 8, 8f, 9f
    uneven nutrition of, 89
PMS (premenstrual syndrome), 79
Polio immunization, 229, 242, 256, 264
    schedule for, 271f, 271–272
Polyhydramnios, 103, 179
Pool safety, 265
Positions, delivery, 144f–145f
Postpartum depression, 152–156
    treatment of, 155–156
Preeclampsia, 125–126
Pregnancy
    airplane flights during, 92–93
    at 8 weeks, 43f, 43–49
    at 12 weeks, 63–74, 64f
    at 16 weeks, 76f, 76–78
    at 20 weeks, 86f, 86–87
    at 24 weeks, 99f, 99–100
    at 28 weeks, 112f, 112–113

    at 32 weeks, 123–124, 124f
    at 36 weeks, 132, 132f
    dental exam before, 20
    diet and, 18–19, 117
    ectopic, 23
    exercise during, 53–61, 56f–61f, 79
    glow of, 63–64, 79, 87, 100, 113
    heightened smell during, 46
    high-risk, 40–41, 51, 68, 102
    honeymoon of, 86–87, 100, 112
    mask of, 32
    maternal age and, 10, 82–83
    medical exam before, 20
    medication risks during, 15–17
    news of, 81–82
    nutrition during, 23–28, 28t
    prenatal care and, 13–28, 28t
    public reactions to, 106–108
    saliva changes in, 44, 65, 79
    sex during, 63
    substance use during, 13–14
    tests for, 22–23, 34
    tobacco use during, 13–14
    water retention during, 31
    weight control during, 18–19, 24–27
    weight gain during, 29–30
Premature labor. See Preterm labor.
Prematurity, 183–187. See also Low birth weight
        babies.
    Apgar test and, 149
    apnea of, 185
    coping with, 134–135
    definition of, 183
    delivery problems with, 181
    ductus arteriosus and, 187
    infant stimulation programs for, 223
    jaundice in, 188
    retinopathy of, 187
Premenstrual syndrome (PMS), 79
Prenatal care, 13–28, 28t
Preterm labor. See also Delivery.
    assessment for, 88
    definition of, 102
    drugs for, 105–106
    fluids for, 104–105

miscarriage and, 53
prognosis for, 106
risks for, 178–179
stories about, 127–130
symptoms of, 103, 104
ultrasonography for, 69, 104
vaginal infections and, 113
Progesterone
ligaments and, 54–55
morning sickness and, 45
Protein
dietary, 28t
low birth weight and, 25
sources of, 26
Proteinuria, 125
Psychosis, 152
Pyridoxine, 28t

Racial factors
genetic disorders and, 23
twins and, 2, 9
Radiation exposure
during airplane flights, 20
from diagnostic tests, 20
Rapid eye movement (REM) sleep, 111
Rash, diaper, 232, 238–239
RDS (respiratory distress syndrome), 184
Reduction, selective, 95–97
Relationships
couples, 93–95, 134–136, 210–214
siblings, 69–71, 174–176, 204–207
Relaxation techniques, 91, 134–135
Respiratory distress syndrome (RDS), 184
Respiratory problems. *See* Breathing
   problem(s).
Retin-A, 16
Retinopathy of prematurity (ROP), 187
Riboflavin, 28t
Ritodrine, for preterm labor, 105
Round ligament pain, 87, 101
Rubella. *See* German measles.
Running, during pregnancy, 55
Ruptured membranes
during labor, 106, 141
preterm labor and, 104

Safety
bathroom, 169, 243–244
bedroom, 245
burn, 256
car, 167–168, 231–232
choking, 256
home, 170–171, 230–231, 242–245, 256,
   265–266
kitchen, 244–245
pool, 265
resources for, 289
Saliva changes, 44, 65, 79
Salt, dietary, 26
Scoliosis, 33
Seizure medicines, 16–17
Selective reduction, 95–97
Selenium, 28t
Sexuality
Braxton-Hicks contractions and, 113
changes in, 63, 79, 87, 100, 113
intimacy and, 134–136
Sexually transmitted diseases (STDs)
family planning and, 22
tests for, 35
Shoes, choice of, 78
Siblings, 69–71, 174–176, 204–207, 216–218
as baby-sitters, 215
Sickle-cell anemia, 65
chorionic villus sampling for, 67
SIDS (sudden infant death syndrome), 233–234
smoking and, 14, 234
Sitz bath, for hemorrhoids, 124
Skiing, 55
Skin
infant's
   diaper rash of, 232, 238–239
   jaundice of, 190
   sunburn of, 257
mother's
   evaluation of, 32
   sensitivity of, 64, 79, 87
SLE (systemic lupus erythematosus), 22, 103
Sleeping
arrangements, 210, 225, 240–241
cycles, 111, 241

Sleeping (*cont.*)
   disturbances, 124, 132
   position, 233–234
   through night, 240–241
Smell, heightened sense of, 46
Smoking. *See also* Tobacco use.
   secondhand, 14
Social Security Income (SSI), 258
Solid food, 252–253
Sonography. *See* Ultrasonography.
Spina bifida
   alpha-fetoprotein test for, 80
   folic acid and, 27
Spinal anesthesia, 146
Spinal curvature, 87, 101, 112
Station, during labor, 139
STDs (sexually transmitted diseases), 22, 35
Steroids
   birth defects with, 16
   for preterm labor, 105–106
Streptococcal infections, 113, 115
Stress management, 91, 134–135
Stretch marks, 64, 79, 87, 101
Strollers, 168, 267, 288, 290
Structural defects, 89, 103
   umbilical cord and, 148
Substance use. *See also* Tobacco use.
   during pregnancy, 13–14
   preterm labor and, 104
Sudden infant death syndrome (SIDS), 233–234
   smoking and, 14, 234
Sugar, in diet, 25
Sunburn
   of infants, 257
   during pregnancy, 64, 79, 87, 190
Support groups, 108–110, 235, 281–285
Support hose, 78, 286–287
Surfactant, 184
Survival laws
   back to basics, 203
   compromise as, 208
   designate as, 197
Swimming, 54–55
Syphilis test, 35
Systemic lupus erythematosus (SLE), 22, 103

Tay-Sachs disease, 23, 65
Teething, 250
Tegretol, birth defects with, 17
Temperament, development of, 239–240, 261–262
Tennis, 55
Terbutaline, for preterm labor, 105
Testosterone, fetal effects of, 16
Tetanus immunization, 225, 229, 233, 242, 256, 264
   schedule for, 271f, 271–272
Thalassemia, 23, 66
Thiamin, 28t
Thyroid disorders
   depression and, 153
   dry skin with, 32
   family planning and, 22
Tobacco use
   dangers of, 234
   infant exposure to, 232–233
   during pregnancy, 13–14
   preterm labor and, 104
   secondhand smoke and, 14
Tocolytic drugs, 105–106
Toxins
   environmental, 19–20
   home, 171, 230–231
Transfusion
   blood, 126
   twin-to-twin, 187, 284
Transient tachypnea of newborns (TTN), 181
Transverse delivery position, 144–145, 145f
Travel arrangements, 83–84
Triceps exercise, 61, 61f
Trichomonas vaginalis, 113
Triple marker test, 80–81
   amniocentesis vs., 80
Trisomy disorders. *See* Down's syndrome.
TTN (transient tachypnea of newborns), 181
Twinning
   genetics of, 10
   influences on, 9–12
   maternal factors in, 10–12
   prevalence of, 8–10
   race and, 2

Twin-proofing. *See* Safety.
Twins
  at 2 weeks old, 209–210
  at 3 weeks old, 199
  at 2 months old, 222–236
  at 4 months old, 237–245
  at 6 months old, 250–257
  at 1 year old, 261–270
  birth order and, 2
  diagnosing of, 8, 29–41
  family impact of, 93–95
  favoritism and, 247–248, 254
  feeding of. *See* Feeding.
  fetal movement of, 31, 86, 99, 111–112
  financial impact of, 257–260
  fraternal, 7f, 7–8, 12
  during gestation
    at 8 weeks, 42f, 42–43
    at 12 weeks, 62, 62f
    at 16 weeks, 75f, 75–76
    at 20 weeks, 85f, 85–86
    at 24 weeks, 98f, 98–99
    at 28 weeks, 111f, 111–112
    at 32 weeks, 123, 123f
    at 36 weeks, 131f, 131–132
  health insurance for, 173–174, 177, 258–259
  hospital discharge of, 194–197, 206
  identical, 7f, 7–8
  as individuals, 228, 247–248, 261–262
  organizations for, 281–285
  parental bonding with, 207–208, 248–249
  placentas for, 8, 8f, 9f
  premature, 102–106, 103f, 104f
  preparing for, 161–164
  publications on, 285–286
  siblings of, 69–71, 174–176, 204–207,
    216–218
  structural defects of, 89, 103
  support groups for, 108–110, 235,
    281–285
  traveling with, 83–84
  vanishing syndrome with, 8, 36–37, 53
  weight gain with, 29–30
Twins Day Festival, 3, 283
Twin-to-twin transfusion syndrome, 187, 284

Ultrasonography
  at 8 weeks, 42f
  at 12 weeks, 62f
  at 16 weeks, 75f, 80
  at 20 weeks, 85f, 86, 88
  at 24 weeks, 98f, 102
  at 28 weeks, 111, 114
  at 32 weeks, 126
  consultant for, 128
  for delivery, 145–146
  diagnostic, 35–37, 36f
  effect of, 68–69
  for preterm labor, 104
Urinary tract infections (UTIs), 44–45
Urination
  decrease in, 87, 101
  frequent, 45, 65, 112, 116
  at night, 76–77
Urine screens, 80, 88, 101, 114, 116
Uterus
  expansion of, 86
  palpation of, 80, 88, 101
UTIs (urinary tract infections), 44–45

Vaccination. *See* Immunization(s).
Vagina
  bleeding from, 149–150
  discharge from, 87, 101, 113
    estrogen and, 76
    labor and, 138
      preterm, 104
  infection of, 103, 104
  preterm labor with, 113
  tests for, 34
  types of, 113
Valproic acid, birth defects with, 16–17
Vanishing twin syndrome, 8, 36–37, 53
Varicella zoster vaccine, 265
Varicose veins, 31
  support hose for, 78, 286–287
VDRL test, 35
Vernix caseosa, 99, 123
Vitamin A
  birth defects with, 16
  dietary, 28t

Vitamin B$_6$, for nausea, 46
Vitamin supplements, 27–28, 28t
Vomiting, 46, 255. *See also* Morning sickness.

Walkers, 265
Walking, for exercise, 54–55, 79
Water retention, during pregnancy, 31
Weaning, 264
Weight gain. *See also* Nutrition.
   dieting and, 79, 115
   during pregnancy, 18–19, 24–27
   rate of, 29–30

Well-baby visits, 165, 228–230
Whooping cough, 225

Yeast infections
   diaper rash with, 239
   scalp, 241
   test for, 34
Yoruba tribe (Nigeria), 2, 9

Zinc, dietary, 28t
Zinc oxide, for diaper rash, 232, 238
Zygote intra-fallopian transfer (ZIFT), 11–12